Beyond Aesthetics

Beyond Aesthetics

Confrontations with Poststructuralism and Postmodernism

Stuart Sim

HARVESTER
WHEATSHEAF

New York   London   Toronto   Sydney   Tokyo   Singapore

First published 1992 by
Harvester Wheatsheaf
Campus 400, Maylands Avenue
Hemel Hempstead
Hertfordshire HP2 7EZ
A division of
Simon & Schuster International Group

Typeset in 10/12 pt Galliard
by Columns Design & Production Services Ltd, Reading

Printed and bound in Great Britain by
BPCC Wheatons Ltd, Exeter

British Library Cataloguing in Publication Data

A catalogue record for this book is available from the British Library

ISBN 0 7450 0909 3 (hbk)
     0 7450 0910 7 (pbk)

1 2 3 4 5   96 95 94 93 92

This book is dedicated to my mother

Contents

Acknowledgements

I was first introduced to this area of discourse back in the 1970s by my then tutor in the Open University, London, Sarat Maharaj, to whom I owe an immense debt of gratitude for his help at various points in my career. I would also like to thank my colleagues in the *Radical Philosophy* editorial collective for many invaluable discussions about poststructuralism and postmodernism over the years, including some memorably frank discussions at editorial meetings concerning two articles I wrote on Lyotard, later published by the journal. Thanks too go to my secretary in the Manchester office of the Open University, Helen Sidlow, for her excellent word-processing skills in the production of the final manuscript from what must have seemed like my endless revisions. Jackie Jones at Harvester Wheatsheaf has been helpful and supportive throughout the entire project.

Earlier versions of three chapters have appeared in article form as follows: ' "De-composing in bad faith": its cause and cure', *Critical Quarterly*, 24 (1982), pp. 25–36 (Chapter 2); 'Deconstructing the pun', *British Journal of Aesthetics*, 27 (1987), pp. 326–34 (Chapter 6); 'Lyotard and the politics of antifoundationalism', *Radical Philosophy*, 44 (1986), pp. 8–13 (Chapter 7).

Last, but most certainly not least, I would like to thank Dr Helene Brandon for suffering through the many trials of this project with me.

· 1 · INTRODUCTION

The Limit of Philosophy?

The poststructuralist and postmodernist projects pose considerable problems for traditional ways of practising philosophy and criticism. With their anarchic procedures, iconoclastic attitudes, preference for rhetoric over logic, and frequently counter-intuitive conclusions, they represent a direct challenge to some of the most fundamental assumptions of philosophical and theoretical discourse: for example, the assumptions that theories must be rule-governed, that rules and concepts must remain constant once defined, that arguments require proof, that proof be logically demonstrable. 'I try to keep myself at the *limit* of philosophical discourse', Jacques Derrida has claimed, adding that, 'I say limit and not death, for I do not at all believe in what today is so easily called the death of philosophy'; but what takes place at this limit point – 'gnawing away at the border', as Derrida has referred to it – hardly looks like philosophy to most of the Anglo-American philosophical establishment, who are more likely to accuse Derrida of the attempted murder of their subject than to applaud his adventurous spirit.[1] Thinkers like Derrida and Jean-François Lyotard have, by their rejection of conventional methods of constructing value judgements, called into question the validity of criticism and succeeded in problematising the whole area of aesthetics: traditionally the site of legislation regarding the art and practice of critical value judgement. 'I judge', Lyotard observes, 'but if I am asked by what criteria do I judge, I will have no answer to give.'[2] This is an astonishing admission for a philosopher to make, and one calculated to call his credentials as a philosopher seriously into question.

The writings of Derrida and Lyotard might be designated as anti-aesthetic in intent, having as their goal the creation of the conditions for a post-aesthetic realm beyond the reach of value judgement. 'He is right not to tolerate explication', Derrida remarks of the poet François Ponge,[3] an assertion that might stand as a motto for Derrida's entire enterprise: he celebrates the right to non-toleration of explication, the right to resist and frustrate the rationalist, rule-bound procedures of standardly constituted academic philosophy and criticism. Avoidance of explication, judgement without specified, or even specifiable, criteria – we certainly appear to be witnessing the death of philosophy and criticism at such points. Philosophy in the West, particularly in the modern era, has tended to press the claims of logic over rhetoric, those of reason over persuasion, and to demand that theoretical discourses be grounded in some logically acceptable, rule-governed manner. The apotheosis of this trend is to be found in modern symbolic logic (propositional calculus onwards), with its grounding axioms and axiom-derived proofing procedures. Axioms provide foundations for logical systems, but they also bring in their wake the vexed question of their own foundation. What might be described as the foundationalist's primary dilemma has been succinctly summarised as follows: 'there is proof, confirmation, evidence – and then there is what grounds proof, and is in itself incapable of being proved.'[4] It is on the basis of that perceived incapability that the poststructuralist and postmodernist projects can begin operations.

Foundationalism can be considered as one of the most persistent imperatives of Western philosophical practice, and although Derrida and Lyotard are by no means the first philosophers of modern times to pursue the antifoundationalist line (Hume and late Wittgenstein also come readily to mind[5]), arguably no one has ever carried it quite so far before, and their work has in consequence created something of a crisis amongst the critical theory fraternity. Whether that work argues the case for 'limit' or 'death' remains to be resolved. This study is designed to confront the claims of poststructuralists and postmodernists like Derrida and Lyotard to have bypassed or transcended the problem of foundations, and to have demonstrated the untenability of traditionally grounded discourses. For all his apparent commitment to respecting limits, going 'beyond' remains one of Derrida's consistent preoccupations: beyond knowledge, interpretation, sexuality, 'beyond the pleasure principle', even 'beyond man and humanism'.[6] 'Let us wage a war on totality', Lyotard has demanded,[7] summing up the poststructuralist/ postmodernist desire to push beyond the absolutes of traditional discourse.

Derrida and Lyotard will constitute the major focus of attention throughout, although space will also be given to some of the Anglo-American poststructuralist/postmodernist network (most notably, Geoffrey Hartman, Christopher Norris and Robert Magliola), as well as to the iconoclastic theories of the sociologist and culture theorist Jean Baudrillard, whose work shows yet another way in which aesthetics can be transcended; indeed, Baudrillard's work might best be described as post-aesthetic in attitude. This is not designed to be a comprehensive survey of the writings of these figures, but rather a series of confrontations in which certain texts will loom larger than others. In the case of Lyotard and Baudrillard, for example, I will be concentrating mainly on their later work, where post-aestheticism is at its most developed. Derrida and Lyotard will be contextualised within the antifoundationalist strain in Western philosophy, since all too often commentary on their work is politically motivated, for or against, rather than historically conscious.[8] Both negative and positive readings of their work will be given over the course of the study, in order finally to assess the role of the anti-aesthetic imperative within current critical debate. What is at stake is the underlying politics of that imperative. It is my contention that the desire to transcend value judgement is ideologically highly suspect, and that the extreme individualism it assumes ultimately is not a tenable position politically as current cultural debates are constituted. Communication – or even the desire for it – effectively breaks down when this extreme individualism is asserted; as we can see in Lyotard's defiant claim that

> When you're trying to think something in philosophy, you don't care less about the addressee, you don't give a damn. Someone comes along and says, 'I don't understand a word of what you say, of what you write': and I reply, 'I don't give a damn. That's not the problem. I don't feel responsible towards you. You're not my judge in this matter'.[9]

Derrida can be equally dismissive of the philosopher's responsibility to conduct a dialogue, remarking of 'the field called "literary"' that 'you make of it what you like or what you can, it no longer concerns me, it has no law, especially scientific law.'[10] In each case this looks far more like the death of philosophy than any mere skirmishing at the subject's limits.

The seductively easy answer to the poststructuralist/postmodernist dilemma is simply to treat these movements as irrelevant to philosophical enquiry: 'not quite philosophy' on 'a path to nowhere', to yoke together two observations on the nature of Derrida's project.[11] Yet there is a positive side to be noted in any confrontation with his project or Lyotard's. The radical scepticism of such thinkers – Derrida being in many ways the inheritor of Hume, for all that he might resist the idea[12] – is an extremely useful corrective to many current trends in philosophy, and I want to argue that it constitutes a significant extension of the debate on foundations: a debate which continues to have considerable mileage left in it.[13] Comforting though it would be, we cannot simply dismiss the work of such figures as Derrida and Lyotard and then return uncritically to traditional positions. The liberating potential of an anti-aesthetics, and the post-aesthetic vistas that it opens up, has to be taken seriously and given its due. While there is a certain air of glibness about the way that poststructuralists and postmodernists claim anti-authoritarian credentials, there is nevertheless a real issue here which deserves to be explored further.

Essentially, the case against poststructuralism and postmodernism is being argued from a broadly socialist, historical materialist position: a position which demands that discourses be made to declare their ideological commitments, unstated or otherwise. As I write, 'socialism' is a term very much under stress, indeed one that many right-wing thinkers would have us think is already consigned to history's dustbin. 'Marxism' is in even worse shape, a term nowadays seemingly inextricably linked in the Western public mind with Soviet-style political systems, and, now that these have collapsed and been discredited, not one to be taken seriously any more, it would seem. The conditions that created socialism and Marxism, however, still obtain, with the socially divisive effects of unbridled free-market competition, and the exploitative relations that it inevitably brings in its train, being no less a factor now in the late twentieth century than they were in the nineteenth. As long as there is widespread, market-created and market-maintained, economic inequality and insecurity, and socio-political hegemony on class and gender lines, then socialism and Marxism will continue to be viable positions to adopt: especially now that socialists no longer have to apologise for the continued existence of Stalinist 'socialism' and its awkward legacy of authoritarian state control. I take both terms ideally to have anti-élitist connotations, and to be concerned with spelling out the likely political consequences for individuals of discourses which, as is the case with poststructuralism and postmodernism, promise some kind of personal liberation. I want to ask: whose liberation?; at whose expense?; for whose benefit? A certain amount of 'reading against the grain' is necessary when considering any discourse claiming to be 'post'. But I want also to stress that Derrida, Lyotard and the poststructuralist/postmodernist network in philosophy, culture theory and criticism leave unresolved problems that point to the need for a realignment of positions within socialist/ Marxist critical theory and aesthetics.[14] The aim of this study is to maintain a sense of tension between the negative and positive readings of the two projects, which keeps the lines open for future dialogue between them and any socialist-oriented aesthetics. The necessary first step to the construction of such a dialogue is to situate poststructuralism and postmodernism within longer-term philosophical debates. Only then can we confront these movements, and their leading figures, in a genuine spirit of enquiry which might reveal the true worth and significance of a 'not quite philosophy on a path to nowhere' within modern philosophical history.

·2· 'ESSENTIAL, SYSTEMATIC, AND THEORETICAL'

Philosophy as Resistance

Another possible way of referring to a 'not quite philosophy on a path to nowhere' is as a 'philosophy of resistance', and it is clear that the resistance factor needs to be borne very firmly in mind in any survey of the poststructuralist and postmodernist projects. The basic stance of any poststructuralist or postmodernist is oppositional. Indeed it is often easier to say what they are *against* in terms of cultural paradigms than what they are actually *for*. I will in consequence talk of there being 'negative' and 'positive' sides to their work, even though such binary oppositions undoubtedly would be rejected by these thinkers. I will also talk on occasion of a Derridean 'critique' of cultural paradigms, on the basis that to go into print arguing against the assumptions of, for example, structuralism, is to be engaged in critique of some description, even though Derrida and his followers dismiss such interpretations of his work: 'in spite of appearances, deconstruction is neither an analysis nor a critique' he warns us (somewhat against the grain in this respect, 'for want of any better term' as he puts it, Norris speaks of 'Derrida's practice of a "philosophical criticism"'[1]). It is all too easy to become tied up in semantic battles when confronting Derrida, and I acknowledge how value-loaded a term 'critique' is for deconstructionists; nevertheless when Derrida is arguing against some phenomenon I see no reason not to call his efforts a critique.

Derrida unmistakably conceives of his project as one of resistance: a constantly re-enacted process of resistance conducted from within philosophy against cultural paradigms and received authority in general. Adopting a conspicuously anti-Althusserian approach, he argues that

I do not believe in decisive ruptures, in an unequivocal 'epistemological break,' as it is called today. Breaks are always, and fatally, reinscribed in an old cloth that must continually, interminably be undone. This interminability is not an accident or contingency; it is essential, systematic, and theoretical. And this in no way minimizes the necessity and relative importance of certain breaks, of the appearance and definition of new structures . . .[2]

In his rejection of the 'epistemological break' explanation of his work – deconstruction as a radical rupture with philosophical tradition, in other words – Derrida situates himself squarely within the bounds of that tradition, for all that he is engaged in its undoing. The limit-point here, to continue Derrida's metaphor, is in the very texture of the fabric, and his act of resistance takes on a quasi-dialectical character. Undoing is presented as a naturally antithetical movement within cultural paradigms. With his talk of subverting authority from within, Derrida gives the impression of edging towards Marxism at such points (if not perhaps Marxism of the Althusserian-structuralist variety). Any approval from that quarter for his oppositional, almost guerrilla-like stance would be swiftly undercut, however, by recognition of the manifestly Nietzschean, 'eternal recurrence', overtones of 'interminability'.[3] Resistance as eternal recurrence, a notion which also has interesting echoes of Sartrean existential choice, would appear to be more negative and self-defeating than subversive to most socialist theorists.[4]

We shall be returning to this idea of 'resistance as eternal recurrence', plus its Nietzschean and Sartrean overtones, later in the work, but for the time being it is enough to have identified a strong resistance imperative in Derrida. It is an imperative clearly present in Lyotard as well, whose approach to cultural paradigms is invariably adversarial:

> to speak is to fight, in the sense of playing, and speech acts fall within the domain of a general agonistics. This does not necessarily mean that one plays in order to win. A move can be made for the sheer pleasure of its invention: what else is involved in that labor of language harassment undertaken by popular speech and by literature. Great joy is had in the endless invention of turns of phrase, or words and meanings, the process behind the evolution of language on the level of *parole*. But undoubtedly even this pleasure depends on a feeling of success won at the expense of an adversary – at least one adversary, and a formidable one: the accepted language, or connotation.[5]

The postmodernist philosopher's task, as Lyotard sees it, is one of disruption; as he notes, 'it is important to increase displacement in the games, and even to disorient it, in such a way as to make an unexpected "move" (a new statement).'[6] Essential, systematic, theoretical 'undoing' on the one hand, agonistics, displacement and disorientation on the other, the resistance factor in Derrida and Lyotard is well to the fore. The primary targets of that resistance are the Western philosophical tradition and modernism, with all the attendant authority those phenomena possess. It is time to consider the background to resistance in Derrida's dialogue with Western philosophy.

Deconstruction's roots lie in phenomenology and semiotics, and Derrida's work is marked by a sense of internal dialogue with Husserl, Heidegger, Saussure and French structuralism. It is worth emphasising Derrida's anti-structuralist bias because it is one of the clearest things to emerge from his work. The essay 'Force and signification' in *Writing and Difference* remains probably the best introduction to this side of his project and it will be considered in some detail in a later chapter. It is sufficient to note for the present the unmistakably poststructuralist, resistance-oriented tone struck by Derrida in his opening remarks on the structuralist enterprise in 'Force and signification':

> If it recedes one day, leaving behind its works and signs on the shores of our civilisation, the structuralist invasion might become a question for the historian of ideas, or perhaps even an object. But the historian would be deceived if he came to this pass: by the very act of considering the structuralist invasion as an object he would forget its meaning and would forget that what is at stake, first of all, is an adventure of vision, a conversion of the way of putting questions to any object posed before us, to historical objects – his own – in particular.[7]

Structuralism is therefore an invasion to be resisted, and Derrida proceeds to probe fairly relentlessly at what he considers to be the questionable assumptions of this imperialistically inclined 'adventure of vision'. The main thrust of his argument is directed against what he calls 'logocentricity', the belief that sounds (of words) are mere representations of meanings already present in a given speaker's mind. Logo-centricity is an assumption that is built into not just structuralism, but the entire Western metaphysical tradition from Plato onwards (Derrida is nothing if not bold in the scope of his operations), and it implies, in Derrida's view, a very restricted theory of meaning. Words are effectively tied to thoughts in a logocentrist scheme, and there is assumed to be a purity of meaning in thought to which words can only approximate – spoken words approximating more closely than written ones (the phenomenon known as 'phonocentricity').

To see words as circumscribed in this way, whether logocentrically or phonocentrically, is to see them as having no independent existence: that is, no capacity to generate either meaning or slippage of meaning on their own. It is to see words as merely representing, with various degrees of imperfection – increasing as one moves from verbal to written utterance – meanings which are present elsewhere (the mind), and fixed elsewhere. Derrida completely rejects such a conception of language, arguing that 'meaning is neither before nor after the act ... the notion of an Idea or "interior design" as simply anterior to a work which would supposedly be the expression of it, is a prejudice: a prejudice of the traditional criticism called idealist.'[8] Derrida's dismissal of the possibility of anteriority of meaning – hence of criticism as an exercise in the *recovery* of meaning (the structuralist mode) – leads him to put forward a rather fanciful view of the process of meaning-creation. Meaning becomes the product of 'the Nietzschean *affirmation*, that is the joyous affirmation of the play of the world and of the innocence of becoming, the affirmation of a world of signs without fault, without truth, and without origin which is offered to an active interpretation'.[9] Rather than the painstaking recovery of meaning – from words acting as expressions of thoughts – there is to be, for reader and critic alike, what Jonathan Culler has called 'the pleasure of infinite creation'.[10] An infinitely creative mode of interpretation, with no fixed points of reference regarding meaning or truth, would represent an ultimate act of resistance not just against logocentricity but also against Western culture's commitment to rationality and linear thought patterns. And when rationality and linear thought are taken on, the stakes of argument are raised quite considerably.

Structuralism is for Derrida one of the most forceful expressions of logocentrism in Western cultural history. At the core of its logocentrism lies the concept of structure. In each artistic artefact there is deemed to be an approximation to an ideal structure present in the artist's mind. An artwork represents that structure in the same way that a word represents a thought. In each case we have an imperfect version of an ideal form that lies elsewhere. Works of art are read through the deep structures of thought by structuralist critics, a practice which Derrida contends puts limits on human creativity:

> Since we take nourishment from the fecundity of structuralism, it is too soon to dispel our dream. We must muse upon what it *might* signify from within it. In the future it will be interpreted, perhaps, as a relaxation, if not a lapse, of the attention given to force, which is the tension of force itself. *Form* fascinates when one no longer has the force to understand force from within itself. That is, to create. That is why literary criticism is structuralist in every age, in its essence and destiny.[11]

The underlying message of the passage above is that formalism inhibits creativity, and that criticism can only be inimical to the practice of 'active interpretation'. It is in the very nature of criticism, Derrida is claiming, to be rationalist: to desire to order, to explain, to reveal how artworks express deep structures of human thought or preconceived artistic intentions. The anti-judgemental imperative in Derrida is clearly the motivating force behind this attack on structuralism.

Structuralism becomes for Derrida a paradigm case of the desire for order and fixity of meaning that lies at the heart of the rationalist tradition – in fact, almost a form of ultra-rationalism. Critics and theorists within that tradition do not seek to interpret 'actively', but instead to analyse phenomena in a methodical manner according to conventionally agreed concepts, rules and procedures. Consistency is the watchword of such a tradition: consistency of application of analytical criteria to cultural phenomena. Active interpretation, however, cultivates inconsistency. Derrida revels in the ambiguity of his 'concepts' – the word has to be placed in quotes because Derrida tends to deny that he *has* any concepts – as in the case of *différance*, with its simultaneous dual meaning of 'difference' and 'deferral'.[12] Pinning down what his 'concepts' actually mean, and hence what they might be considered to *do* in the cause of undoing, can be the most frustrating of tasks. 'The *supplement*', we are informed, 'is neither a plus nor a minus'; 'the *gram* is neither a signifier nor a signified';[13] *différance* is 'neither a *word* nor a concept', but is instead 'strategic' and 'irreducibly multivalent'.[14] Derrida's disciples are quick to support this anti-analytical strain in his work; thus Robert Magliola can picture Derrida's project as a sustained meditation 'on what he has called the "and/or" between "and/or"'.[15]

What Magliola has dubbed Derrida's 'anguished off-rationalism'[16] consistently gives the impression of avoiding such standardly analytical devices as logical inference and deduction, cultivating instead a style of writing heavily based on word-play and linguistic ingenuity. Geoffrey Hartman has claimed that every pun in Derrida's work is 'philosophically accountable',[17] which is true in the limited sense that punning is an integral part of the strategy to create a non-logocentrist style. Puns work in an associative rather than a linear way, and since Derrida is not in the business of explication but of active interpretation, then their importance to the deconstructionist enterprise becomes fairly obvious. In Derrida's writing, to quote Hartman, 'interpretation no longer aims at the reconciliation or unification of warring truths.'[18] To refuse to analyse or to specify a consistent method of interpretation, to be off-rational in other words, is once again to call one's philosophical credentials seriously into question. The off-rationalism of a 'not quite philosophy on a path to nowhere' has to be seen as distinctly unpromising territory for a philosopher to inhabit.

To see why deconstructionists find it desirable to challenge analytical modes of thought it helps to consider Derrida in terms of the phenomenological movement in modern philosophy. Husserl and

Heidegger are among the earliest preoccupations of Derrida's work (as in his edition of Husserl's *Origin of Geometry*), and there is, as I have noted, an internal dialogue with these thinkers running throughout his writings. Husserl enjoins the phenomenologist 'to stand like a blind man before ideas';[19] Derrida, entering into the spirit of things, describes deconstruction as 'blind tactics'.[20] The major concern of Husserl is to find a method of analysis free from presuppositions; that is to say, a method free from any *a priori* metaphysical commitments. The proper attitude for philosophers to adopt, in Husserl's view, is one of a 'radical lack of prejudice', that enables them to operate 'without the apparatus of premises and conclusions' that traditionally clog up philosophical enquiry.[21]

There are clear echoes of Cartesianism in Husserl's search for something indubitable on which to base an epistemology. In Descartes's case the proposition *cogito ergo sum* provided that something which, in his view, did not need to be justified elsewhere. It formed for him a ground, or foundation, for a theory of knowledge. For Husserl the ground was to be located in the phenomenal experience of the individual; to quote Howard Gardner,

> For the phenomenologists, one's perception of the self and body was central; interest inhered in the content of objects, in essential qualities, in the appearance of things: intention, organization, directedness, attractiveness were accepted as valid phenomena which required no demonstration except, perhaps, to satisfy stubborn scientists.[22]

What this method involved was a suspension of most of the concerns of the Western philosophical tradition. Husserl bracketed these concerns, concentrating his attention instead on phenomenal experience, which in effect became foundational to his philosophy. A presuppositionless starting-point is thus achieved by the expediency of 'putting the world in brackets'; that is, by the reduction of the world-out-there to the individual's stream of experiences – the process known as *epoché* in Husserl.

As various commentators have pointed out, bracketing is a somewhat suspect philosophical method since it involves a kind of trick: a suspension of inconvenient data as it were. 'The phenomenological method with its ultimate appeal to intuition, not to the logic of language, makes *argument* impossible. As a way of *proving* anything, it is simply inadequate', as George Nakhnikian dismissively notes in an introduction to Husserl.[23] (There is, I would claim, a similar appeal to intuition in Derrida, as well as a commitment to rendering argument impossible, and I will return to these phenomenologically derived aspects of his work later.) What is required in phenomenological analysis is a suspension of our disbelief that we can simply ignore inconvenient data in this cavalier way. Given the concern traditionally displayed in philosophy with proof and logical consistency, this suspension has not been so easy to achieve, although its virtue is certainly easy to appreciate; as Edo Pivčević has remarked, the gist of Husserl's *epoché* is that

> We do not have to deny the existence of the fact-world; in fact, we do not have to deny anything at all. All we have to do is to refrain from making any judgements concerning the 'things out there' in their spatio-temporal existence.[24]

The inconvenience of rule-governed value judgement is, convincingly or not it remains to be seen, sidestepped by the phenomenologist.

Derrida plays the bracketing card too with regard to the entire Western tradition of metaphysics, with its belief in logocentricity and rational structures of argument. In this case the inconvenient data to be subjected to *epoché* are the conventional conceptions of the structure of thought, the nature of meaning and the role of language. The 'innocence of becoming', with its suggestion of the perpetual creation, and just as perpetual transcendence, of meaning, has definite connotations of presuppositionlessness. Culler has summed up the Derridean approach to interpretation as follows: 'However broad the spectrum of possibilities on which one bases an analysis, it is always possible to go beyond them.'[25] Foundations, in other words, are always breachable to a deconstructionist, always ultimately incapable of delimiting meaning. While freely admitting the 'theoretical attractions' of such a view, Culler sounds a very traditional note of caution as to its 'practical difficulties', remarking that 'The analysis of cultural phenomena must always take place in some context, and at any one time the production of meaning in a culture is governed by conventions.'[26] These conventions might be pragmatic in nature rather than logical of course, and Culler is not necessarily expounding a foundationalist line here, at least not a *strict* foundationalist line. Not many philosophers will now argue for strict foundationalism, although within their own limited sphere some logicians doubtless still would, but that is not to say that strict foundationalism has ceased to be a significant factor in philosophical and critical discourse. I would argue that it still forms the horizon of such discourse, tacitly rather than publicly acknowledged, and that the conventions Culler refers to, whatever they may be at any one point, will eventually be seen to rely on some strict foundationalist principle such as the law of identity. While a wide range of positions is possible between strict foundationalism and radical antifoundationalism, with a variety of pragmatisms inhabiting the middle ground between, much of the time there is an unacknowledged, what one might call 'in-the-last-instance', commitment to strict foundationalist principles to be noted. Presuppositions regarding meaning are in this 'last-instance' sense ultimately reducible to grounds. Deconstructionists effectively bracket this presupposition-oriented view in favour of celebrating what Hartman has called 'the strength of the signifier vis-a-vis a signified (the "meaning") that tries to enclose it'.[27] From such a perspective as this, words are characterised, not by fixed meaning, but instead by 'a certain indeterminacy of meaning'.[28] The insistence on the necessity for presuppositions confronts the demand for their bracketing across the logocentrist divide. On the one hand we have thought constrained by convention; on the other, intuitions given free rein to create meaning in an endless succession of instants that resist the claims of order and fixity.

The roots of this particular debate are to be found in Saussure's work on the semiotics of language, and his insistence on the arbitrariness of the sign: 'The bond between the signifier and the signified is arbitrary. Since I mean by sign the whole that results from the associating of the signifier with the signified, I can simply say: *the linguistic sign is arbitrary.*'[29] Saying that the bond between signifier and signified is arbitrary is saying that these elements stand in a purely contingent relationship to each other, thus raising the spectre of meaning becoming unfixed, and perhaps even unfixable. Saussure is quick to counter any idea that arbitrariness leads to a situation of anarchy, pointing out that 'the individual does not have the power to change a sign in any way once it has become established in the linguistic community.' Nevertheless, the fact that the signifier is deemed to have 'no natural connection with the signified'[30] has such potentially alarming implications for his theory of meaning that he settles for a 'relative' arbitrariness instead, in an attempt to exorcise what Roland Barthes has referred to as 'the terror of uncertain signs'.[31] There are therefore held to be 'degrees of arbitrariness', and '*the sign may be relatively motivated.*'[32] Saussure begins to sound almost militantly logocentrist when he calls for 'the limiting of arbitrariness'. The fear here is of a collapse into precisely the kind of active interpretation that Derrida is at pains to promote, Saussure arguing that

> In fact, the whole system of language is based on the irrational principle of the arbitrariness of the sign, which would lead to the worst sort of complication if applied without restriction. But the mind contrives to introduce a principle of order and regularity into certain parts of the mass of signs, and this is the role of relative motivation.[33]

Saussure is too much a product of the logocentrist tradition to tolerate for long a world where irrationalism and arbitrariness hold sway, hence those highly emotive appeals for limiting, order and regularity. In the process of doing so, however, he reveals the weak link of the logocentrist system, and it is a weak link that Derrida goes to work on with a vengeance. Far from experiencing any 'terror of uncertain signs', Derrida embraces the possibility wholeheartedly. The enclosure of the signifier by the signified, on which so much of structuralist analysis depends, can be called into question without going outside Saussure himself: undoing proceeds from within.

The theory of the strong signifier is, therefore, embedded within the *Course of General Linguistics*, and it receives a further boost from Saussure's theory of relations. In the latter case relations between linguistic terms are held to depend on the syntagmatic/associative distinction. Saussure believed that language was by nature linear, and that words acquired relations between each other by the fact of being chained together in linear sequence. The syntagm, a combination of words consisting of two or more consecutive units ('human life' being one such example offered by Saussure), was the basic sequence involved, and 'in the syntagm a term acquires its value only because it stands in opposition to everything that precedes or follows it.' Saussure speaks of syntagmatic relations as being 'inside discourse', but a different, non-linear, kind of relations is to be found 'outside discourse'. These 'associative relations' (now more usually referred to as 'paradigmatic') come about through the operation of memory. They 'are not supported by linearity', and are unique to the individual, being 'a part of the inner storehouse that makes up the language of each speaker'.[34] (To belong to the inner storehouse of experience of the individual is, in Saussure's view, to be outside discourse.) This opens up the intriguing possibility of words triggering off very different chains of association in individual minds – the stream-of-consciousness process that we know as 'association of ideas'[35] – and thus undermining the process of 'limiting of arbitrariness'. Where meaning is diffused in this way the strong signifier comes into its own. Derrida's method of textual analysis relies considerably on associative relation as a means of resisting signifier enclosure, and it is also worth noting that, as we shall see, he refuses to recognise Saussure's inside/outside distinction as regards discourse. Puns are essentially associative and non-linear by nature, and therefore form an ideal medium for the strong signifier. With the extensive use made of the pun in deconstructive active interpretation we reach a clear break with the concept of linearity of thought – that concept on which both logocentrism and the Western philosophical tradition so manifestly depend. The line of resistance concerning the production of meaning is sharply drawn.

Philosophy as resistance in Derrida follows the route of the strong signifier, and its objective is to disrupt and displace the fixed points of reference on which logocentrism is structured. Derrida has accused the 'structural consciousness' of being no more than 'a reflection of the accomplished, the constituted, the *constructed*';[36] that is, of engaging in classification of meaning at the expense of its creation. Opt for the strong signifier, however, and creation becomes the order of the day: a creation that breaks down the claims of the accomplished, the constituted and the constructed to exert any sort of authority over time. If meaning is as diffused and transitory a phenomenon as Derrida's dialogue with semiotics seems to reveal, then the authority associated with logocentrism simply evaporates into 'a world of signs without fault, without truth, and without origin'. At that stage of the proceedings countless acts of resistance become possible, including, as a case in point, Christopher Norris's 'revenge of literary theory'[37] against philosophy, where the latter discipline is somewhat unceremoniously subjected to a radical linguistic critique in the name of the strong signifier. As a victim of what has been described as the 'endless accidence of language'[38] philosophy loses its legislative function for Norris, to become another form of rhetoric; in this case a rhetoric concerned to disguise 'its own inescapable predicament as written language'.[39]

The revenge of literary theory on philosophy is essentially the revenge of the strong signifier, but the question does have to be asked as to whether the strong signifier ultimately undermines itself – and in the process undermines the philosophy of resistance. What legitimates resistance if resistance is a celebration of the inadmissibility of legitimation? What is left after the application of a negative critique (I feel it is justifiable to call it that given the way that Derrida carefully and systematically sets out to uncover the hidden assumptions of, for example, structuralist discourse) which calls into question the very foundations of the art of critique? Derrida could very well stand accused of being parasitic on the tradition that he is busily engaged in deconstructing, although his defenders have been at considerable pains to deny that this is in fact so. The comments below are typical of the line taken to the charge by such defenders:

> The usual superficial criticism of Derrida is that he questions the value of 'truth' and 'logic' and yet uses logic to demonstrate the truth of his own arguments. The point is that the overt concern of Derrida's writing is the predicament of having to use the resources of the heritage that he questions.[40]

Is the criticism such a superficial one as Madan Sarup is claiming? The possibility remains that the resources Derrida both uses and abuses may be an accurate reflection of the world of signs, rather than the conspiracy against creativity that he likes to pretend they are. Predicaments can be of one's own making after all. It makes little sense to rail against the constraining effects on human beings of physical processes, for example, nor to complain about being forced to operate from within those same constraints, if physical processes (regardless of how these are explained by science at any one point) are simply a fact of existence that just has to be accepted by finite creatures such as ourselves. Sarup's 'superficial criticism' may be much harder to bracket than his dismissive tone would seem to imply.

What deconstruction offers critics is the opportunity to break free from many of the constraints of academic convention: from *explication de texte*, sober style and painstaking scholarship in general (although on the latter score Derrida's casual aside about the possible presence of 'false citations' in his work might ring some warning bells as to what a deconstructive liberation might sanction[41]). To take up the offer is to move from what has been called 'care and rationality' (in the compilation of one's citations, for example) to 'playfulness and hysteria'.[42] 'Critics in the Anglo-American tradition are arbiters of taste, not developers of ideas', Hartman has complained,[43] and the deconstructive mode, in its witty, word-playing, iconoclastic way, offers endless scope for the enthusiastic developer willing to kick over the traces of an academic training. Value judgement, an activity requiring much careful, and time-consuming, marshalling of proof, evidence and citation, can be bracketed in favour of an exploration of the phenomenal experience of the individual critic, where strong signifiers propel stream-of-consciousness in unpredictable directions. 'It is easy to slip from metaphor to metaphor in describing this book', Hartman writes of Derrida's *Glas*,[44] signalling the form that an anti-judgemental, strong signifier-led playfulness might take. It is not only easy, one might remark, it is also necessary, otherwise rational argument might reassert itself, and this is to be avoided at all costs by critics of the Hartman persuasion. M. H. Abrams, in a generally highly critical essay on the subject of deconstruction, has rather loftily maintained that 'in the course of time, the way of reading that we have in common with our critical precursors will assimilate what the new ways have to offer of valid insights into the complexities of the interpretive process';[45] but it is hard to see how the strong signifier can be so easily appropriated to the cause of logocentrism. The '*différance* . . . is neither a *word* nor a concept' mentality actively resists any such quasi-imperialist attempt at absorption by its perceived enemy. When Hartman derides traditional – that is, non-deconstructive – criticism for its obsessive 'wish to "solve the phenomena"',[46] he reveals just how wide a gulf separates the protagonists in this debate. To all intents and purposes, 'solving' and 'creating' belong to different universes of discourse. Derrida makes this crystal clear when he insists that, in engaging with a text, the deconstructionist critic 'should neither comment, nor underscore a single word, nor extract anything, nor draw a lesson from it'.[47]

Lyotard is no less firm in his refusal to play the value judgement game: 'I judge. But if I am asked by what criteria do I judge, I will have no answer to give.' Lyotard's philosophy of resistance has a more explicitly political edge to it than does Derrida's. To quote Samuel Weber, 'Lyotard's argumentation is undoubtedly directed against the totalitarian pretensions of totalizing thought',[48] and it is politically influential thought of the Marxist or Hegelian variety that Lyotard is particularly concerned to confront: 'We no longer have recourse to the grand narratives – we can resort neither to the dialectic of Spirit nor even to the emancipation of humanity as a validation for post-modern scientific discourse.'[49] It would not be difficult to identify other likely candidates for 'grand narrative' status, almost any form of religion or nationalism would qualify. What they all share is a desire, as well as a claim, to 'solve the phenomena'. The postmodern sensibility is, therefore, a resistance-oriented one directed against authority, or, to be more precise, the authority assumed by its supporters to reside in any of the grand narratives: 'if a metanarrative implying a philosophy of history is used to legitimate knowledge, questions are raised concerning the validity of the institutions governing the social bond: these must be legitimated as well.'[50] We are back with the problem of foundations: 'there is proof, confirmation, evidence – and then there is what grounds proof, and is in itself incapable of being proved'.

Lyotard, like Derrida and Hartman, feels that the 'solve the phenomena' imperative inevitably has to encounter the foundationalist dilemma, and that its claim to be able to overcome this obstacle and maintain its totality of operation cannot be upheld. It is the goal of the poststructuralist and postmodernist projects to reveal, with a guerrilla-like sense of persistence, the gaps in the totality, and it is no accident that so much of the resistance is inspired by the foundationalist dilemma: here is an area where aporias are an ever-present occupational hazard and the 'terror of uncertain signs' is never far below the surface – perfect conditions indeed for the pursuit of multivalency.

Much of what I shall go on to say about Derrida in the chapters to come, indeed have already said so far, runs counter to Norris's reading of his project as outlined in a number of books, notably *The Deconstructive Turn*, *The Contest of Faculties*, *Derrida*, and, most recently, *What's Wrong with Postmodernism?* Given that Norris has become one of the most persuasive, and fair-minded, apologists for Derrida over the last decade or so, it is advisable for anyone entering the debate to situate himself/herself in terms of 'Norris's Derrida'. Derrida is no prophet of unreason, critical anarchy or millenarian visions in Norris's view – even though it requires some special pleading to rescue him from such charges, as we shall see – but instead a rigorous scrutiniser and dissector of texts, whose writings 'are always aimed at locating the stress points or moments of self-contestation where texts come up against the ineluctable limits of their own ideological projects'.[51] *What's Wrong with Postmodernism?* deals at some length with what Norris considers to be a profusion of misreadings of Derrida in the recent literature, both by his detractors (for example, Habermas in *The Philosophical Discourse of Modernity*) and his supporters (mainly the American deconstructionist school of literary criticism). In the former case Derrida is misread as propounding 'a species of latter-day Nietzschean irrationalism', and in the latter as offering 'a handy pretext for dispensing with the effort of conceptual critique'.[52] Norris's Derrida, in contrast, sounds surprisingly more like a philosopher in the traditional mould – 'there is no question of simply revoking the Kantian paradigm and declaring a break with that entire heritage of enlightened critical thought', we are warned – than the wild man of legend with his fabled ability 'to allure to transgression', and Derrida himself can be called on to reinforce Norris's case: 'the value of truth . . . is never contested or destroyed in my writings', Derrida claims at one point, 'but only reinscribed in more powerful, larger, more stratified contexts', where one can happily 'invoke rules of competence, criteria of discussion and of consensus, good faith, lucidity, rigour, criticism, and pedagogy'.[53] It becomes hard to see why Derrida's work has created the fuss that manifestly it has if Norris's Derrida is the whole story. Why has there been such wholesale misreading?

But of course it is *not* the whole story, as even Norris, surely the most scrupulously honest of Derrida's defenders, is forced to acknowledge. Habermas's criticisms are granted some force as long as one restricts oneself to certain texts in the Derrida canon:

> The favoured texts for this purpose would include Derrida's response to John Searle on the topic of speech-act theory; the closing paragraph of 'Structure, sign and play', with its apocalyptic overtones and Nietzschean end-of-philosophy rhetoric; and, more recently, the 'Envois' section of *La Carte Postale*. . . . One could then go back to Derrida's earliest published work – his Introduction to Husserl's 'The origin of geometry' – and cite the well-known passage where he appears to encounter a moment of choice between 'philosophy' and 'literature', or the quest for some pure, univocal, self-present meaning (Husserl) as opposed to the prospect of a liberating 'freeplay' of the signifier glimpsed in such writings as Joyce's *Finnegan's Wake*.[54]

To this list could be added, and will be by me in the chapters that follow, the numerous 'beyonds' that litter the pages of Derrida's writings. Norris can give no very convincing argument for the presence of this anarchic–apocalyptic streak in Derrida, other than to claim that most of the time his subject observes the protocols of rules of competence, criteria of discussion and of consensus, good faith, lucidity, rigour, criticism and pedagogy. Since the revolutionary side of Derrida's work resides in the *problematisation* of just such conventional phenomena, this leaves us with an oddly reduced, rather tame figure, whose project sounds all but indistinguishable from that of such 'reading against the grain' theorists as Pierre Macherey.[55] One might also add that when one turns to the pages of Derrida he rarely looks this tame and consensus-oriented; as Llewelyn has remarked, Derrida is not so easily domesticated.[56] What Norris's reading ignores, or at least fails to communicate, is the sheer strangeness and alienating quality of Derrida's writing and general textual concerns. Taken on those terms of strangeness and alienation Derrida is a much more awkward customer, and it is essentially that awkward Derrida that I deal with in this study. It may well be that Derrida cannot deliver what his more radical utterances seem to promise, but I see that as no reason for claiming that they are somehow marginal to his real project. I regard them, instead, as the very core of Derrida, at once enticing and politically dubious, and my attention is accordingly directed firmly at the role of those many 'beyonds'.

·3· 'PROOF, CONFIRMATION, EVIDENCE'

Foundationalism and Antifoundationalism

'There is proof, confirmation, evidence – and then there is what grounds proof, and is in itself incapable of being proved': finding that elusive starting-point from which one's philosophical system can be constructed has been a continual preoccupation of Western philosophy. Much of the impetus for the debate in modern times has come from Cartesian scepticism, and, given its prominent place at the beginnings of modern philosophy, it is worth dwelling on what is at stake here for a moment. Working his way back through the contents of his knowledge, Descartes decides that much of it can be called into question. He describes himself as being 'embarrassed by so many doubts and errors, that it seemed to me that the only profit I had had from my efforts to acquire knowledge was the progressive discovery of my own ignorance'.[1] Those recurring 'doubts and errors' lead him to a method featuring a high degree of Husserl's desired 'radical lack of prejudice':

> Some years ago now I observed the multitude of errors that I had accepted as true in my earliest years, and the dubiousness of the whole superstructure I had since then reared on them; and the consequent need of making a clean sweep for once in my life, and beginning again from the very foundations, if I would establish some secure and lasting result in science.[2]

The 'clean sweep' of Descartes's scepticism eventually reaches an apparent barrier: the fact of his own thinking. 'I could not feign that I was not',[3] he notes, and there follows in due course the foundation that he seeks: 'Thus I have now weighed all considerations enough and more than enough; and must at length conclude that this proposition "I am", "I exist", whenever I utter it or conceive it in my mind, is necessarily true.'[4]

Cogito ergo sum is for Descartes the elusive starting-point that the committed foundationalist strives to attain: the point at which philosophical scepticism must admit defeat – 'enough and more than enough'. Before long a body of knowledge is being compiled on the basis of that starting-point, including certain knowledge as to God's existence: 'On all counts, the conclusion must be: from the mere fact that I exist, and have in me some idea of a most perfect being, that is, God, it is clearly demonstrated that God also exists.'[5] The transition from certainty as to phenomenal experience to certainty as to divine existence is a questionable one – Descartes being, in C. H. Whiteley's words, 'seriously sceptical only about sense-perception, and indecently credulous about some theological arguments'[6] – but the rationale for it is clear enough. Behind Descartes's proofs lies a foundational principle, *cogito ergo sum*, on which he feels he can depend: a foundational principle which resists doubt. It is not a case of the *cogito* being incapable of being proved, but rather of the *cogito* being deemed to lie beyond the *need* for any such proof. It is self-evidently in this latter category, in Descartes's view, and at that point scepticism simply ceases.

At least, scepticism ceases if it is indeed self-evidently so that the *cogito* is foundational. There is a vast philosophical literature, running from Descartes's own time to the present day, devoted to demonstrating that it is in fact *not* so.[7] This is not the place to assess such a literature: what is important for our present purpose is the assumption made by the respective camps. On the Cartesian side, the assumption that once the elusive starting-point has been located, epistemological certainty follows; on the anti-Cartesian side, that once the starting-point has been called into question then the entire edifice of post-sceptical Cartesian philosophy – proofs for the existence of God, mind–body duality, etc. – must be considered to be in a state of collapse. Cartesians see the promised land of secure and lasting results, whereas their opponents see only the unjustified circumscription of the promised clean sweep. The debate is a highly symbolic one in demonstrating what is at issue regarding foundations. Foundations enable one to construct philosophical systems, 'whole superstructures', and then to defend them with confidence. They enable one to keep scepticism, that recurrent virus in the philosophical body, at bay. In the absence of foundations, the sceptic has considerable room for manoeuvre, and when that happens it is not just our knowledge which ends up with a question mark hanging over it: the philosophical enterprise in general can begin to look very dubious.

The more radical that scepticism is, the more dubious institutional philosophy can look. Whiteley has noted that what he calls 'thorough and pervasive' scepticism 'is usually directed against some entrenched intellectual Establishment', and that 'being an uncomfortable position, it is tolerable only if it can be employed to make self-important people still more uncomfortable.'[8] These sentiments very much apply to the work of Hume, who is plainly concerned to spread as much discomfort as he can amongst the philosophical establishment of his day:

> It is easy for one of judgement and learning, to perceive the weak foundation even of those systems, which have obtained the greatest credit, and have carried their pretensions highest to accurate and profound reasoning. Principles taken upon trust, consequences lamely deduced from them, want of coherence in the parts, and of evidence in the whole, these are everywhere to be met with in the systems of the most eminent philosophers, and seem to have drawn disgrace upon philosophy itself.

Hume's thorough and pervasive scepticism regarding causality and personal identity undermines many of the certainties of our world-view, and can make philosophy very difficult to practise. As such it is one of the most important sources for modern antifoundationalism, although Hume himself was clearly unhappy about the antifoundational implications of his researches: 'I cannot forbear feeding my despair with all those desponding reflections, which the present subject furnishes me with in such abundance.'[9] Nevertheless, in pinpointing with such clarity what follows from 'weak foundations' – in effect, unreliable proof, confirmation and evidence – as well as the apparent pervasiveness of such weakness throughout the philosophical enterprise, Hume strikes an authentically antifoundational note.

Hume's scepticism leads him to deny the validity of many of the inferences that we make habitually on the basis of our experience: for example, that we can have knowledge of the future; that nature is uniform; that there is a necessary connection between cause and effect; that we have a fixed personal identity that endures over time. In each of these cases, Hume feels, the inference can be challenged. We do not in fact *know* that a given effect will follow a given cause as it has in the past. At best we can *predict* this on the basis of past experience; that is, we can assume a degree of probability as to the occurrence, but no sense of certainty about it. The inductive gap yawns wide. Certainty would require there to be a necessary connection between causes and effects, but in his observation of causal sequences, such as the famous example of the billiard balls, Hume can find no such connection.[10] He is compelled to the following conclusion by his researches:

> The idea of necessity arises from some impression. There is no impression conveyed by our senses which can give rise to that idea. It must, therefore, be derived from some internal impression, or impression of reflection. There is no internal impression which has any relation to the present

business, but that propensity, which custom produces, to pass from an object to the idea of its usual attendant. This, therefore, is the essence of necessity. Upon the whole, necessity is something that exists in the mind, not in objects.[11]

'Custom' is hardly the kind of concept to endear itself to the foundationalist. It is patently inadequate as a means of bridging the inductive gap and establishing secure and lasting results. In many ways custom is, philosophically speaking, a gesture of despair, as well as being a highly instructive example of the uncomfortable positions into which scepticism can lead the philosopher. Whiteley spells out just how much further potential for discomfort the custom 'solution' contains when he observes that

> Hume wanted to hold that the conclusions of physicists were sounder than those of theologians or astrologers, despite the fact that his theories gave no warrant for this distinction: if inductive inference is not the work of reason, we have no *reason* for preferring the Nautical Almanac to Old Moore's Almanac, and might quite well select our creeds for their emotional appeal or their entertainment value.

Whiteley is on the side of reason, his brief being to establish his own doctrine of 'confirmationism' as a technique for 'discriminating between stronger and weaker evidence, superior and inferior opinions';[12] but what is intended by him as a warning against the dangers of what has since come to be called an 'anything goes' approach to epistemology could equally well be read by some, less committed perhaps to such implicitly foundationalist notions as stronger/weaker and superior/inferior, as an open invitation to indulge in experiment.[13] Deconstruction and postmodernism unashamedly exploit emotional appeal and entertainment value; what is punning if not entertaining? When Lyotard notes that 'I judge, but if I am asked by what criteria do I judge, I will have no answer to give', we might hazard a guess that emotional appeal and entertainment value are the most likely candidates; Norris suggests as much when he assigns philosophy to the level of rhetoric (where emotional appeal and entertainment value are acceptable objectives) on the basis of 'its own inescapable predicament as written language'. In a world without foundations, 'a world of signs without fault, without truth, and without origin', emotional factors will almost inevitably come into play. Hume may feel unhappy at the prospect ('all those desponding reflections'): poststructuralists and postmodernists clearly are not.

The inductive gap revealed by Hume need not lead to an 'anything goes' epistemology, but one can see its potential for exploitation by radical sceptics and antifoundationalists. Hume provides yet more ammunition for the antifoundationalist cause when he turns to the subject of personal identity. When it comes to self and identity, the stakes are extremely high: 'nor is there anything of which we can be certain if we doubt of this.' Given the stakes, Hume's conclusion is not a comfortable one: 'I may venture to affirm of the rest of mankind, that they are nothing but a bundle or collection of different perceptions, which succeed each other with an inconceivable rapidity, and are in perpetual flux and movement.'[14] There is, in other words, no fixed personal identity that holds over time, and when we consider the immense weight laid on personal experience by empiricists like Hume, we can appreciate just how uncomfortable a conclusion this is for him to reach. Whatever grounds for certainty we may think we have will be remorselessly undercut by the passage of time. The elusiveness of the starting-point reasserts itself with a vengeance. Derrida's attack on the metaphysics of presence will depend on a similar analysis: given such 'perpetual flux and movement' meaning can never be fully present to itself, nor ever perceived as being so. Each 'now' we experience is simultaneously a 'not-now', thus destroying the possibility of there being any enduring foundations of discourse:

> the presence of the perceived present can appear as such only inasmuch as it is *continuously compounded* with a nonpresence and nonperception. . . . As soon as we admit this continuity of the now and the not-now, perception and nonperception, in the zone of primordiality common to primordial impression and primordial retention, we admit the other into the self-identity of the *Augenblick*; nonpresence and nonevidence are admitted into the *blink of the instant*.[15]

Whereas to Hume being condemned to the 'blink of the instant' induces a sense of despair, to Derrida it opens up a world of exciting possibilities. The 'active interpretation' which 'affirms play and tries to pass beyond man and humanism'[16] derives its force from, and can hardly be countenanced without, that 'blink of the instant' which eclipses foundations.

Hume is no system builder, and generally speaking antifoundationalists are to be found in the non-system-building camp in philosophy. Two possible exceptions to this tendency suggest themselves, and those are Hegel and Marx. On the face of it this may seem to be an odd claim to make: philosophical systems surely demand foundations if they are to retain any credibility, and Hegel is one of the arch-system builders in the history of philosophy, with Marx not very far behind.[17] How then can they be appropriated to the cause of antifoundationalism? The line I am going to pursue is that the notion of 'dialectic' employed by each thinker has significantly antifoundational implications. This is particularly so in

Marx's case, although given his debt to Hegel we need to bear the work of both in mind in order to gain a proper understanding of the dialectic's antifoundational potential. The lines of communication between deconstruction and socialist aesthetics will largely depend on the extent of that potential to put traditional, foundation-dependent, systems of thought under perpetual stress.

The Hegelian dialectic of thesis–antithesis–synthesis, in which the first part of the triad generates the second, its contradictory, which is then synthesised with the first term into a new thesis beginning the process all over again, takes place in the realm of ideas. Hegel is a dialectical idealist whose work traces the process by which the 'World Spirit' (or 'universal mind') finally achieves its goal of self-understanding and self-realisation:

> The word of reconciliation is the *objectively* existent Spirit, which beholds the pure knowledge of itself *qua universal* essence, in its opposite, in the pure knowledge of itself *qua* absolutely self-contained and exclusive *individuality* – a reciprocal recognition which is absolute Spirit . . . it is God manifested in the midst of those who know themselves in the form of pure knowledge.

The progress of spirit is teleological and would seem to assume a foundational principle. Hegel is certainly critical of a sceptical tradition which leaves us with no basis to construct such a teleologically oriented system. The 'sceptical self-consciousness', he advises us, 'is the *absolute dialectical unrest*, this medley of sensuous and intellectual representations whose differences coincide, and whose identity is equally again dissolved . . . a purely casual, confused medley, the dizziness of a perpetually self-engendered disorder.'[18] This is Hume's 'perpetual flux and movement' restated, but with a different solution offered. A dialectic teleologically directed towards the absolute replaces custom, with inevitability promising the secure and lasting result that mere convention alone patently cannot.

Despite its sense of inevitability, however, Hegel's dialectic has antifoundational possibilities while it is still in the process of unfolding and the absolute is no more than a distant horizon. J. N. Findlay insists on the dialectic's ability to create new and unexpected states of affairs:

> Dialectic is, in fact, a richer and more supple form of thought-advance than mathematical inference, for while the latter proceeds on lines of strict identity, educing only what is explicit or almost explicit in some thought-position's content, dialectic always makes higher-order comments upon its various thought-positions, stating relations that carry us far beyond their obvious content.[19]

The claim to go 'beyond' – in this case beyond mathematical truth, that paradigm of reasoning to so many philosophers over the years – opens up some tentative lines of communication to the world of Derrida. Findlay's argument, which is one often advanced by critics of modern logic, is that mathematics, with its commitment to strict logical identity (the cornerstone of most philosophical system-building), yields only tauto-logies. Dialectics, by implication, involves a much looser form of identity that is not tied to the rules of classical logic. Dialectical identity is fluid and constantly exposed to change – at least in its pre-absolute state of operation – and points towards Derrida's foundation-free 'innocence of becoming' condition. While *in medias res*, the dialectic appears to be offering a challenge to the metaphysics of presence, where strict identity certainly applies, through its ability to surpass the tautologies of foundation-bound reasoning and to generate the unex-pected. The first step in the project to go beyond man and humanism is to go beyond classical logic and strict identity, and the Hegelian dialectic makes precisely that move. The teleology of the system ultimately differentiates it from Derrida's enterprise, but at some level both are calling the metaphysics of presence into question, and with it the foundational imperative.

There may be the secure and lasting result to end all secure and lasting results awaiting us on the horizon of Hegelian philosophy, but the method of reaching it contains, at any one point, considerable flux and movement. Inside ultimate certainty lies local uncertainty in the sheer suppleness of the dialectic's movement.[20] Similar points can be made about the Marxist version of the dialectic, although in this case we are operating in the realm of matter rather than ideas. Marx situates the dialectic in human action as it occurs within human history, thus converting Hegel's dialectical idealism into dialectical materialism (although it should be noted that Hegel's 'philosophy of history' had already made notional gestures in the latter direction[21]). It is no longer a conflict between ideas that we are witnessing, but a conflict between human beings: 'The history of all hitherto existing society is the history of class struggles', as the *Communist Manifesto* declaims. Thesis and antithesis have become transformed into material entities, into social classes engaged in a power struggle. The dominant class in any historical period generates opposition from the economically exploited and politically suppressed class underneath it, until that latter class overcomes it – as the bourgeoisie did with the feudal nobility – thus creating the synthesis of the power struggle that begins the cycle anew. Like Hegel, Marx prescribes an ultimate end to the dialectic: in this case it will arrive once the current conflict of the bourgeoisie and the proletariat is resolved:

If the proletariat during its contest with the bourgeoisie is compelled, by the force of circumstances, to organise itself as a class; if, by means of a revolution, it makes itself the ruling class, and, as such, sweeps away by force the old conditions of production, then it will, along with these conditions, have swept away the conditions for the existence of class antagonisms and of classes generally, and will thereby have abolished its own supremacy as a class. In place of the old bourgeois society, with its classes and class antagonisms, we shall have an association, in which the free development of each is the condition for the free development of all.[22]

This is the Marxist utopia where history effectively has ceased, but until that point is reached the dialectic has a greater degree of fluidity than Hegel's does. One notes the repetitive 'if' – 'if the proletariat', 'if, by means of a revolution' – which seems to allow at least some scope for unpredictability. There is not quite the acute sense of inevitability about the process that we find in Hegel. In Marx, the dialectic has to be interpreted by human beings before the appropriate action to bring about its resolution can be instituted. Given that 'if factor', the Marxist dialectic falls even further short of the metaphysics of presence than does its Hegelian counterpart.

One might not wish to push the point too far – there are always absolute resolutions on the horizon to be taken into account – but while it is actually in *operation* the dialectic, particularly the Marxist one, has 'innocence of becoming' connotations, hence a pretension towards the antifoundational. The 'negation of the negation' aspect of the dialectic provides further justification for that pretension. In Engels' reading of the notion the stress is very firmly on the breach of the classical law of identity that is involved: 'life consists precisely and primarily in this – that a being is at each moment itself and yet something else.' The negation of the negation, the process by which a material entity, or historical phenomenon, continually experiences the negation of its previous state as the dialectic unfolds in time (thesis spawning antithesis, the resulting conflict then spawning in its turn a synthesis/new thesis), is to Engels a law 'unconsciously operative in nature and history',[23] and it has antifoundational connotations. As long as dialectical change is occurring, as long as each 'now' is simultaneously a 'not-now', then the law of identity is being negated. We are back in the world of the 'blink of the instant'.

Negating the law of identity and thus problematising the validity of classical logic (and all those formal logics that follow on from it in the twentieth century) can be a mixed blessing, even for a Marxist. It can problematise dialectics itself. 'If we want to comprehend the real relations of the classics of Marxist dialectics to the principle of contradiction', Adam Schaff has pointed out, 'we must follow up how they make use of it in the course of reasoning, thus tacitly acknowledging its validity.' Further pursuing the 'superficial criticism' route against dialectics, Schaff suggests that

> a Marxist judge, confronted with the declaration of a defendant that he was and at the same time was not at home on the night in question, would not consider this contradiction as a reflection of the objective contradictions inherent in reality itself but as a proof that the defendant is lying.[24]

Superficial or not, these are still useful arguments to turn back against Sarup and apologists for antifoundationalism in general. The metaphysics of presence has a nasty habit of undermining opposed discourses in this way.[25]

How successful the dialectic is in evading the demands of proof, confirmation and evidence is arguable, but it holds out the promise of antifoundationalism in its mode of operation. At some point of the process, for all that teleology ultimately must divide them, the dialectic gestures towards deconstruction. Negating and undoing have at least a family resemblance. We have already noted a family resemblance between undoing and eternal recurrence, and the latter provides another apparently antifoundational route out of the Hegelian dialectic in the way that it dispenses with the notion of teleological progress towards the absolute. The 'transvaluation of all values' in which Nietzsche is engaged leads to the conclusion that there are no longer any absolute truths about the world (as there were assumed to be in Hegel) but only interpretations:

> Against positivism, which halts at phenomena – There are only facts – I would say: No, facts is precisely what there is not, only interpretations. We cannot establish any fact 'in itself': perhaps it is folly to want to do such a thing.
> Everything is 'subjective,' you say; but even this is interpretation. The 'subject' is not something given, it is something added and invented and projected behind what there is. – Finally, is it necessary to posit an interpreter behind the interpretation? Even this is invention, hypothesis.

Nietzsche's 'perspectivism' precludes foundations and takes us one step nearer the deconstructive goal of a world of signs without truth, fault or origin.[26]

There is, as we have seen, an even stronger gesture towards deconstructionist antifoundationalism in Husserlian phenomenology and its call for a 'radical lack of prejudice' on the part of the individual before ideas and intellectual history. 'To one truly without prejudice', Husserl notes, 'it is immaterial whether a certainty comes to us from Kant or Thomas Aquinas, from Darwin or Aristotle, from Helmholtz or Parcelsus.' When he goes on to assert that 'What is needed is not the insistence that one sees with his own eyes: rather it is that he not explain away under the pressure of prejudice what has been seen',[27] Husserl strikes an authentically deconstructionist note; resisting the pressure of prejudice, of preconceived notions and schemes of interpretation, is precisely what the Derridean project is about. In this more radical version of Cartesianism there are at least intimations of antilogocentricity to be noted.

Despite the 'radical lack of prejudice', Husserl still feels that he has a foundational principle to fall back upon. The *epoché* isolates that elusive starting-point in phenomenal experience, an area where traditional philosophy's 'apparatus of premises and conclusions' is held to be largely irrelevant. In opting for the *epoché* we have, in effect, stepped outside discourse, and, as Pivčević has noted, it is a position that we can maintain only at the expense of making any value judgements. Moving outside discourse, turning a blind eye to foundational philosophy and appealing to intuition, all suggest an antifoundational perspective, for all that they are being employed in the search *for* a foundation. To bracket is to opt out of the foundational game as it is conventionally played, even by sceptics, and to provide the conditions for active interpretation. Husserl's foundation, ironically enough, prepares the ground for the most radical form of antifoundationalism in modern philosophy.

Later phenomenologists, Heidegger and Sartre for example, have an even more dramatic way of stating the conditions of the *epoché* than does Husserl. For Heidegger,

> This characteristic of Dasein's Being – this 'that it is' – is veiled in its 'whence' and 'whither', yet disclosed in itself all the more unveiledly; we call it the '*thrownness*' of this entity into its 'there'. . . . Even if Dasein is 'assured' in its belief about its 'whither', or if, in rational enlightenment, it supposes itself to know about its 'whence', all this counts for nothing as against the phenomenal facts of the case: for the mood brings Dasein before the 'that-it-is' of its 'there', which, as such, stares it in the face with the inexorability of an enigma.[28]

The 'phenomenal facts of the case', that is, the lack of any transcendental quality to being, dictates as its appropriate response, anxiety. In similar fashion in Sartre, we experience anguish on the realisation that we are 'abandoned' into an existence where the phenomenal facts of the case are 'the absolute contingency of being, its indifferent irreducibility' and the constant 'nihilation' of its 'past being'.[29] Radical lack of prejudice is built into our ontological state in both these cases, and seems to preclude the possibility of foundations. As in Hume, a gap opens up between our expectations, product of a long-standing tradition of the metaphysics of presence, and the reality of an intuition-based, 'blink of the instant' existence where 'all this counts for nothing'. This is territory where the antifoundationalist can flourish, and Derrida is clearly exploiting those gaps bequeathed to him by the phenomenological movement. Sartre's existentialism in particular carries that sense of the remorseless creation, and just as remorseless annihilation, of meaning that marks out Derrida's world of signs: even if it is the case that Sartre gives us anxiety, rather than innocence, of becoming.

If radical scepticism almost inexorably moves down an antifoundational path, its negative critique leaving us with no fixed points of reference by which to construct systems of thought with any real sense of confidence, then dialectics and phenomenology, initially at least, seem to provide a resolution of the foundationalist dilemma. The resolution is, however, obtained at a considerable cost: foundations which can exist only by breaching or suspending traditional philosophical rules of discourse. We are not so much beyond proof, confirmation and evidence, as in a state of war with them. One could argue that there is eventually more for the antifoundationalist than the foundationalist in either of these philosophies.

An antifoundationalist case of a different kind can be drawn from the later work of Wittgenstein. The move here is back into language, particularly into language-use. For Wittgenstein, meaning, and by extension whatever it is that is held to ground meaning, is in the main to be subordinated to linguistic usage: 'For a *large* class of cases – although not for all – in which we employ the word "meaning" it can be defined thus: the meaning of a word is its use in the language.'[30] The antifoundationalist credentials of such a position are easily identified. As David Pears has pointed out, for later Wittgenstein, 'outside human thought and speech there are no independent, objective points of support, and meaning and necessity are preserved only in the linguistic practices which embody them.'[31] The shift of focus from meaning to use elides the problem of foundations. If analysis of use alone is enough to determine meaning, then there is no need to seek meaning's foundation: the foundational dilemma is essentially a false one from a Wittgensteinian perspective. What Wittgenstein does, according to Staten, is to dissolve the 'metaphysical mystery about meaning',[32] and, it could be added, about foundations too.

Dissolving 'metaphysical mystery' has been a long-time preoccupation of Richard Rorty, who is similarly concerned to keep us inside language and to call idealism and the search for 'objective points of support' into doubt: 'It is the impossible attempt to step outside our skins – the traditions, linguistic and other, within which we do our thinking and self-criticism – and compare ourselves with something absolute.' Rorty feels that the 'Platonic urge to escape from the finitude of one's time and place'[33] has bedevilled Western philosophy to no particular purpose. His deconstruction of the foundational imperative is yet another exercise in elision: 'liberal culture', he argues, 'needs an improved self-description rather than a set of foundations.' The question to be asked of the foundationalist, for Rorty, is not 'How do you know?', but 'Why do you talk that way?'[34] Pragmatically conducted debate amongst equals replaces the search for supremacy in philosophical and critical enquiry; the give-and-take of the academic common-room or seminar-room the urge for final solutions.

Scepticism, suspension, elision, there is a range of options for the antifoundationalist to adopt. Yet perhaps the 'usual superficial criticism' can be registered in each case, that logic, and hence foundations, is being relied on at some point of the proceedings – otherwise why believe the claims of the sceptic, the phenomenologist or the pragmatist? On what *grounds* should we accept the judgement that 'liberal culture needs an improved self-description rather than a set of foundations'? Or that use takes precedence over meaning? The dilemma continues to lurk in the background of even the most determined efforts to destabilise it or render it irrelevant, a point made with some force by that self-confessed 'card-carrying antifoundationalist' Stanley Fish in *Doing What Comes Naturally*. In claiming 'to provide us with a perspective on what we have been doing such that we are now in a position either to do it better or to do something we have not been able to do before', antifoundationalism, for Fish, ends up as 'nothing more or less than a reinvention of foundationalism by the very form of thought that has supposedly reduced it to ruins'. Fish is here pursuing another version of his famous 'theory has no consequences' line of argument, and he sees no particular issue of political importance in the foundationalist dilemma: 'Not only does being converted to anti-foundationalism bring with it no pedagogical pay-off', he asserts, 'being opposed to anti-foundationalism entails no pedagogical penalty.' Practice wins out in Fish, a card-carrying pragmatist no less than a card-carrying antifoundationalist, who seems happy enough to leave things as they are in the best-of-all-pedagogical worlds, where 'practice has nothing to do with theory' and antifounda-tionalism 'offers you nothing but the assurance that what it is unable to give you – knowledge, goals, purposes, strategies – is what you already have'.[35]

There is a certain air of smugness about Fish's above-the-battle pose, the antifoundationalist amused at the pretensions of antifoundationalism, which is unlikely to please either side in the debate, and his answer to the foundationalist dilemma seems to be to disregard it and continue on happily with your own 'practice', whatever it may be. In Derrida's terms of reference, however, the breaks are being reinscribed in an old cloth, and doubt, suspension and elision in their turn must be undone. What needs to be considered now is whether Derridean essential, systematic, theoretical undoing succeeds in being anything other than yet another reinscription; whether a philosophy of resistance can genuinely go beyond simply confirming both the problem and the problem of its solution. Derrida's world of signs seems to hold out just such a promise of transcendence; how real is that promise?

I say 'needs to be considered now', which reveals that I am still in some sense operating from within the horizon of foundationalism. This is immediately to give hostages to fortune to the antifoundationalist camp, and I will just have to live with this, hostages to fortune being an occupational hazard in the foundationalism debate. Other than Fish's highly pragmatic route out of the debate, the other available options to what I can only call a 'reluctant foundationalism' would appear to be uncritical acquiescence with Derrida's claim to have problematised foundationalism – which is to beg the question of what is at stake – or, alternatively, silence in the face of the apparently intractable foundationalist dilemma. So I will proceed with a reluctant foundationalism, which no doubt on occasion will sound more confident in its critique of the Derridean project of problematisation than is probably either justifiable or defensible – although it is hoped nothing like as confident as John Ellis's straight-down-the-line analytical reading of Derrida in *Against Deconstruction*. Ellis, as Norris notes, sets out to counter the claims of deconstruction by means of 'a healthy anti-Gallic commonsense rationalism, plus a fortifying dose of elementary logic'; in other words, from a position of fairly uncritical acceptance of strict foundationalism and its principles.[36] At the risk of sounding like wishing to have one's cake and eat it, I ask the reader to assume a healthy degree of un-Ellis-like scepticism regarding my own foundational position at any one point, which nevertheless falls short of uncritical acquiescence, silence or Fish's 'false problem' approach. The reluctant foundationalist takes refuge in the 'unacknowledged horizon' argument, in the belief that horizons of discourse are not so easily transcended – although they can of course be pushed back. Nor can the political consequences of dispensing with those horizons be glossed over: both foundationalism and antifoundationalism entail political consequences, and, no matter how reluctantly, I opt for the consequences of foundationalism for the most part of the critique that follows. I want to be as fair to Derrida as one can be from within foundationalism, and a reluctant foundationalism seems a not unreasonable attitude to adopt towards this particular attempt at problematisation, enabling one to move in and out of sympathy with a thinker who both attracts and repels in almost equal measure.

·4· 'EXTRAVAGANT METAPHORICAL WHIMSY'

Derrida and the Deconstruction of Metaphysics

Derrida's writing, suggests Christopher Norris, 'will strike most philosophers . . . as a style of extravagant metaphorical whimsy . . . a kind of sophistical doodling on the margins of serious, truth-seeking discourse'. Norris's concern is to defend Derrida against charges of this nature, and to present a picture of deconstruction as a rigorous and revolutionary intellectual discipline, in manner 'closely allied to certain present-day forms of psychoanalytical criticism', which destabilises logocentrist discourse from the inside: a discipline with the 'habit of uncovering a disjunct relationship between logic and language, the order of concepts and the order of signification'.[1] Most philosophers would be content simply to accept Norris's 'whimsy' assessment at face value, however, and quickly pass on to more pressing, truth-seeking, problems. The pursuit of whimsy and the pursuit of truth are not normally viewed from within the philosophical profession as being compatible activities. Faced with an apparently wilful refusal to address, never mind attempt to solve, the phenomena, academically trained philosophers can experience the greatest difficulty in deciphering Derrida. When it comes to deconstruction, as Lorna Sage has wryly remarked of the Anglo-American intellectual establishment, 'we de-compose, most of us, in rather bad faith.'[2] Given our training in the art of solving the phenomena, it is probably hard for us to do otherwise.

Yet if Derrida is out there on the margins, it should be noted that he is there deliberately and with a very specific sense of purpose. From those margins he is conducting a thorough and pervasive campaign of scepticism against the centre of Western metaphysics: a campaign which has as its goal the liberation of language and discourse from the supposedly constraining effects of logic and logocentrism. Instead of presence there will be a 'will to effacement' on the part of signs that are internally, ineradicably, marked by *différance*:[3] and when it comes to the latter, 'there is no subject who is agent, author, and master of *différance* . . . the relationship to the present, the reference to a present reality, to a *being* – are always *deferred.*'[4] Presence assumes authority: in the endless deferment of that presence – a presence which is necessary in order to guarantee the validity of foundations – lies the death of authority, and a consequent release into a world of signs without truth, fault or origin.

The desire to dismantle and then pass beyond metaphysics and all that it stands for in our culture, particularly the authoritarian implications of presence, runs deep in Derrida. 'I am not simply a philosopher', he warns us, and indeed the scope of the deconstructive project is far wider than what Derrida would see as the relatively parochial concerns of most metaphysicians.[5] 'Deconstruction', he claims, 'is not a discursive or theoretical affair, but a practico-political one';[6] and that practico-political, inherently anti-metaphysical imperative seems constantly to strive for the destabilisation of the act of value judgement. There is, Derrida insists, 'another story, always already begun, at the moment where it begins',[7] therefore the objective of the philosopher must be 'not to respond but to resonate' in his writing.[8] The parallel columns of *Glas*, the parallel texts of 'Living on: Border lines', are designed to resound against each other in just such an unpredictable manner, with readers being invited to find their own route through this maze of echoes, where 'one procession is superimposed on the other, accompanying it without accompanying it', as best as they can:

> What has happened, if it has happened, is a sort of overrun [*débordement*] that spoils all these boundaries and divisions and forces us to extend the accredited concept, the dominant notion of a 'text,' of what I still call a 'text,' for strategic reasons, in part – a 'text' that is henceforth no longer a finished corpus of writing, some content enclosed in a book or its margins, but a differential network, a fabric of traces referring endlessly to something other than itself, to other differential traces. . . . Whatever the (demonstrated) necessity of such an overrun, such a *dé-bordement*, it still will have come as a shock.[9]

Resonance leads us away from logic and resolution to the complexities of infinite regress, to what Derrida has called the *mise en abyme*, the 'infinite reflection, for example, the shield in the shield in the shield'.[10] This is an entirely characteristic Derridean image or 'concept', shifting, partial, inconclusive, resistant to resolution on an infinite scale. By its very nature it defies metaphysics, since it precludes even the *possibility* of any debate about origins and closure, or the nature of presence. In the face of *mise en abyme* and *différance*, foundations simply cannot be formulated.

The practico-political side of deconstruction, its subversively conducted campaign against authority and authoritarianism, can be seen to
particular advantage in Derrida's attack on structuralism and its
'adventure of vision'[11] in 'Force and signification'. Structuralism is
pictured in this essay as a culmination of the logocentrist tradition in
Western metaphysics, as a totalitarian method of analysis whose
essentialism arbitrarily delimits meaning and inhibits imagination and
creativity. Neither its 'technical ingenuity' nor its 'mathematical subtlety'
can be considered to mask the sterility that lies at the heart of the
enterprise. 'The relief and design of structures', argues Derrida in a
devastating denunciation of the formalist ethic, 'appears more clearly
when content, which is the living energy of meaning, is neutralized.
Somewhat like the architecture of an uninhabited or deserted city,
reduced to its skeleton by some catastrophe of nature or art.'[12] The
emotive contrast of life and death is carefully calculated and typical of
Derrida's practice throughout 'Force and signification', where structuralism is invariably regarded as an enemy to the production of meaning
– a dead hand laid on the creative urge. To a structuralist, meaning is
something to be recovered, something that has taken place before the act
of criticism begins. Against this essentially archaeological mode of
analysis Derrida poses, and celebrates the virtues of, writing, in his
formulation of the concept a perfect exemplar of the innocence of
becoming in action:

> It is because writing is *inaugural*, in the fresh sense of the word, that it is
> dangerous and anguishing. It does not know where it is going, no
> knowledge can keep it from the essential precipitation toward the meaning
> that it constitutes and that is, primarily, its future.[13]

If writing does not know where it is going, if no knowledge can shape or
alter its progress, then it lies beyond the reach of authority. It cannot be
controlled or reduced to a mathematical form or system; neither can it be
apprehended in its totality. Indeed it is ontologically incapable of *being* a
totality, since it cannot stop unfolding into an unknown future. Writing
marks the site of the guerrilla movement within logocentrist language
and criticism that is deconstruction: it never begins, it never ends, and at
any given now it is always simultaneously an identity-destroying not-now.

Structuralism becomes a totalitarian exercise by turning structure into
'the object itself, the literary thing itself', such that 'the framework of
construction, morphological correlation, becomes . . . the critic's sole
preoccupation . . . the very being of the work.' Where this totalitarian-
minded formalism, or 'ultrastructuralism' as Derrida calls it,[14] can lead is
to be seen in the case of the critic Jean Rousset, and his book *Forme et*

Signification: Essais sur les structures littéraires de Corneille à Claudel, the particular focus of Derrida's antistructuralist tirade in 'Force and signification'. While professing a certain degree of admiration for Rousset's book, 'this series of brilliant and penetrating exercises intended to illustrate a method',[15] Derrida is scathing about what he considers to be its excessively geometrical approach to formal analysis: 'The geometry is only metaphorical, it will be said. Certainly. But metaphor is never innocent. It orients research and fixes results.' Geometry is, in effect, backdated into the author's intention, an intention obeying the deep structures of thought for a structuralist:

> Not only does the geometric structure of *Polyeucte* mobilize all the resources and attention of the author, but an entire teleology of Corneille's progress is coordinated to it. Everything transpires as if, until 1643, Corneille had only gotten a glimpse of, or anticipated the design of, *Polyeucte*, which was still in the shadow and which would eventually coincide with the Corneillean design itself, thereby taking on the dignity of an entelechy toward which everything would be in motion. Corneille's work and development are put into perspective and interpreted teleologically on the basis of what is considered its destination, its final structure. *Before Polyeucte*, everything is but a sketch in which only what is missing is due consideration, those elements which are still shapeless and lacking as concerns the perfection to come, or which only foretell this perfection.[16]

It is worth examining this passage in some detail for what it reveals about the value-system behind Derrida's crusade against logocentrism. He is particularly critical of the way that ultrastructuralist formalism marginal-ises creativity (the 'force' that Derrida keeps referring to throughout the essay). There are no surprises to be found in Rousset's universe, preformed structures have already set the agenda and artists can be no more than agents of those structures – mere channels by which the structures realise their predetermined development. No innocence of becoming is possible under the circumstances – in this world truth, fault and origin hold sway – and the artist has no choice but to progress to a prearranged goal: a goal that is prearranged from beyond the realm of human effort. Derrida scents determinism at work in Rousset's analysis, as artworks are read through a structural scheme which imposes a specific geometrical form on them (the 'ring and the helix' of the supposed Corneillean grand design) in terms of the logocentre of 1643 and *Polyeucte*, at which latter point the structure is finally present to itself with all *différance* dissolved. The critic's task, as the ultrastructuralist conceives it, is to mark the stages by which that logocentre is reached: to catalogue how deep structure comes to its teleologically directed fruition.

Metaphor is clearly not innocent in Rousset's case. If 'the ring and the helix' are taken to Corneille's work as analytical tools, then, given what amounts to the radical *excess* of prejudice that such a move involves, it is only to be expected that the works will coincide with the geometry to a greater or lesser degree: the research-orienting preconception will yield the required result. What Derrida elsewhere in the essay refers to as the 'circularity and traditionality of Logos' applies.[17] The critic will find what he seeks, but at the expense of backdating a programme on to the author which renders him a virtual prisoner of deep structure. *Polyeucte* writes Corneille; deep structure provides the geometry by means of which *Polyeucte* writes Corneille. From such a perspective, form exists in order to realise its own perfection in the metaphysics of presence, where interior design and anterior meaning conspire to prevent signs from offering themselves up to an active interpretation. *Polyeucte* is inhibited from becoming anything other than ultrastructuralist method dictates it must be; closure of the imagination has been effected, and at such points Derrida's line of argument takes on a noticeably political dimension. First of all structure, and then the critical method that celebrates its pre-eminence, are seen to operate in an authoritarian manner, and the thrust of Derrida's argument is firmly against the authoritarian impulse.

Rousset is made to bear the weight of Derrida's displeasure with a long tradition of structuralist analysis on the logocentrist principle. It is a tradition where the most characteristic move is to locate the logocentre, the moment of full presence, such that a hierarchy of related works can then be constructed in terms of that logocentre. Thus Lévi-Strauss feels motivated to argue of a group of South American Indian myths (Bororo, Ge and Sherente) that 'in all these instances we are dealing with the same myth . . . the apparent divergences between the versions are to be treated as the result of transformations within a set.' The unifying logocentre acts to organise even the rogue elements in its field of analysis, its 'unique and most economical coding system', according to Lévi-Strauss, 'working to reduce messages of a most disheartening complexity, and which previously appeared to defeat all attempts to decipher them'. Structuralist logocentrism has distinctly imperialist tendencies: 'Either structural analysis succeeds in exhausting all the concrete modalities of its subject', Lévi-Strauss insists, 'or we lose the right to apply it to one of the modalities.'[18] Since he continues to apply it, Lévi-Strauss clearly feels that it *does* exhaust all, divergences included. Deconstructionists would most likely fall on the reference to 'apparent divergences', reading these as quintessential moments of *différance* artificially absorbed into a suspect teleology, whose objective is the 'proliferation of schematizations'[19] at the expense of the free play of meaning. Within structuralist method, Derrida would argue, lies a drive to curb expressive freedom and to elide *différance*: and it is a drive wholly lacking in justification if, as Derrida claims elsewhere in *Writing and Difference*, 'the center is not the center'.[20]

A similar commitment to unity and the logocentring power of structure can often be noted in the work of Roland Barthes, as in the essay 'Introduction to the structural analysis of narratives':

> How is novel to be set against novella, tale against myth, drama against tragedy (as has been done a thousand times) without reference to a common model? . . . is not structuralism's constant aim to master the infinity of utterances [*paroles*] by describing the 'language' ['*langue*'] of which they are the products and from which they can be generated. Faced with the infinity of narratives, the multiplicity of standpoints – historical, psychological, sociological, ethnological, aesthetic, etc. – from which they can be studied, the analyst finds himself in more or less the same situation as Saussure confronted by the heterogeneity of language [*langage*] and seeking to extract a principle of classification and a central focus for description from the apparent confusion of the individual messages . . . either a narrative is merely a rambling collection of events, in which case nothing can be said about it other than by referring back to the storyteller's (the author's) art, talent or genius – all mythical forms of chance – or else it shares with other narratives a common structure which is open to analysis, no matter how much patience its formulation requires.[21]

The elision of *différance* is again very noticeable, with Barthes actively seeking to unify 'the apparent confusion of the individual messages' much as Lévi-Strauss did the apparent divergences of his set of myths, and Rousset the deviations from the ring and helix structure in Corneille's pre-*Polyeucte* dramatic output. In each case Derrida would see the imposition of a teleology which cannot be defended, a desire for order whose authoritarian impulses – Barthes's determination to bring infinity, chance and rambling narrative to heel, for example – are to be resisted. To Derrida the unity of presence is a rather desperately maintained fiction. Structuralism seeks the *Polyeucte* in every author's oeuvre, the *Polyeucte*-effect in every phenomenon brought under scrutiny. Research is oriented, results fixed, force neutralised: it is the 'circularity and traditionality of Logos' in operation and it signals the intrinsic totalitarianism of the structuralist enterprise.

To oppose this critical totalitarianism, where structure is always 'a receptive one, waiting, like a girl in love, ready for its future meaning to marry and fecundate it',[22] Derrida typically calls for a strategically minded guerrilla campaign within criticism itself:

> Emancipation from this language must be attempted. But not as an *attempt* at emancipation from it, for this is impossible unless we forget *our* history. Rather, as the dream of emancipation. Nor as emancipation from it, which would be meaningless and would deprive us of the light of

meaning. Rather, as resistance to it, as far as is possible. In any event, we must not abandon ourselves to this language with the abandon which today characterizes the worst exhilaration of the most nuanced structural formalism.[23]

The philosophy of resistance, that essential, systematic and theoretical activity, must work from within the metaphysics of presence, remaining constantly aware of the latter's considerable residual power over us, of the sheer seductiveness of notions of unity and order in the face of chance and confusion. Yet unity and order remain illusions to the deconstructionist: illusions insidiously directed against the creative urge:

> Why is there more beauty in *Polyeucte* than in 'an ascending movement of two rings'? The force of the work, the force of genius, the force, too, of that which engenders in general is precisely that which resists geometrical metaphorization and is the proper object of literary criticism. . . . Rousset sometimes seems to have 'little interest in art'. . . . Why then, once more, this geometer's privilege? Assuming, in the last analysis, that beauty lets itself be espoused or exhausted by the geometer, is he not, in the case of the sublime – and Corneille is said to be sublime – forced to commit an act of violence?[24]

The violence done by ultrastructuralism to literary objects – the preformationist tendencies, the refusal to countenance any deviation *from* these preformationist tendencies – is countered by Derrida's appeal to a *différance* that is beyond the reach of such violence:

> But is it by chance . . . that the meaning of meaning (in the general sense of meaning and not in the sense of signalization) is infinite implication, the indefinite referral of signifier to signifier? And that its force is a certain pure and infinite equivocality which gives signified meaning no respite, no rest, but engages it in its own *economy* so that it always signifies again and differs? Except in the *Livre irréalisé* by Mallarmé, that which is written is never identical to itself.

The centre is not the centre; presence is not presence, but instead a now/not-now caught up in an inexhaustible network of exchange. Structuralism's attempt to impose finitude on literary objects, to reduce 'everything not intelligible in the light of a "preestablished" teleological framework . . . to the inconsequentiality of accident or dross',[25] is doomed to failure given the restlessness and sheer evasiveness of *différance*. It will be *différance* that leads the way out of the closed system of the structural consciousness to the realm of active interpretation: the route, in effect, out of metaphysics. And structuralism, with its 'more or less avowed dependence upon phenomenology', is, for Derrida, 'a tributary of the most purely traditional stream of Western philosophy, which, above and beyond its anti-Platonism, leads Husserl back to Plato'.[26]

Derrida's point is that all metaphysics is, eventually, a metaphysics dependent on presence. Few philosophers in the Western tradition are capable of thinking themselves out of the orbit of presence, fewer still are capable of living with the implications of the loss of presence – Nietzsche perhaps is up to a point, Hume, as we saw, ultimately is not. With *différance* on his side, Derrida feels he can retire to the margins, the better to conduct his campaign against the false credentials of the centre. The *différance* that is inscribed within writing effectively destroys the claims of imperialist ultrastructuralism. 'Structure then', as Derrida notes, 'can be *methodically* threatened.'[27]

As a negative critique of structuralism – and I feel that 'critique' is an entirely justifiable term to use to describe this series of attacks on logocentrist assumptions – 'Force and signification' can be fairly devastating: structuralism's teleological tendencies and radical excess of prejudice have perhaps never been more clearly identified. The implication of ultrastructuralism, Derrida declares persuasively, is that when 'confronted with a literary work, one should always be able to find a line, no matter how complex, that accounts for the unity, the totality of its movement, and all the points it must traverse.' And Rousset, in Derrida's reading the entirely representative ultrastructuralist, *is* always able to find that line, such that one is left wondering when the structural logocentre finally is located in *Polyeucte*, 'whether the credit is due Corneille or Rousset'.[28] The arrow is well aimed and does considerable damage to its target.

It is when we come to ask ourselves what is being offered positively in the wake of the negative critique that the problems begin in earnest with Derrida's poststructuralism. Values are there in abundance in the essay: Derrida is anti-authoritarian, anti-totalitarian, a libertarian, a rebel against conformity, a risk-taker, a breaker of new ground, a subversive guerrilla, a transgressor of dead rules – but what does all this iconoclasm add up to in terms of a programme against the evils of logocentrism? The answer from Derrida's side is that one must commit oneself to writing, the active means by which structure can be methodically threatened; but writing proves to be the most slippery of activities to pin down:

> Writing is the outlet as the descent of meaning outside itself within itself: metaphor-for-others-aimed-at-others-here-and-now, metaphor as the possibility of others here-and-now, metaphor as metaphysics in which Being must hide itself if the other is to appear. Excavation within the other toward the other in which the same seeks its vein and the true gold of its phenomenon. ... Writing is the moment of this original Valley of the other within Being. The moment of depth as decay. Incidence and insistence of inscription.[29]

This is Derrida in his millenarian mode, as we saw him appear earlier in his call for a world without truth, fault or origin, and while it has a considerable rhetorical appeal – those uncharted regions of thought to be explored, those collapses of authority to be observed at first hand when structure undermines itself in depth suddenly revealed as decay – it is hard to see how the occasion for that millenarianism can be controlled for polemical effect. Writing appears more as something that happens to us than as something that we can turn against teleology and logocentrism. We can resurrect the 'usual superficial criticism' at such points, and query how Derrida's 'writing' can escape the implosion of meaning – 'the descent of meaning outside itself within itself' – that seems to be an inevitable consequence of any sustained engagement with language. Writing is simultaneously our only means of escape from a repressive authority, and a vicious circle that undermines our act of resistance at source. To claim that Derrida is yet again drawing attention to 'the predicament of having to use the resources of the heritage he questions', while acting as an agent of writing, a concept that instantly unweaves what he says while remaining forever beyond his power to control, comes perilously close to a despairing argument on the 'human condition' model. Who can control writing? If no one, then what is its practico-political dimension, other than being a medium for the registration of individual angst?

Dangerous and anguishing as it is, writing simply seems to call attention to our ineffectiveness and weakness, and as David Wood has remarked, 'the risk of sterilizing the reader, too anxious to lift his frozen pen, is very real.'[30] It could be said that Derrida rescues us from the determinism of structure only to land us in the abyss between signifier and signified – the abyss where signifier can never meet signified. How we are to continue our anti-metaphysical programme from there is not too clear, and for all that Robert Magliola can proclaim that 'overhead the vaulted dome of the metaphysical heavens is cracking',[31] Derrida shows himself well aware in 'Structure, sign and play' of just how difficult it can be to prosecute a campaign against logocentrist metaphysics while remaining true to one's subversive principles:

> But all these destructive discourses and all their analogues are trapped in a kind of circle. This circle is unique. It describes the form of the relation between the history of metaphysics and the destruction of the history of metaphysics. There is no sense in doing without the concepts of metaphysics in order to shake metaphysics. We have no language – no syntax and no lexicon – which is foreign to this history; we can pronounce not a single destructive proposition which has not already had to slip into the form, the logic, and the implicit postulations of precisely what it seeks to contest.[32]

Trapped in the logocentrist circle, we have no option but to make use of its resources: but to what extent does this succeed in really shaking metaphysics? More to the point, does shaking make the structure fall?

'Beyond opposition, *différance* and rhythm. Beyond a beyond whose line would have to divide, that is to oppose entities, beyond the beyond of opposition, beyond opposition, rhythm': Derrida often sounds as if the fall of structure and its empire has already taken place. Yet in one of his most characteristic gestures he concludes the postscript to *The Post Card*, from where the above quotation is taken, with the promise that, 'This is to be continued.'[33] Perhaps deconstruction is more interested in the act of shaking than the fall? In the negative critique where an adversarial posture, if persisted in, brings to our attention the sheer mutability of our structures and contexts of thought, structure can be made 'to reveal not only its supports, but also the secret place in which it is neither construction nor ruin but lability'.[34] The 'secret place' is where the centre is not the centre, and each now is simultaneously a not-now; a world of constant flux in which, to relate Derrida back to one of the earliest debates on the metaphysics of presence in Western philosophy, we can never step into the same river *once*, never mind twice.[35] Deconstruction becomes an act of revelation, but an act of revelation which has to be conducted, can *only* be conducted, from within the enemy's language and concepts. The apparently intractable problem facing the guerrilla is how to use the enemy's discourse while managing to avoid that discourse's metaphysical commitments. Deconstruction revels in such paradoxes, in its ability, as Norris approvingly notes, 'to argue with the utmost *logical* rigour to conclusions which may yet be counter-intuitive or at odds with commonsense (consensual) wisdom'.[36] 'This is to be continued': the enemy's concepts are simultaneously to be used and avoided by means of that convenient bracketing device derived from Heidegger's phenomenological armoury, *sous rature*:

> Heidegger . . . in *Zur Seinsfrage* . . . lets the word 'being' be read only if it is crossed out. . . . That mark of deletion is the final writing of an epoch. Under its strokes the presence of a transcendental signified is effaced while still remaining legible. Is effaced while still remaining legible, is destroyed while making visible the very idea of the sign.[37]

If we use a concept from the history of metaphysics, according to Derrida, 'we can only use it under erasure . . . its necessity felt before letting itself be erased.'[38] Courtesy of *sous rature*, the linguistic guerrilla can have his or her cake and eat it, combining the opposed virtues of logocentricity and *différance* in an ingenious – perhaps also cynical – way that is very difficult to counter. Experience can be erased: it 'has always designated the relationship with a presence'.[39] The past can be erased: it 'can no longer be understood in the form of a modified presence, as a present-past'.[40] Perhaps even time itself can be placed *sous rature*: 'one may indeed wonder by what right all that is in question here should still be called time, now anterior present, delay, etc.'[41] *Sous rature* catches Derrida at his most whimsical; saying, but then again *not* saying, what his theories cannot allow him to say; using, but then again *not* using, the enemy's concepts with the express purpose of undermining them. 'The Outside is the Inside', Derrida can claim, entirely counter-intuitively, taunting all truth-seeking philosophers with that still-resonant 'is', its necessity fleetingly felt, only to evaporate the moment one decides to subject it to any form of logical analysis.[42]

The impulse seems to be to propel us beyond history and knowledge, which, Derrida argues, 'have always been determined (and not only etymologically or philosophically) as detours *for the purpose* of the reappropriation of presence'.[43] At that point doubts again begin to surface concerning the direction of Derrida's practico-political programme. Leaving aside for the time being the politics of the rhetoric, the erasure of history seems an unnecessarily extreme, and ultimately unwise, step for the deconstructionist to take. To be removed from history is to be removed from conventional political process: a gesture which effectively surrenders that process to one's enemies, who can continue to trade on the considerable attractions of order and unity over those of the abyss. There is a note of desperation about a call for the end of history, which goes well beyond the practical. The end of history is also the end of discourse – 'no account of Time; no Arts; no Letters; no Society', as Thomas Hobbes remarked of that paradigmatic ahistorical state, the 'state of nature'[44] – and exile from all discourse seems a very high price to pay for liberation from metaphysics. It is one thing to plead for a loosening-up of the criteria governing interpretation, another thing entirely to suggest that we embrace the end of interpretation. That way lies solipsism and silence. Take us outside history and the lines of communication to socialism are stretched to breaking point. Marxism, it is true, views the end of history as a desirable aim ('we shall have an association, in which the free development of each is the condition for the free development of all'), but only as the culmination of a long and complex dialectical process which has to take place in and through history. Derrida's end of history, on the other hand, precludes process, as if the desired state could be achieved by act of will or critical fiat: with one bound the antifoundationalist was free . . ..

This is perhaps to take the metaphor too literally. We do not, after all, accuse Barthes of incitement to murder when he calls for 'the death of the author'.[45] But metaphor, as Derrida has reminded us, is never innocent, and where it seems to be pointing us here is beyond practical politics. Deconstruction's drive to transcend any and all authority breaks down at times into a politics of gesture, which is most unlikely to bring down entrenched structures of power. Sometimes the gesture is whimsical: the pun that free-associates its way merrily through sober discourse can have considerable entertainment value. At other times the gesture is closer to despair: as it is in the rejection of a history that provides the conditions for collective action and the amelioration of solipsism – the necessary conditions for socialism, in other words. To put concepts under erasure is yet another gesture; indeed Derrida's oeuvre abounds in gesture. It is a bold gesture to dispense with experience; perhaps the boldest gesture of all to dispense with time. Whether gestures alone are enough to deliver you into the world of signs without truth, fault or origin is another matter. The gestures do, however, have considerable rhetorical force, being directed unequivocally against constraint in all its various manifestations. Derrida's liberationist credentials are clearly evident in his choice of adversaries: no structure, no system, no phenomenon is too large or too powerful to lie beyond Derrida's gestures of dissent. He wages a campaign of resistance which has a distinctly messianic ring to it, and while it can never promise to remove all the obstacles that block the path to complete release from authority – Derrida can give us only 'the dream of emancipation' from within the circle where the history of metaphysics confronts the history of the destruction of metaphysics – it can by gesture and metaphor build up a formidable rhetorical head of steam against the foundationalist establishment. 'Overhead the vaulted dome of the metaphysical heavens is cracking' graphically communicates to us what that head of steam is designed to precipitate: even if the image it conjures up belongs more to 'the dream of emancipation' than to the real, political, world.

Behind the rhetoric, the gestures, the strategies and the blind tactics lies a desire to render the creation of meaning value-free – beyond aesthetic or moral judgements of any kind. The deconstruction of metaphysics is the deconstruction of all those phenomena that prohibit this antifoundationalist dream from being realised. High on this list of phenomena is intentionality. 'There is no getting away from intentionality', John Searle claims,[46] in exemplary logocentrist fashion, a sentiment which can be fleshed out as 'there is no way of *meaning* getting away from intentionality'. In the deconstructionist scheme of things, however, *différance* insistently intrudes between intention and meaning, and if meaning cannot be present to intention then the logocentrist enterprise is in deep trouble. The intentionality issue has a particular resonance in the field of literary aesthetics. The role of authorial intention has been hotly debated from the days of New

Criticism and Wimsatt and Beardsley's 'intentionalist fallacy' argument onwards.[47] In a recent intervention into the intentionality debate, Steven Knapp and Walter Benn Michaels, in fiercely antitheoretical mode, declare that

> all theoretical arguments on the issue of authorial intention must at some point accept the premises of anti-intentionalist accounts of meaning. In debates about intention, the moment of imagining intentionless meaning constitutes the theoretical moment itself. From the standpoint of an argument against critical theory, then, the only important question about intention is whether there can in fact be intentionless meanings. If our argument against theory is to succeed, the answer to this question must be no.[48]

Knapp and Michaels are attacking logocentrist critical theory no less than its antilogocentrist counterpart (E. D. Hirsch's hermeneutics is a particular target), but their reference to 'intentionless meanings' has a particular appropriateness to the Derridean project. Intentionless meaning is indeed the ultimate objective of deconstruction, and intentionless in a far stricter sense than a theorist like Hirsch is arguing for. Hirsch simply wants the creation of meaning to extend past the author, the argument being that 'An author almost always means more than he is aware of meaning, since he cannot explicitly pay attention to all the aspects of his meaning.'[49] There are therefore intentionless meanings as far as the author is concerned, but they are not to be construed as free-floating in the desired deconstructionist manner – they belong instead to the reader. Hirsch carefully discriminates between the 'author's meaning' and the 'reader's meaning'.[50] There is an act of will on the part of both author and reader/interpreter which prevents meaning from getting away from intention entirely, and in the process delimits the range of possibilities that is open to meaning at any one point:

> But if a determinate work sequence does not in itself necessarily represent one, particular, self-identical, unchanging complex of meaning, then the determinacy of its verbal meaning must be accounted for by some other discriminating force which causes the meaning to be *this* instead of *that* or *that* or *that*, all of which it could be. That discriminating force must involve an act of will, since unless one particular complex of meaning is *willed* (no matter how 'rich' and 'various' it might be), there would be no distinction between what an author does mean by a word sequence and what he could mean by it. Determinacy of verbal meaning requires an act of will.

Intentionless in this context clearly does not mean indeterminate: *this* will always predominate over the claims of *that* or *that* or *that*. Extension of meaning-creation past the author does not mean extension into the uncharted, value-free realm of signs without truth, fault or origin: 'meaning', Hirsch insists, 'is an affair of consciousness.'[51] Determinacy, the key to logocentricity, continues to assert itself even when authorial intention is breached. 'Rich' and 'various' meaning may well be, but it is rich and various within boundaries and relative to *somebody's* intention. Author *and* reader are centres of power over meaning: both keep it safely within the bounds of presence.

With Derrida, however, *this* is *always* simultaneously *that* – and *that* and *that* and *that* without check (and even more complicatedly, as Llewelyn points out, 'both-this-and-that-and-neither-this-nor-that'[52]). The Knapp/Michaels critique of Hirsch reveals some fissures in the logocentrist position, but only over the degree to which authorial intention is considered to circumscribe textual meaning. For one side it circumscribes totally: 'Meaning is just another name for expressed intention';[53] for the other it does not: 'An author almost always means more than he is aware of meaning.' But neither party is embracing anything like radical linguistic indeterminacy on the Derridean model, where *this* and *that* become all but interchangeable at any given point. Between Knapp/Michaels and Hirsch, and their respective advocates,[54] lie matters of emphasis (even Hirsch allows an 'almost always' qualification regarding intentionless meaning); between them all, theorist and antitheorist alike, and Derrida, however, lies a gulf that gives the appearance of being unbridgeable. As Derrida uncompromisingly puts it, when it comes to modes of interpretation, 'I do not believe that today there is any question of *choosing*.'[55]

Meaning will always be narrowed down to a *this* by the logocentrist, who maintains a faith in the power and stability of presence that Derrida cannot share. When Derrida analyses the history of presence, he finds a series of what are to him increasingly desperate attempts to narrow down 'to a point of presence, a fixed origin':[56]

> the entire history of the concept of structure . . . must be thought of as a series of substitutions of center for center, as a linked chain of determinations of the center. Successively, and in a regulated fashion, the center receives different forms or names. The history of metaphysics, like the history of the West, is the history of these metaphors and metonymies. Its matrix . . . is the determination of being as *presence* in all senses of this word. It could be shown that all the names related to fundamentals, to principles, or to the center have always designated an invariable presence – *eidos, arche, telos, energeia, ouisa* (essence, existence, substance, subject) aletheia, transcendentality, consciousness, God, man, and so forth.[57]

We can easily add intentionality and determinacy to this list of fundamentals, and the extent of the gulf that separates Searle, Knapp,

Michaels, Hirsch *et al.*, from Derrida becomes all too obvious. Where the logocentrists see boundaries, Derrida sees metaphors and metonymies unsuccessfully trying to mask the radical instability of presence. Holding on to presence and the idea that meaning can be kept under control by intention amounts to a fear of the unknown, of the 'as yet unnamable which is proclaiming itself and which can do so, as is necessary whenever a birth is in the offing, only under the species of the nonspecies, in the formless, mute, infant, and terrifying form of monstrosity'.[58] Intentionless meanings to which neither author nor reader/interpreter can lay any claim certainly would be prime candidates for the 'monstrosity' label as far as most logocentrists are concerned. In the face of the 'as yet unnamable', aesthetic and moral judgement breaks down and active interpretation is sanctioned.

Knapp and Michaels may believe that 'whatever positions people think they hold on language, interpretation, and belief, in practice they are all pragmatists. They all think language is intentional'.[59] Derrida, however, can counter with *différance*, that eternal intrusion, as he sees it, between intention and meaning. In 'the movement of *différance* . . . the subject is constituted only in being divided from itself, in becoming space, in temporizing, in deferral.'[60] Constantly deferring the conjunction of signifier and signified, intention and meaning, *différance* is intrinsically antifoundational; in Spivak's words, 'a structure never quite there' that 'never produces presence as such'.[61] The 'fixed origins' and 'points of presence' on which logocentricity so crucially depends can never occur as long as *différance* is at loose within discourse: and where there are no fixed origins or points of presence, then aesthetic and moral judgements evaporate even as they are being made. *Différance* enables Derrida to be openly disdainful of the whole business of constructing judgements according to criteria of presence: 'the field called "literary"; you make of it what you like or what you can, it no longer concerns me, it has no law, especially scientific law.' 'What you can', when your judgements are dissolving all around you, does not seem like very much at all. This is the language of someone who believes he has gone beyond intentionality into the state of infinite play – 'the play of the world and of the innocence of becoming' – where any gestures towards teleology are simply futile. In this realm there is neither need, nor indeed much scope, for interpretation in the logocentrist style, since 'Nothing, neither among the elements nor within the system, is anywhere ever simply present or absent. There are only, everywhere, differences and traces of traces.'[62]

Where there are traces of traces going back in infinite regress, the pun comes into its own as an agent of *différance*. The pun, which has precisely the present/absent, 'never quite there' relationship to meaning that active interpretation seeks, resonates rather than responds – always suggesting something other than it is actually saying. For the deconstructionist the pun has that marvellous quality of being 'beyond good or evil'.[63] It is *différance* in operation, with its ontologically guaranteed incapability of taking on, or unambiguously expressing, centred meaning. The pun is a veritable treasury of intentionless meaning that deconstructs judgement as it goes, and it will be considered, along with the politics it entails, in more depth in Chapter 6.

Derrida's language points towards escape, while simultaneously acknowledging its plight of being entangled within the history of metaphysics: 'he is after all caught and held by the metaphysical enclosure even as he questions it', as Spivak notes.[64] Thus the desire for innocence of becoming, for 'beyonds', has continually to be balanced against the pressing need for the essential, systematic, theoretical unweaving that the deconstruction of metaphysics demands. Derrida sees himself as engaged in a 'simultaneously faithful and violent circulation between the inside and the outside of philosophy'.[65] This is consistent with his expressed intention to remain at 'the *limit* of philosophical discourse', and his promise regarding his 'strategy without finality',[66] that 'This is to be continued'. Nevertheless, for all the balancing, the 'beyonds', those areas of the unnameable, exert a considerable fascination on Derrida, lending his work on occasion a millenarian air. This can pose problems for commentators who wish to give us Derrida the rigorous deconstructor of Western philosophy. Thus Spivak can ask why the opening chapter to *Of Grammatology* is 'full of a slightly embarrassing messianic promise', and continue, bearing in mind Derrida's dislike of the idea of epistemological breaks,

> How reconcile ourselves with this break between the world of the past and the world of the future? It seems an empiricist betrayal of the structure of difference and postponement, and any deconstructive reading of Derrida will have to take this into account.[67]

What this future reading will have to take into account is Derrida's apocalyptic-sounding references to the 'exhaustion' of language, the 'death of the civilization of the book', the 'death of speech', and his erasure of history and knowledge.[68]

Even more messianic in tone is the 'Exergue' to *Of Grammatology*:

> The future can only be anticipated in the form of an absolute danger. It is that which breaks absolutely with constituted normality and can only be proclaimed, *presented*, as a sort of monstrosity. For that future world and for that within it which will have put into question the values of sign, word, and writing, for that which guides our future anterior, there is as yet no exergue.[69]

The desire for 'beyond' gets the better of Derrida at this point, and he sounds like someone on the very threshold of the millennium, but, frustratingly for him, not quite able to break through. All he can do is to 'designate the crevice through which the unnameable glimmer beyond the closure can be glimpsed'.[70] The prophetic mode, with its Nietzschean overtones of the revaluation of all values, is reproduced in 'Force and signification', and is right at the limits of philosophy: further than this one cannot go without leaving the discourse behind entirely. Some would argue that Derrida eventually *does* leave the discourse behind. René Major, commenting on *Glas*, complains that

> I would say that you make Knowledge and the Body (yours, mine) submit to a treatment which makes them cave in on themselves, coil themselves, box themselves into a cavity in which they grind themselves, fragment themselves, dislocate themselves. Caught in a '*dessein si funeste*' one does not emerge, if one ever does emerge, intact.[71]

Despite Major's scepticism at the effect of Derrida's liberationist tendencies, and Spivak's evident embarrassment at them, many other commentators have been drawn to this side of Derrida that offers a tantalising glimpse beyond closure. Robert Magliola, for example, embraces the messianic liberationism wholeheartedly in *Derrida on the Mend*, pushing deconstruction deep into the realms of both Eastern and Western religious mysticism in the process.[72] Mysticism, like deconstruction, ultimately lies beyond questions of judgement, and Magliola's cross-referencing between the two areas of discourse is interesting and imaginative. He develops some complex strategies to defend Derrida's antifoundationalism and rejection of the law of identity, but once again the question arises as to what the ideological implications of such an ostensibly anarchic method of critique are. Magliola-style deconstruction poses much the same kind of political problems noted with Derrida earlier. Mysticism is not, I intend to argue, the most satisfying of directions for an avowedly practico-political programme to take.

Magliola directly confronts that side of Derrida that Spivak prefers discreetly to bracket for the time being:

> If one assembles the apocalyptic passages in Derrida, the scenario is a sort of erased eschatology: mankind is on the flatland and overhead the vaulted dome of the metaphysical heavens is cracking; mankind is on *this side* of the opening, so his 'thought' of differance is 'blank' – the face that is open to view is the opening on the inside of the closure and is thus 'a necessarily indeterminate index' ... some reference to the current situation in astronomy, and so on, begs mention. ... Is Derrida's *la faille*, the fissure or crevice at the metaphysical closure, analogous to astronomy's own vaunted 'black hole', the black hole which because it opens on *this side* of

science's closure, is for the astronomer a 'necessarily indeterminate index'?[73]

The image of the black hole is perhaps just too apposite. It is the unnameable towards which Derrida is so inexorably drawn, the ultimate act of erasure where discourse will disappear, the break from constituted normality from which there really is no way back. Most of the time Derrida gives the impression of being someone marooned on the threshold of the metaphysically unnamable, still in thrall to the history of metaphysics that he has taken to the brink. Magliola, who wants him to take that next step into what is for philosophy the black hole of religious mysticism, regards this as evidence of a failure of vision on deconstruction's part:

> Perhaps one way of describing the poststructuralist quandary is to say that Derridean deconstruction can 'cross-out' (i.e., it can place even the best of conclusions *sous rature*), but it cannot 'cross-over', or better, 'cross back-and-forth' BETWEEN the comportments of presence and alterity.[74]

Such crossing back-and-forth is possible, Magliola argues, using the perspectives of Nagarjunist Buddhism and Christian differential mysticism. When deconstruction is exposed to these traditions then the longed-for exergue finally can be achieved, liberating deconstruction from the circle containing the history of metaphysics and the destruction of the history of metaphysics:

> Derrida wends/rends the off-way, the anguished off-rationalism of the natural man. It shall be my claim that there is a mystical off-rationalism, an off-rationalism which comports a security and liberation, and even enables – at will – a transaction between the differential and the logocentric.[75]

Mystical off-rationalism might be seen as a more effective form of erasure, one drawing on a tradition which has never been comprehended by the circle just mentioned and therefore carrying none of its complicating commitments.

Nagarjunist Buddhism is presented by Magliola as a large-scale exercise in *différance*:

> The juncture of 'our epoch' and Derrida's own sustained task, is 'meditation' cautious and concentrated, on what he has called the 'and/or' *between* 'and/or'. Nagarjuna, an Indian thinker who flourished in the second century after Christ and developed the Madhyamikan approach in Buddhism, tells us the following: 'In the Katyayanavavada-Sutra the Lord [Buddha], who had the right insight into both bhava [existing] and abhava

[non-existing], rejected both the extremes of 'is'. . . . . Nagarjuna's Madhyamika 'philosophy', as we shall see, teaches the 'and/or' which is *between* the 'and/or' of existence and non-existence, identity and non-identity, causality and non-causality.

The 'and/or' which is between 'and/or' is clearly not a state of presence. There is no centre to organise around here: like *mise en abyme* it will continue to disclose other versions of itself *between* itself, presumably down to infinity. This is the 'Middle Path' of Nagarjuna, which, Magliola holds, 'tracks the Derridean trace', and even goes 'beyond Derrida' in frequenting 'the unheard-of-thought'.[76] When we are confronted by 'the unheard-of-thought' we reach once again, as with Derrida's 'unnamable', a limit-point for philosophy, where neither cross-over nor cross-back-and-forth look achievable. The projected solution to the apparent stalemate is '*tathata* (thusness/suchness), the capability which is differentially between'. Pinning down what *tathata* *is*, however, and precisely *how* it allows one to conduct transactions between the differential and the logocentric as promised, proves to be extremely difficult. Very conveniently for the 'and/or' theorist, *tathata* 'is neither finite nor infinite, neither limited nor unlimited, neither conventionally between the former, nor conventionally between the latter: *tathata* is, somehow, off/finite and off-limit'. The 'somehow' is slightly worrying, since *tathata* is considered to be 'enabling'. Its use 'frees the differential mystic to shift to and fro between the logocentric and the differential according to what the situation-at-hand requires'.[77] Taking a cynical view one might hazard the opinion that *tathata* appears to have the handy status of A. N. Prior's 'tonk' logical operator: it is exactly what you need to make your theory work at any given point, taking on whatever commitment you choose to ask of it.[78] This looks more like anarchy than liberation, the prosecution of doodling and whimsy well out on the margins. (When Leitch remarks of the trace that it 'inhabits everything', but that, 'seemingly subatomic', it is 'generically intractable, unnatural, and untrackable', there is a similar sense of the theorist being allowed to make things too easy for himself.[79])

One reaches a state of acceptance under the influence of *tathata* (Magliola speaks of the differential mystic as being 'happy'), but that raises doubts again as to the direction of the practico-political programme in question. We seem to have slid imperceptibly from revolutionary sentiments to quietism to, finally, gnomic utterance:

> Beware of gnawing the ideogram of nothingness [devoidness]:
> Your teeth will crack. Swallow it whole, and you've a treasure
> Beyond the hope of Buddha and the Mind.

The east breeze fondles the horse's ears:
How sweet the smell of plum.[80]

Christian differential mysticism can take us no further than this towards understanding our role in the liberation of meaning. The exergue will have to rely on rhetoric to make its point that it has transcended metaphysics, and that is a poor basis for the deconstructionist brave new world of signs without truth, fault or origin. We are being offered nothing more substantial as yet than the dream of emancipation.

We began the chapter with 'extravagant metaphorical whimsy' and we seem to be ending with it too: *tathata* and the 'ideogram of nothingness' are well beyond the concerns of serious, truth-seeking discourse. This is not to deny that Derrida has succeeded in shaking logocentrist metaphysics. Structuralism is most definitely shaken after its encounter with Derrida. Emotive though it can be to make accusations of totalitarianism, ultrastructuralism does seem to force meaning to fit preconceived schemes of predeterminist intent. Creativity *is* inhibited, the human factor *is* marginalised by such an approach. Derrida's objections are powerful and succeed in capturing a certain moment in critical history with great accuracy. A certain critical pretension is dismantled, probably beyond recall, with great skill. It is when we move from the objections (the negative critique) to the programme for subsequent critical action that the doubts begin to crowd in. The more we pursue that programme the more we seem to be in danger of exiling ourselves from participation in the discourse of political power: with the qualification, of course, that those who never felt they *were* participants in such a discourse (women, ethnic minorities, etc.) will see the programme in an altogether more positive light. And if metaphor is never innocent, then what are we to make of deconstruction as 'the dream of emancipation'? That it can only isolate us from each other and any possibility of collective action? That it can never have any practical effect in the only, political, world where emancipation would actually *mean* anything? Again, this way lies solipsism and silence, and those are highly problematical states, politically speaking. The force of the rhetoric can be considerable – Derrida constructs a powerful discourse of liberation out of his various 'beyonds' – but it dissipates when we cross over into the cloudy realms of mysticism, and Derrida provides the conditions for that transfer with his messianic promises and apocalyptic-sounding pronouncements.

So metaphysics shakes but does not fall. Nevertheless meaning is in *some* sense unshackled, logocentricity in *some* sense called into question, foundationalism in *some* sense problematised. Fissures have been revealed in our system of values which allow for the possibility of a very different kind of critical practice than hitherto, for all that the politics involved can seem questionable and on occasion perhaps even naive. It is time to see how Derrida's own critical practice (I will elaborate on my use of this term shortly) responds to such challenges.

·5· 'NEITHER COMMENT, NOR UNDERSCORE . . ., NOR EXTRACT'

Derrida as Critic

If one wanted a 'mission statement' for deconstructive criticism, one could do worse than turn to the pages of 'Living on:Border lines':

> Shall we leave this text on its own power? We should neither comment, nor underscore a single word, nor extract anything, nor draw a lesson from it. One should not, one should refrain from – such would be the law of the text that gives itself, gives itself up, to be read [*qui se donne à lire*]. Yet it also calls for a violence that matches it in intensity, a violence different in intention, perhaps, but one that exerts itself against the first law only in order to attempt a commitment, an involvement, with that law. To move, yieldingly, towards it, to draw close to it fictively. The violent truth of 'reading'.[1]

Derrida has a specific text in mind at this point, *L'arrêt de mort* by Maurice Blanchot, but the sentiments expressed have a general relevance to deconstructive critical practice. No commenting, no underscoring, no extracting, no drawing of lessons equals no interpretation, in the *explication de texte* sense. On the active side, the deconstructionist critic is encouraged towards violence (I shall return to the problem of Derrida's imagery at a later point), and the techniques of fiction writing: in other words, shaking of structure and resonance are to be our consolation for the loss of *explication de texte*. This is an anti-aesthetic that directs us away from evaluation, and I will explore Derrida's own critical practice to see whether its non-interpretative but violent stance really does succeed in problematising logocentricity and rational structures of thought. The main texts under discussion will be 'Living on:Border lines' and *The Truth in Painting*, with some closing remarks about *The Post Card*.

I call it 'critical practice', although it is likely that Derrida would reject such a description, on the grounds that deconstruction involves breaching the conditions required for criticism as we traditionally conceive of that activity. Nevertheless, there are at least family resemblances to criticism to be noted. Magliola refers to Derrida's 'off-rationalism', and we might extend this idea to suggest that what is being called for in the mission statement is an 'off-criticism'. The commentator is being asked to stand at an oblique angle to the text, an angle where one engages less with the text than with its 'law'. The sense of being off-centre from the text, of never as such fully entering into the critical act, is characteristic of Derrida's writing on the arts, his off-critical practice as we might better term it. It is never quite there with regard to the text it is ostensibly discussing, and Derrida is a past-master at the art of deferring the moment of criticism, the moment of commenting, underscoring, extracting and lesson-drawing. Derrida situates himself 'Between the outside and the inside, between the external and the internal edge-line, the framer and the framed, the figure and the ground, form and content, signifier and signified, and *so on* for any two-faced opposition',[2] where *explication de texte*, the coincidence of critical interpreter and textual meaning, can never take place. In the spirit of his not-quite-philosophy we are now confronted by a not-quite-criticism: 'I have amassed references (to "things," and "texts" they would say) but in truth what I have just written is without reference. Above all, to myself or to texts that I have signed in another language.'[3] Text and critical act will be kept at arm's length by means of a writing 'without reference', deliberately refraining – the self-denying ordinance of deconstructive criticism – from comment, etc.

Derrida's off-criticism is consistently oblique in approach. He may start with a text – Shelley's *The Triumph of Life* in 'Living on:Border lines', for example – but soon he is voicing what is to traditional criticism very peripheral concerns:

> I wish to raise the question of the *bord*, the edge, the border, and the *bord de mer*, the shore. . . . If we are to approach a text, it must have an edge. The question of the text, as it has been elaborated and transformed in the last dozen or so years, has not merely 'touched' 'shore', *le bord* (scandalously tampering, changing, as in Mallarmé's declaration, '*On a touché au vers*'), all those boundaries that form the running border of what used to be called a text, of what we once thought this word could identify, i.e., the supposed end and beginning of a work, the unity of a corpus, the title, the margins, the signatures, the referential realm outside the frame, and so forth.[4]

Textual analysis is bracketed before it has been given a chance to begin, and we are considering instead the question of textuality: but even that point of reference is dissolving around us, as the boundaries of textuality are being put into question. Both critical act and actual text are fast receding. 'I write four times here, around painting', Derrida informs us in *The Truth in Painting*,[5] and his off-criticism displays a remarkable talent for delaying engagement with the centre of any discourse ('*The Triumph of Life*, which it is not my intention to discuss here', signals just how far off the criticism will be in this instance[6]). 'I continually ask what *must* be done or not be done (for example in reading, writing, teaching, and so on)', we are warned, 'to find out what the place of that which takes place, is constructed upon (for example the university, the boundaries between departments, between one discourse and another, and so on).'[7] Boundaries, margins, frames, signatures, our attention is systematically displaced from the text in its narrative guise. The violence Derrida repeatedly speaks of lies in that act of displacement, whereby we are wrenched away from contemplation of the text and its particular narrative sequence.

In its avoidance and problematisation of value judgement, Derrida's off-criticism might be viewed as an exercise in frustrating the reader. Whenever *explication de texte* seems to be looming on the horizon, Derrida will invoke his self-denying ordinance:

> I register, I record this remark on the shore of what is called the unfinishedness of *The Triumph of Life*, at the moment when Shelley is drowned. I do so without claiming to understand what people mean in this case by 'unfinished,' or to decide anything. I do so only to recall the immense procedures that should come before a statement about whether a work is finished or unfinished. Where are we to situate the event of Shelley's drowning? And who will decide the answer to this question? Who will form a narrative of these borderline events (*événements de bord*). At whose demand?[8]

J. Hillis Miller has remarked of *The Triumph of Life* that it 'contains within itself, jostling irreconcilably with one another, both logocentric metaphysics and nihilism. It is no accident that critics have disagreed about it'.[9] Off-criticism, however, never brings us to the stage of fully entering into such a debate – 'not my intention to discuss here'. Critical questions in Derrida are rarely more than 'preliminaries to the posing of such a question'.[10] Even the 'immense procedures' that are placed in our path by Derrida, to delay us from reaching the point where the debate could *begin*, hardly seem to come within the sphere of literary enquiry. It could be argued that questions like 'Where are we to situate the event of Shelley's drowning?' come perilously close to 'How many children had Lady Macbeth?' territory. Before we can contemplate textual analysis we must be in possession of a narrative of borderline events, but the action of *différance* precludes such a possibility. Not for the last time in Derrida, a barrage of questions drives us down a blind alley from which there seems to be no obvious way back. The reader may well feel that to be caught up in the toils of blind tactics in this way is to be reduced to the plight of I. A. Richards' philosopher in the search for universals: 'A blind man in a dark room chasing a black cat which is not there.'[11] Off-criticism is, and deliberately and provocatively so, an exercise in that kind of frustration.

Derrida is well aware of his considerable potential for frustration, and he actively cultivates it: 'This telegraphic band produces an untranslatable supplement', he claims of 'Border lines'; adding, in partial self-defence, 'whether I wish it or not' – Derrida being no more the master of *différance* than anyone else is presumed to be. 'Living on:Border lines' sets out quite systematically to frustrate the reader's expectations of what critique should be by superimposing texts on one another, in defiance of convention and without regard to the supposed integrity of the individual texts and authors in question:

> This operation would never be considered legitimate on the part of a teacher, who must give his references and tell what he's talking about, giving it its recognizable title. You can't give a course on Shelley without ever mentioning him, pretending to deal with Blanchot, and more than a few others. And your transitions have to be readable, that is, in accordance with criteria of readability very firmly established, and long since.[12]

'Living on:Border lines' cuts loose from all such considerations of legitimacy, and its parallel texts certainly represent a challenge to readability. Footnotes have always had a *différance*-like ability to interrupt the flow of textual argument, but a footnote which is co-extensive with its text turns interruption into an art form. Each text is a constant source of resonance to the other, thereby calling its autonomy into question. Strategic footnoting of this nature works to disrupt logocentric reading of Derrida, pushing us even further back from the texts initially held up for inspection into the hinterland of preliminaries.

Keeping the reader at the level of preliminaries is a major objective of these texts. From the beginning, Derrida's argument gives the impression of constantly folding back on itself, of disclosing problems within problems within problems in a monotonous seriality:

> But who's talking about living? In other words on living? This time, 'in other words' does not put the same thing into other words, does not clarify an ambiguous expression, does not function like an 'i.e.' It amasses the powers of indecision and adds to the foregoing utterance its capacity

for skidding. Under the pretext of commenting upon a terribly indeterminate, shifting statement, a statement difficult to pin down [*arrêter*], it gives a reading or version of it that is all the less satisfactory, controllable, unequivocal, for being more 'powerful' than what it comments upon or translates. The supposed 'commentary' of the 'i.e.' or 'in other words' has furnished only a textual supplement that calls in turn for an overdetermining 'in other words', and so on and so forth.[13]

Each attempt to set up a question for consideration merely generates a previous question to be addressed (Derrida refers to his work in general as 'the displacement of a *question*'[14]), and if we are skidding anywhere in this passage we are skidding backwards. The act of criticism, the 'i.e.' or 'in other words' that would need no further explanation, recedes into the distance. Any word, given its infinite network of traces, can hold up our progress almost indefinitely: 'Forever unable to saturate a context, what reading will ever master the "on" of living on? For we have not exhausted its ambiguity: each of the meanings we have listed above can be divided further.'[15] The 'and/or' between 'and/or' relentlessly will defer the conditions required for the practice of value judgement.

A similar movement of doubling back and folding in on itself can be seen in the opening stages of the argument in *The Truth in Painting*:

Someone, not me, comes and says the words: 'I am interested in the idiom in painting'. ... Does he mean that he is interested in the idiom 'in painting', in the idiom itself, for its own sake, 'in painting' (an expression that is in itself strongly idiomatic; but what is an idiom?)? That he is interested in the idiomatic expression itself, in the words 'in painting'? Interested in words in painting or in the words 'in painting'? Or in the words 'in painting'? That he is interested in the idiom in painting, i.e., in what pertains to the idiom, the idiomatic trait or style (that which is singular, proper, inimitable) in the domain of painting, or else – another possible translation – in the singularity or the irreducible specificity of pictorial art, of that 'language', which painting is supposed to be, etc.? Which makes, if you count them well, at least four hypotheses; but each one divides again, is grafted and contaminated by all the others; and you would never be finished translating them. Nor will I.[16]

Confronted by strategic manoeuvring of this sort (wending/rending of the off-way with a vengeance) we can begin to understand the sense of bewilderment that Derrida can induce in his audience on occasion: 'I asked you where to begin, and you have led me into a labyrinth', being one typically despairing response from an interviewer.[17] As Derrida comments shortly after the passage above, in what to many of his readers will be the bleakest of phrases, 'Performative supplementarity is thus open to infinity':[18] another case of 'you can never step into the same river once'. Almost any phrase in the language (*any* language) could begin to take on hitherto undreamt of depths of complexity under such questioning, whose persistency suggests a particularly militant form of psychoanalysis (Derrida's 'violence' expressing itself yet again). Presence is systematically undermined in the relentless displacement of the question, and it is interesting to note in this context that we are dealing with a writing which divides itself off from the possibility of spoken utterance. Those aggressively handled diacritical marks demand *reading*, refusing to take on the character of second-order speech. They manifestly do not 'depend upon my pure and free spontaneity' of thought or utterance, as Derrida argues is the case with the phonocentric signifier in Saussure.

We are confronted by writing with a life of its own, but which is constantly collapsing in on itself and the possibility of stable meaning. It is thoroughly disorienting to the reader, and it reveals no more cheering a prospect than the abyss with its 'interminable chain of differences'.[19]

Restricting readers to the level of preliminaries, and keeping them in a state of perpetual frustration as to the moment when engagement with the text will begin, might be seen as acts of power. In other words, there may be a disguised political agenda at work in Derrida's off-criticism. Derrida denies possessing such power or intent – 'And if you were to bide your time awhile here in these pages, you would discover that I cannot dominate the situation'[20] – but one wonders just how seriously to take such a disclaimer from such a consummate master of tactics and strategy. In one of his articles on deconstruction, David Wood quotes 'a sceptical friend' of his as follows:

> everything I read of Derrida's has one consequence – the production of an invulnerable discourse – a kind of postmodern omnipotence. It is said that deconstruction is not a position. So it cannot be attacked! It is said that deconstruction 'is' not, at all, that it is not an 'is'. All the better, for that makes 'it' completely immune to criticism.[21]

There is more than a grain of truth to this: performative supplementarity, well reinforced by periodic bouts of unanswered and unanswerable questions, at the very least defers criticism of one's position. Derrida is somehow never quite there to be attacked, his guerrilla instincts have always already taken him somewhere else inside the discourse ('Before any other preliminary, I jump suddenly to the middle of the text', he notes disarmingly in an aside in an article on Heidegger[22]), most likely to inspect something or other puzzlingly irrelevant to the art of textual enquiry, as traditionally practised: at once 'cagey and oblique', as Culler has put it.[23] The novelist Nicholson Baker has been caricatured as the sort of person who would probably spend his time at a party 'measuring the depth of the sherry glasses or numbering the stages of puff-pastry disintegration in the vol-au-vents',[24] and Derrida's obsession with frames, borders, margins, signatures, etc., can often seem to the bemused reader similarly tangential to the business at hand. Wood asks, 'what is it for the critical reader to *follow* Derrida?', and the answer might be that it is to put oneself in the service of a performative supplementarity that stands to traditional academic textual analysis much as puff-pastry disintegration does to party-going. This is criticism so far off that it can hardly be countered: and that is a position of power for the theorist to be in. Derrida can move freely around in your discourse creating havoc as he goes, you cannot in his, except according to his rules. Just as it is notoriously difficult to turn the resources of philosophy against not-quite-philosophy, so it is to turn those of criticism against not-quite-criticism. There *is* a political agenda at work here. The immense procedures that Derrida puts in our way to delay the onset of the critical act and engagement with the texts are not neutral, and perhaps, as David Wood has suggested, 'the question of its [deconstruction's] own power, vulnerability, desire, might prove to be its Achilles' heel'.[25] Derrida reveals himself to be no mean manipulator of reader response, and he can be called to account for that, given his stated intention to free us all from the manipulations of ultrastructuralism. The antagonist of closure is capable of producing some very closed texts himself in terms of debate. And all those references to violence that punctuate his theory and off-criticism hardly bespeak neutrality. It may only be *linguistic* violence that is being called for, but the image is not innocent and indicates that as far as Derrida is concerned a serious power struggle is being waged.

Derrida has warned us that deconstructive writing involves 'a reduction of the [phenomenological] reduction' that 'opens the way to an infinite discursiveness',[26] and the systematically pursued divisions of the opening pages of both 'Living on:Border lines' and *The Truth in Painting* seem to be enacting that discursiveness. There is rigour here – the single-minded reduction of words and phrases to reveal the multitude of aporias hidden beneath the apparently unproblematical surface – but it is not the kind of rigour normally associated with critical thought. What is happening in these two texts can make 'Force and signification', with its determinate objective and analytical approach to the object of enquiry, look like very traditional philosophical critique indeed. Something far more radical is being offered in the off-criticism, where the entire process of value judgement, the very heart of logocentric critique, is being kept in a state of suspension, never permitted to confront its textual object. The rapid-fire, tonally violent reiteration of the division testifies to the strength of Derrida's desire to prevent the conditions for critique from ever being allowed to form: the desire to aspire instead to a certain kind of unreadability which will maintain the invulnerability of the deconstructionist enterprise:

> the double invagination of this narrative body in deconstruction overruns and exceeds not merely the oppositions of values that make the rules and form the law in all the schools of reading, ancient and modern, before and after Freud; it overruns a delimitation of the fantasy, a delimitation in the name of which some would here abandon, for example, the mad hypothesis to 'my' fantasy-projection, to that of the one who says 'I' here, the narrator, the narrators, or me, who am telling you all this here. The unreadability will have taken place, as unreadable, will have become readable (*se sera donné à lire*) right here, as unreadable, from the very bottom of the crypt in which it remains. . . . From here on it's up to you to think of what will have taken place, to work out both the conditions for its possibility and its consequences. As for me, I must break off here, interrupt all this, close the parenthesis, and let the movement continue without me.[27]

Despite the disclaimers of a power relationship – 'From here on it's up to you' – it is Derrida who has led us into this labyrinth of unreadability by means of a ruthlessly prosecuted active interpretation. 'It's up to you' may sound democratic, but it has sinister implications nevertheless. The critical reader following Derrida is abandoned, beyond aesthetics, where the concepts 'you' and 'I' appear to have little purchase, and the textual movement that continues is a movement that endlessly defers the working out of any conditions for judgement. It is rather like being in the position of existential choice minus the choice: solipsism and silence seem to have re-entrenched themselves in individual existence. Derrida has succeeded admirably in demonstrating the power that deconstruction can give one over the reader.

The forced superimposition of the two texts in 'Living on:Border lines' means that we can never be sure where Derrida's comments are being addressed. At any one point in an off-critical exercise like this, the referent of the argument can always be located in the other text – or anywhere at all, come to that:

> One text reads another. How can a reading be settled on (*arrêter*)? For example, we can say that *The Triumph of Life* reads *L'arrêt de mort*, among other things. And, among other things, vice versa. Each 'text' is a machine with multiple reading heads for other texts. To read *L'arrêt de mort*, starting with the title in its endless mobility, I can always be guided by another text.[28]

If a reading cannot be settled on, then no 'reading' by Derrida can be called into question, of course, and the 'vice versa' neatly problematises critical value judgement because it would never be clear where the judgement was meant to apply (*that* or *that* or *that?*). In Derrida's terms of reference it would be free floating, a judgement whose home was forever elsewhere in another text: 'half of it always "not there" and the other half always "not that"' in Spivak's formulation. In truth, Derrida does not have a great deal to say about *The Triumph of Life* ('not my intention to discuss here'), and *L'arrêt de mort* is certainly much more to the fore; but the largely absent *Triumph* appears often enough, is endlessly and subversively available to be called on if need be, to keep the *L'arrêt de mort* commentary under erasure. Textual integrity disappears in the face of the off-critic's practised ability always to 'be guided by another text'. Textuality rapidly becomes the most amorphous of phenomena when placed under such duress ('An edgeless textuality destructures and reinscribes the metaphysical motif of the absolute referent, of the thing itself in its final instance', as Derrida puts it[29]), and this is precisely what the cult of active interpretation, and the post-aesthetic world of signs without truth, fault or origin require it to be. It is not just the superimposition of Shelley and Blanchot that we have to contend with either, but the superimposition of 'Living on' and 'Border lines'. Here too it is a case of half of it always not there and the other half always not that. The complex pattern of resounding between Shelley and Blanchot is further complicated by its context, the structurally divided, but themselves resounding, pages of 'Living on:Border lines'. The strong signifier is at its most elusive under such circumstances, Derrida at his most tactically acute.

True to his promise, Derrida does move towards the narrative of *L'arrêt de mort*: indeed he quotes from it at considerable length on several occasions as if to preserve the text from the intrusion of the critic as much as possible. Also true to his promise, the closer he comes to the text the more he leaves it on its own power – 'In the interval between the first occurrence, event, coming of the "Come" in the story and the first quotation of it, an interval that I'll leave you to read, that I'll let you read', being the model of non-commenting critical practice – until finally Blanchot himself is allowed to take over, and 'Living on' ends with several pages of *L'arrêt de mort*. It seems appropriate that a text that set out to demonstrate the almost insuperable difficulties of entering into the critical act should conclude in the pre-critical state of the bare presentation of the fictional narrative. It is as if we have regressed over the course of 'Living on:Border lines' even further away from the possibility of *explication de texte*. I say 'Living on' only at this point because 'Border lines' survives, living on past the death of its parallel text as a ghostly kind of echo. But that is to argue that quotation is not *really* part of a text, which, apart from its unwelcome implications for logocentric critical practice, is to make Derrida's point for him about the effect of *différance* on the sign – half of it always not there, the other half always not that. Whatever else we might think of 'Living on:Border lines', we have to acknowledge it as a highly successful enactment of Derrida's linguistic theories and his desire for a 'truth beyond truth . . . the supplement of truthless truth'.[30]

Such a desire clearly motivates Derrida in *The Truth in Painting*, a similarly oblique exercise in off-criticism. It is possible to make this book sound quite undisturbing. It is a book about the nature of painting, about aesthetic theory (Kant, Hegel and Heidegger in particular), about painters and paintings (Adami's *Studies for a Drawing after 'Glas'*, Titus-Carmel's series *The Pocket Size Tlingit Coffin*, Van Gogh's *Old Shoes with Laces*). It reiterates some of the concerns of 'Force and signification', as when it confronts traditional philosophical aesthetics:

> If, therefore, one were to broach lessons on art or aesthetics by a question of this type ('What is art?' 'What is the origin of art or of works of art?' 'What is the meaning of art?' 'What does art mean?' etc.), the form of the question would already provide an answer . . . the philosophical encloses art in its circle but its discourse on art is at once, by the same token, caught in a circle.[31]

This is the anti-ultrastructuralist argument revisited – orients research, fixes results – and it can be a powerful one in its anti-authoritarian intent. The practico-political side of the exercise is stressed too: 'It is because deconstruction interferes with solid structures, "material" institutions, and not only with discourses or signifying representations, that it is always distinct from an analysis or a "critique".'[32] This is Derrida at his most approachable, but it would be to misrepresent the strangeness and subversiveness of this text to deal with it on this level only. The opening pages, with their alarming divisions of words and phrases, their batteries of disorienting questions, indicate that we are not going to be offered standard aesthetic critique in what follows, and once again there is to be much superimposition of text on text to keep us permanently off-balance. This is to be a journey '*around* painting', and 'around' proves to be a prime source of extravagant metaphorical whimsy and sophistical doodling for Derrida.

For example, there is the matter of the number of drawings in *The Pocket Size Tlingit Coffin* series. The question of the border, the edge of the work, again exercises Derrida, as it does throughout *The Truth in Painting*. In this case Titus-Carmel's series consists of 127 dated drawings of the same object, the coffin. The number 127 is thus taken to be the work's boundary with the world. Derrida is curious about why the artist chose this limit: 'Must we take into account the dates or the number of articles? . . . What will this number – 127 – have satisfied to stop desire from going further? Why not one coffin more?'[33] We are still within the bounds of traditional criticism at the point of asking this question. Intentionalists would know precisely where to take it from here, into author's meaning, etc., but Derrida immediately leaps well beyond aesthetics with his off-critical speculations (of which I list only a small sample):

> 127: 12+7. 12: 3×4 (hours, months, seasons, anything at all, you choose), 7 = 3+4 or again 1+2+3+4 = 10 and 1+2+7 = 10. Pythagorean tetractys (I talked about it too much in *Dissemination*. I let it drop, not without recalling that the proportions of the coffin no. 0 (–1 or +1) correspond to the golden number (10×6.2×2.4cm.) and therefore to the same register of arithmopoetic speculations).

> This morning on my table, I've a little 'electronic pocketable calculator' (model Ur-300, serial no. 27932) next to the typewriter. I compute, with a somewhat distracted hand.

> And here it is: 127 is a *prime number*.

> That's not all, but it's very important. A prime number, by definition, is *only divisible by itself.* By no other whole number. The coffin, in its generic unicity, is thus entire, intact, invulnerable, divisible by nothing other than itself. Nothing will affect it again from outside. . . . The prime number of the coffin thus resists all analysis, that's what it's for, it doesn't resolve itself into fantasies, it does not divide itself. It does not split.[34]

Numerology is a perfectly respectable field of enquiry for the critic to engage in (Renaissance literature, for example, is rich in such significance), but it is rarely handled in such an anarchic way as this. The sequence suggests nothing so much as numerological *punning* in its associative movement, although it should also be pointed out that this is very serious, one might even say violent, free-play. It is as if Derrida were locating *différance* in numbers, a radical act when we consider the crucial role allotted to mathematics by the rationalist tradition in Western philosophy, and subjecting numbers to the same 'violent truth of reading' as words must suffer under a deconstructionist regime. Even though something like an 'i.e.' or 'in other words' comes at the end of the sequence, it could hardly be said to *follow* from the steps of that sequence. It is in a very real sense without reference to what went before, given the violent wrenching, dislocation and displacement of the material that has just taken place. And all of this effort, of which I have included only a fragment, is being expended *before* we reach the drawings themselves. It is another example of the 'immense procedures' ploy to keep *explication de texte* at bay.

The obliqueness of approach we note here can also be seen in Derrida's treatment of Van Gogh's *Old Shoes with Laces*. Initiating the act of engagement causes Derrida the usual problems:

> We should return to the thing itself. And I don't know yet where to start from. I don't know if it must be talked or written about. Producing a discourse/making a speech on the subject of it, on the subject of anything at all, is perhaps the first thing to avoid.[35]

A discourse of a sort is produced, although almost by reflex what transpires on such occasions is a series of questions:

> Here it is. Questions about awkward gait (limping or shifty?), questions of this type: 'Where to put one's feet?' 'How is it going to work (*marcher*)?' 'And what if it doesn't work?' 'What happens when it doesn't work (or when you hang up your shoes or miss them with your feet)?' 'When – and for what reason – it stops working?' 'Who is walking?' 'With whom?' 'With what?' 'On whose feet?' 'Who is pulling whose leg?' (*qui fait marcher qui?*)' 'Who is making what go?' (*qui fait marcher quoi?*) 'What is making whom or what work?' etc., all these idiomatic figures of the question seem to me, right here, to be necessary.[36]

To Derrida these questions are a necessary development of the questions with which he began the essay on Van Gogh – 'What of shoes? What, shoes? Whose are the shoes? What are they made of? And even, who are they?'[37] – but again, to most critics this will seem like a gratuitous elaboration of the peripheral. We continue to skirt *around* painting, generating 'immense procedures' that leave us far short of the conditions for the critical act. Thus in the closing stages of the Van Gogh piece, Derrida can have the following exchange with himself:

> But did this spectral analysis concern the real shoes or the shoes in the painting? – The ones that remain, according to the restance of which I speak. The spectral character of the analysis defies the distinction between the real shoes and the shoes in painting.[38]

It is as if we have lost the original object of enquiry on the way, and are left with nothing but that 'edgeless textuality' referred to earlier. With the object of enquiry in suspension, we reach point zero for criticism.

Recurrent formal patterns emerge from Derrida's off-criticism in 'Living on:Border lines' and *The Truth in Painting*: the clusters of momentum-destroying, self-referential questions (especially in the text's early stages); the concentration on peripheral textual details, such as signatures, frames, borders, etc.; the superimposing of works on works such that we are never quite sure of where the argument's referent lies; the chains of associative reasoning that ceaselessly and relentlessly alter the focus of the argument; the 'immense procedures' constantly being erected between the critic and the text; the periodic disclaimers of authority or control on Derrida's part. The objective is to defer *explication de texte*, permanently if possible, and value judgement is studiously avoided by Derrida, its necessary conditions continually problematised. The end result is a discourse displaying a strong internal desire for invulnerability, and it is no accident that this is what Derrida's off-criticism so often finds, and most prizes, in the texts it chooses to supplement. *L'arrêt de mort*'s 'unreadability', the resistance to analysis of *The Pocket Size Tlingit Coffin*'s prime number, the edgeless textuality of the Adami and the Van Gogh works, in each case analysis apparently is confounded.

In many ways Derrida is at his most radical in his off-criticism, and also at his most questionable. Invulnerable discourses have an air of authoritarianism about them in the way that they inhibit dissenting voices, and raise grave doubts about the political implications of their tendency to reduce their audiences to solipsism and silence. These are not desirable attributes to socialism. Deconstruction interferes rather than analyses or critiques, Derrida claims, but even interference proves to have its limits:

> As for painting, any discourse on it, beside it or above, always strikes me as silly, both didactic and incantatory, programed, worked by the compulsion of mastery, be it poetical or philosophical, always, and the more so when it is pertinent, in the position of chitchat, unequal and unproductive in the sight of what, at a stroke (*d'un trait*), does without or goes beyond the language, remaining heterogeneous to it or denying it any overview.[39]

The tone here is dismissive, almost imperious in the way that it invites us to withdraw from interpretative discourse. It is another one of Derrida's characteristically sweeping rhetorical gestures, with yet another 'beyond' (Derrida seems to have an endless stock of them to hand) being wheeled in to deflect any criticism of his position that may be offered. We might detect more than a hint of the 'compulsion of mastery' that Derrida affects to despise on display in this 'discourse on discourse on painting'. The invulnerability tactic has a distinctly political edge. It is worth repeating that, for a theorist, invulnerability equals power over others.

Wood has argued that 'the continuing power of deconstruction' rests in large part on its ability 'to excite, to allure to transgression, to open up texts to previously unheard of readings, to raise questions where none had appeared before, and to preserve the space of questioning where others (such as Heidegger and Levinas) have opened it up';[40] but while the off-criticism of Derrida raises its fair share of questions, it is more arguable whether it always preserves the space of questioning in the democratic manner implied by Wood. Derrida can be very manipulative in protecting his position of invulnerability, and we can often note a contrary movement in his off-critical writings, which shows its power in the way that it prevents the critical reader from reaching the stage of transgression, reading or questioning. It is not so much a case of opening up texts to us, as of leading us in circles:

> I give up. Discouragement. I'll never get to the end of it, I'll never be quits, I'll have to start again after treating as residues, more than once, all the words I've just used, I shall have to use a lot of them, consume them, gnaw them to the bone or wear them threadbare, put them back into perspective, turn them round in all directions through a series of deviations, variations, modulations, anamorphoses. And then stop at a given moment . . . in an apparently arbitrary fashion . . .[41]

This is deconstruction as eternal recurrence, invulnerability at the price of exile from discourse. It is another rhetorical gesture on Derrida's part because he never will give up – 'This is to be continued' – but it signals a Nietzschean sense of nihilism at the centre of his project, which the off-criticism has a particular talent for foregrounding. Nihilism is, of course, in the eye of the beholder. To those who have never felt included in discourses of power, exile and relative political powerlessness are hardly states to be feared. Radical feminism can therefore regard any game-playing with logocentricity, which, given patriarchy's stranglehold on most discourses, effectively means *phallogocentricity*, with approval. Placing under erasure that which has never taken your wishes into account, and which views you as the necessarily inferior side of a loaded binary opposition into the bargain, must be a very satisfying manoeuvre to perform. The off-critical refusal to play the value-judgement game takes on a whole new political dimension under such circumstances. That would be the positive reading of deconstruction's meaning for feminism. Could it not also be said, however, that deconstruction amounts to a moving of the goalposts as far as feminism is concerned? Its message might be put as follows: 'do not bother to seek for power because power is illusory.' An entire historical campaign to combat *exclusion* from significant discourses, the critical included, is thereby rendered problematical. Just when you think you are on the verge of righting a historical wrong, males do not so much shift the goalposts as abolish them altogether. Off-criticism does not, as such, show how discourses have been used and abused for political purposes, surely one of the primary goals of feminism no less than of socialism. There are times when commenting, underscoring, extracting or drawing of lessons – all of them activities that socialist aesthetics in its various guises has turned to political account – are necessary processes to show how texts might be re-read to very different effect. 'Reading against the grain' has been notably successful in just this regard, subjecting texts to critical interrogation in order to bring to light their hidden ideological assumptions.[42]

The aesthetic world of signs is an easier target for Derrida than its philosophical counterpart, because aesthetic artefacts trade heavily on ambiguity in a way that traditional philosophy has always chosen not to. Derrida does not play the critical game – no commenting, underscoring, extracting or drawing of lessons to be found in his off-criticism – but this can seem less of an act of violence against its objects than can his refusal to play the philosophical game, given that the texts at the end of the respective lines are doing very different things and looking for very different responses. There is a certain logic to constructing an off-critical discourse which seeks to cultivate the ambiguity of the discourse of aesthetic artefacts in its own supplemental way, paying tribute to art's 'making strange' qualities rather than trying to demystify them. Perhaps that latter discourse has *always* been closer to the world of signs without truth, fault or origin than metaphysics ever could be, has always had a vested interest in a slippage that problematised foundationalism in its harder-edged forms. Off-criticism celebrates that slippage – the strong signifier in action – and it may well be that it is the condition to which all of Derrida's researches tend: in which case claims might be made for *The Post Card* as the ultimate refinement of the process.

It may seem strange to introduce *The Post Card* into a discussion of Derrida's off-critical writings, but it is, amongst many other things, a work of aesthetic enquiry. On the basis of the medieval illustration of Plato and Socrates, reproduced as a Bodleian Library postcard, Derrida is able to engage in some dazzlingly inventive 'performative supplement-arity' about the relations between those two figures and their respective roles in the history of Western metaphysics. Speculations on the postcard, which shows Socrates acting as Plato's scribe in a curious piece of role-reversal, are refracted through a series of postcards from Derrida to various correspondents, enabling him, as Norris puts it, 'to keep philosophical issues in play, but also to prevent them from settling down into a fixed agenda for debate'.[43] Derrida can superimpose the personal on the philosophical, and vice versa, in a way that blurs the boundaries of each in the now characteristic half-not-there/half-not-that style:

I have not yet recovered from this revelatory catastrophe: Plato behind

Socrates. Behind he has always been, as it is thought, but not like that. Me, I always knew it, and they did too, those two I mean. What a couple. Socrates turns his *back* to Plato, who has made him write whatever he wanted, while pretending to receive it from him. This reproduction is sold here as a *post card*, you have noticed, with *greetings* and *address*, Socrates writing, do you realize, and on a postcard. . . . I wanted to address it to you right away, like a piece of news, an adventure, a chance simultaneously anodine, anecdotal, and overwhelming, the most ancient and the last . . . a kind of personal message, a secret between us, the secret of reproduction.[44]

The refinement that *The Post Card* makes is to take the off-criticism into *narrative*, the area where it will be the least vulnerable to any attacks mounted by the metaphysicians. It is possible to make a case for *The Post Card* as an epistolary novel of ideas:[45] whether Derrida is describing real events or not, whether his correspondents are real or imaginary, matters not at all in the final event. That would make the text both supplement *and* narrative, the best of both worlds as far as the deconstructionist is concerned. This is the logical conclusion to moving yieldingly towards, and drawing fictively close to, the aesthetic artefact. In this challenging hybrid of genres, Derrida makes one of his most sustained, and inventive, bids to reach a position of invulnerability beyond analysis. From whatever angle analysis is attempted it will have to contend with a slippage of *genre* that leaves most analysts stranded, 'between the outside and the inside'. And to acknowledge this of Derrida, constructing a narrative around Plato, is to be forced to acknowledge the same of the narratives that appear under Plato's name. Philosophy's predicament as written language is neatly deployed to frustrate would-be hostile analysts. Once again, Derrida manoeuvres himself into a position of power.

Derrida's off-critical writings constitute some of his most adventurous work, certainly some of his most illuminating in terms of showing how free-play and performative supplementarity can set about problematising logocentric, and for feminists phallogocentric, value judgement. Off-criticism also illuminates the less satisfactory side of his project: the latent authoritarianism, the periodic air of nihilism, the drive towards solipsism and silence.[46] The desire to go beyond aesthetics is a questionable one politically as far as most socialists are concerned, and when probed it soon reveals some very complicated motives. Derrida does indeed lead us into the labyrinth, and at some point one has to start asking whose interests that serves.

·6· 'WE SHALL CATCH AT THAT WORD'

Hartman, the Pun and Deconstructive Criticism

The pun has a special place reserved for it in the methodology of deconstructionist criticism. In 'the system of differences and the movement of *différance*', Derrida writes, 'the subject is constituted only in being divided from itself, in becoming space, in temporizing, in deferral',[1] and the pun is a classic example of the divided subject: it is never quite there, it can never quite achieve presence. Its subversive implications within discourse are considerable, and the deconstructionist critic is expected to surrender to its lure. It is, as Spivak remarks, a 'question of attitude' on the part of the critic:

> If in the process of deciphering a text in the traditional way we come across a word that seems to harbor an unresolvable contradiction, and by virtue of being *one* word is made sometimes to work in one way and sometimes in another and thus is made to point away from the absence of a unified meaning, we shall catch at that word. If a metaphor seems to suppress its implications, we shall catch at that metaphor. We shall follow its adventures through the text and see the text coming undone as a structure of concealment, revealing its self-transgression, its undecidability.[2]

We shall catch at that word, but of course we shall never reach it: it will divide, defer, persistently elude us in space and time. The pun is just such a case of unresolvable contradiction, an endlessly resourceful creator of intentionless meaning, and substantial claims are made for its deconstructing abilities. It is, Geoffrey Hartman insists, 'beyond good and evil', therefore beyond judgement. The pun is the critic's passport to the post-aesthetic realm that lies beyond logocentricity. I want now to explore one critic's use and defence of that passport.

In the question of attitude Geoffrey Hartman ranks very high. The most linguistically exuberant of the Yale school, Hartman can follow a word's adventures through a text with a sense of commitment bordering on the obsessive. *Saving the Text* abounds with examples of Hartman in this mode:

> The broken phrase 'je m'ec. . .' implies that the wish to find a classic point of repose must fall into an infinite if calculable disorder. For the meanings of 'je m'ec. . .' (see also chap. 2) cannot be computed. I equalize or equilibrate myself, even I square myself (EC: *Ecke*, the German word for *carré*). *Ecke* also means corner, or (French) *coin*, and may introduce a bilingual pun via the English *coin*, which is what circulates in an economy. But *Ecke* is also the word for angle, or (German) *Winkel*. All these meanings (except English 'coin'), and some others (e.g., the German word *Stuck*, in French *pièce* or *morsure*, *pièce* reintroducing the idea of coin money) are joined in the Wartburg dictionary to the matricial word *Canthus*, from which also the German word for board or edge, *Kante*, and, by antonomasia, *Kant*, the philosopher, who now emerges as Winckel-man (Angle-man).[3]

The abrupt shifts of register, topic and language in the passage above can only serve to have a disorienting effect on an audience expecting critique, although Hartman does warn us that, like Derrida, he is no longer really interested in *explication de texte*.[4] We are never permitted to find a point of rest in such writing, or gain our bearings. The author ceaselessly, disorientingly, changes our frame of reference by pushing puns to their limits – and then seemingly beyond into other languages. At which point logical critical discourse, as our tradition broadly understands the term, begins to collapse and post-aesthetics to beckon. This is active interpretation at its most active.

This recourse to the pun, and the heavily allusive style that invariably accompanies it (cultural references fall thick and fast in Hartman), conspires to alienate the vast majority of Anglo-American theorists and critics, most of whom would be only too ready to agree with Freud's assessment of the pun as 'the lowest form of verbal joke'.[5] Most of them would probably argue as well that the verbal joke has only a minimal role to play in critical discourse anyway. The aim in such discourse is generally taken to be a transparent style of writing, a style accessible to one's fellow scholars and other interested parties without being in any very radical way unsettling or disturbing. The critic 'represses his own artistic impulses' in what Hartman has referred to as a

> type of judiciousness . . . almost always linked to a strong sense for the vernacular: more precisely, to the idealization of the vernacular as an organic medium, a language of nature that communicates ideas without the noise or elaboration of extraverted theory.[6]

Hartman, on the other hand, believes strongly in critical noise, and just as strongly in the powers of the pun. 'Every pun, in Derrida', he writes in *Saving the Text*, 'is philosophically accountable, every *sottie* or *sortie* must contribute to the *déniaisement* of the European Mind, still so virginal after all the attempts on it: by Sade, Rousseau, Nietzsche, Marx, Freud, Sartre, Genet, Bataille.' This sounds suspiciously like according the pun a value, but Hartman proceeds to make several claims for punning which characterise it as a value-free activity.

I am going to test these claims by analysing the following statements from the text:

1. I must pun as I must sneeze.
2. There is no such thing as a good pun.
3. Puns are the only thing beyond good and evil.[7]

All three statements involve judgements about the nature of the pun, in terms of both its reception and its production: judgements, I want to claim, that cannot be sustained. The attempt to posit a physiological basis for punning, ingenious though it is and potentially of considerable moment for the deconstructive enterprise, ultimately is doomed to failure. Punning, as will be shown by reference to the psychological literature on the subject of humour, is a highly complex mental activity requiring a considerable knowledge of language and its codes on the part of both the producer and the receiver. It cannot realistically be equated with a physiological reflex, where, epistemologically speaking, innocence obtains and value judgements are inapplicable. Where knowledge is concerned, value judgements of some description always *are* applicable and innocence is little better than a chimera. The move into physiology represents an attempt to circumvent foundations and values (in the sense that, if no foundations, then no absolute values). In fact, we might say that physiology is functioning in a quasi-foundational way for Hartman: once we reach involuntary reflex we need seek no further explanations, having gone beyond the domain of epistemology. The theory can then build outwards from this pre-interpretative (and pre-epistemological) point. Yet ingenious though the manoeuvre is, it cannot be considered to satisfy the antifoundational requirement for a starting-point totally free of epistemological commitments, as we shall soon discover.

There is an extensive historical literature on the subject of humour stretching back to Aristotle at the very least, but for our present purposes it is sensible to start with Freud and the beginnings of modern psychological theory on the topic. Freud's work on jokes has to be seen in the wider context of his study of the subconscious and its drives, although I do not intend to go into this aspect in any detail here. All that has to be borne in mind is that, for Freud, there is no such thing as an innocent or uncoded joke; meaning is always present in the humour process. This is made quite clear in Freud's treatment of jokes dependent on linguistic experience, where he differentiates between the pun and the play upon words. Puns are 'the lowest form of verbal joke, probably because they are the "cheapest" – can be made with the least trouble'. Freud further argues that puns 'do in fact make the least demand on the technique of expression just as the play upon words makes the highest'.[8] 'Least demand' is still demand, however, and it will be seen to draw on the past linguistic experience of both the pun-maker and the audience. Clearly, Hartman would be in disagreement with such sentiments when it comes to the production of puns – 'I must pun as I must sneeze' – but it has to be pointed out that, for all the divergences of opinion on the subject of humour we can find in the literature since Freud, there does seem to be general agreement concerning the relationship between punning and experience. Puns are therefore considered by psychologists to be coded, and unquestionably dependent on our previous linguistic experience. Thus they are to be regarded as value-laden. Far from being a reflex reaction on the physiological model as Hartman wants them to be, they are in fact a highly self-conscious mode of expression.

As a case in point, plunging into the relevant post-Freudian literature, Shultz and Scott lay stress on the factor of self-consciousness in humour, arguing that the creation of jokes such as puns

> involves an order of cognitive processing which is just the reverse of that involved in the reception of jokes. The creator proceeds from the resolution to the incongruity while the recipient proceeds from the incongruity to the resolution. Paradoxically, it seems that the creator of a joke has an idea of how the incongruity will be resolved even before he constructs the incongruity.[9]

The process involved hardly seems analogous to sneezing, with both the production and reception ends involving a conscious mental effort foreign to physiological reflex mechanisms. In a very similar vein, Rapp speaks of puns as requiring 'more involved and complicated techniques' than most other types of humour, and as being correspondingly 'more difficult to analyse'.[10] Far from being epistemologically *undetermined*, as Hartman wants us to believe, the argument here is that puns are epistemologically *overdetermined*.

Recent psychological literature contains several general theories of humour. Giles and Oxford's 'Multidimensional theory of laughter causation' is an excellent example of such a general theory, with some interesting reflections on puns and their social context. A taxonomy of 'laughter situations' is postulated, the authors arguing that 'it would appear that laughter principally occurs under seven mutually exclusive conditions, giving rise to the following forms of laughter: humorous, social, ignorance, anxiety, derision and apologetic laughters and the phenomenon of tickling.' Puns are placed in the first category of 'humorous laughter', which is regarded as 'an overt expression of "rebellion" to social pressures, codes and institutions'. Such rebellion is necessary, the authors feel, because

> individuals in probably all civilized cultures are continually active social conformers to an almost infinite system of diverse codes of conduct, including legal codes, occupational constraints, marital–familial ties and moral–ethical restrictions – all of which appear drastically to limit individual freedom, sometimes to an almost insufferable degree.

Laughter, seen by Giles and Oxford as a response to the violation of a code, becomes the channel by which frustration is displaced so that a 'reasonably adequate level of sanity' can be maintained in a society.

Violation of a code, and recognition of same by the participants, also takes place in the context of punning: 'laughter at a pun is elicited since a contradiction of regular socially acceptable semantic usage has occurred.' By way of such contradiction the socially repressed individual attains ' "revenge" on all the restrictions and limitations which society and civilization have imposed on him'.[11] Punning, it could be argued, has similar connotations of 'revenge' for the deconstructionist: revenge on what is felt to be the tyranny of logocentricity and its system of diverse codes, which serve to restrict and limit individuals in their search for proliferation of meaning. When Christopher Norris speaks of 'the revenge of literary theory on that old tradition of philosophical disdain or condescension stretching back at least to Plato's *Republic*',[12] he indicates vividly the cast of mind involved. Violation of discourse by the pun could hardly be said to be a value-free activity either. If puns are part of a strategy of revenge, then they cannot be considered as lying 'beyond good and evil'. They are operating in a coded, valorised context. They are in fact deliberately being introduced into discourse in order to undermine its authority – as well as the authority of those who control the discourse – in an act of cognitive processing.

Psychologists who espouse the 'incongruity theory' of humour would seem to be similarly committed to coding. Incongruity has come in for quite a lot of attention in twentieth-century psychology. Gestalt theory, for example, utilises it in such a way as to leave no doubt of the code-recognition that it entails: 'Incongruity generally implies lack of harmony between what we expect (on the basis of past experience) and what we see or what actually happens.'[13] The identification of past experience as a key element in the process again tends to suggest flaws in Hartman's theories. From the point of view of pun-reception, the identification of incongruities is inconceivable without a fairly sophisticated grasp of codes, and it would seem at the least unlikely that incongruity was not also intuitively recognised in the act of pun-production (cognitive processing would be present yet again). In neither case do we appear to be dealing with a value-free activity. Whether the move is from incongruity to resolution or resolution to incongruity seems quite incidental. What is important to note is that in both instances it is a code-dependent move that is occurring. Deckers and Kizer see humour as 'a function of the degree of incongruity between stimuli',[14] which identifies the mechanism of discrimination operating in reception. Kenny goes even further, extending the argument about stimuli into the creation end of the process: 'Regarding humour as an affective response, any theoretical account of humour appreciation must take into consideration not only the stimulus-confirmation of a joke-ending expectancy, but also the dynamic "tendency", i.e. wit content of jokes.'[15] This directs our attention back not just to the creation of wit but to the consciously taken decisions lying behind the activity.

Apter and Smith's 'Theory of psychological reversals' comes into the category of incongruity theory, and provides yet more ammunition against Hartman. On this occasion we have a general theory designed to cover 'non-rational experience and behaviour' (such as humour and the arts), which argues that behaviour of this type results from 'the action of psychological processes which display bistability rather than homeostasis'. A bistable system 'has two rather than one preferred state', and these two states are defined as telic and paratelic in nature:

> at any time an individual will tend to be either in a telic or a paratelic state: that is, this is a bistable dimension. When the individual is in a telic state he strives for goals which phenomenologically are seen by him as essential to him and imposed on him, either by the requirements of his own body (e.g., hunger drive) or by the requirements of society (e.g., to pass an examination). When the individual is in a paratelic state he behaves because he enjoys the behaviour in itself and, where goals are involved, these are seen by him as being freely chosen or adopted by him and in some sense inessential (e.g., climbing, to reach the top of a mountain). In other words, in the telic state behaviour is chosen to achieve goals, in the paratelic state goals are chosen (where they are chosen at all) to provide a raison d'être for the behaviour.

In the condition we know as humour, 'identity synergy' is reached: synergy being 'the bringing together of two cognitive opposites so as to enhance each other's phenomenological qualities' (as when red and green colours in close proximity 'enhance each other's vividness'); while identity synergy is the state in which 'that opposition and identity are perceived concurrently'. When such an event occurs the individual undergoes a reversal to a paratelic state of heightened arousal, which, in the authors' view, 'represents an escape, or at least a playful escape, from logic'.[16] The latter sounds very much like the desired state of mind in the deconstructionist scheme of things, where Derrida is constantly seeking to engineer ways of escape from the conceptual thought of the Western metaphysical tradition into his own version of a paratelic state; but again we should note the stress on the *conscious* nature of the process under review, which cannot really be said to feature the involuntariness associated with sneezing.

The psychological literature on humour provides little in the way of evidence for Hartman's claims for the pun. None of the analyses we have considered supports the idea that punning is a quasi-physiological activity, indeed all seem to be at pains to point out just how sophisticated a mental process the activity actually is. Statement (1) can be called into question, therefore, particularly when we refer to the work done on incongruity theory. Statements (2) and (3) are similarly questionable, in the sense that they present puns as being beyond value judgements (whether of an aesthetic kind as in (2), or a moral one as in (3) makes no difference to the argument). The pun may be one of the prime agents of subversion in deconstructive criticism, but it cannot be seen as physiologically spontaneous and hence as removed from the sphere of influence of epistemological commitments. Quick though wit may be, it is nevertheless the end-product of processing undertaken in the cause of a practico-political programme. Not only does Hartman not pun as he sneezes, it would probably be most unwise of him to do so. Reflex spontaneity would be less open to his control and therefore less effective as a strategy of subversion. Puns are not value-free and hence not antifoundational. They have hidden epistemological commitments that do not allow us to escape from logic in any but a playful way.

As far as the nature of puns and punning goes, Hartman's claims would appear to have no scientific basis, but perhaps we need to reflect a little longer on their role in deconstructionist criticism before passing any final judgement on the virtue of the strategy as a whole. Puns work by association of ideas, with the strong signifier's adventures taking the individual in unpredictable directions. We have here both tactics – punning is continually resorted to by deconstructionist critics as a method of breaking down syntagmatic sequences and challenging readers to think in a subversively non-linear fashion – and blindness: who knows where the adventures will end? Who knows *if* the adventures will end?

Wherever the word is located in space and time, there will be found the trace and 'another story, always already begun, at the moment where it begins'. It would obviously be of great benefit to deconstructionists such as Hartman and Derrida if punning *were* a spontaneous reflex on the physiological model, because then there would be no problem with logocentrist presuppositions. Locating the pun in reflex cuts out the world of values entirely and contrives to 'naturalise' punning. To naturalise punning would be to naturalise deconstruction – and that would be a notable coup were it possible. Similarly, if puns were indeed beyond good and evil – that is, beyond the scope of value judgement – then they would have considerable subversive significance when set loose within the confines of syntagmatically structured discourse. They would be checking the linear progress of that discourse from the inside, acting as tactical devices to blur meaning at any given point in the unfolding of the sequence. Under such circumstances discourse could never build up any sense of authority: the centre manifestly could not hold with the strong signifier in constant attendance.

Hartman's adventures with the pun in *Saving the Text* amount to a riotous celebration of the strong signifier. A cascade of allusion and imagery, the currency of active interpretation, confronts the reader on almost any page:

> Near the beginning of *Glas* Derrida asks: 'What does the death knell of the proper name signify?'(27b) We can now answer: it signifies the birth of the literary text. The fading of the name leaves no legacy ('legs', homonym of '*lait*' and near-anagram of 'glas', as in 291b) except for the paronomasia of a text. 'Reste ici ou glas qu'on ne peut arrêter' (287b). Yet this movement without terms incorporates 'terms' that displace the proper name. These terms are fixed or frozen particles (*glas* into *glace* and *classe*), coagulations in the stream of discourse, milk-stones (*galalithes*) or even body-stones ('le calcul de la mère' refers also to the organic, pathological kidney stone, *caillou*). They grow in language as in a culture; they are formed by a process analogous to introjection or incorporation; and there is a radical ambivalence about their value, whether they are blockage and detritus, or seminal and pregnant tissue. The letter *L*, signifying the pronoun 'Elle', is a mock-up of such a term; so is the reduction of 'savoir absolu' to *Sa*, which could be confused with another pronoun in the possessive case, also pointing to the feminine gender. 'L'a, similarly, combines in Lacan's algebraic manner this capital *L* with what seems to be the *petit objet a* (standing for 'autre' instead of 'Autre', here within the feminine sphere).[17]

The length of the extract above is significant: it is extremely hard to check Hartman once he is in full flow, skipping from text to text, discourse to discourse, language to language, one half-articulated thought to another. It is not a text in its own right – it has no desire to be – but a resonating supplement to *Glas*, and the caving in, boxing in, grinding, fragmenting and dislocating that René Major identified in the operation of the Derrida text echoes through its supplement. This is scarcely commentary, and neither is it linear argument in our normal understanding of the term: although it is interesting that it remains within, and obeys, the rules of formal grammar – surely a prime target for deconstruction? One might assume that active interpretation would lie beyond syntax as well as beyond meaning, but although the pun shifts and squirms away from presence in Hartman, it does so within formally structured sentences.[18] The strong signifier would in fact lose most of its impact if it were not constrained by grammar and syntax – which might be turned into an argument against deconstruction in its high messianic mode. Indeterminacy can only be appreciated – one is tempted to say can only be *understood* – within a context of determinacy: that is, as a violation of a code. The idea of a radical indeterminacy, and that is what the world of signs without truth, fault or origin is assuming, is self-defeating. Staying within the bounds of syntax may be a tacit admission by deconstructionists of an inescapable binary relationship within discourse – determinacy/indeterminacy. Equally, deconstructionists can claim that determinacy entails indeterminacy, and so continue their tactical subversion in the manner of Hartman above. This is to reduce deconstruction, however, to the status of a playful escape from a logic to which it is symbiotically connected, rather than viewing it as the path to a brave new world where determinacy is excluded. It is to say that the strong signifier is bounded, that *rebellion* is bounded.

If it is bounded it is nevertheless very allusive within those boundaries. 'We are tempted to become associative and metaphorical',[19] Hartman remarks, and it is a temptation that he rarely resists. Derrida, Lacan, French puns and play-upon-words, this is all very knowing discourse, and one that assumes a very knowing audience. Whether such a display of knowledge can ever be free of value is another question. The sheer fluency of the allusion positively radiates knowledge and authority. If metaphor is never innocent then neither is the talent to be associative and metaphorical. Catching at words is tactical, certainly, but perhaps not so blind as it likes to pretend to be. Once again the point can be made about the high degree of cognitive processing required of all the participants in the punning process. Allusion may defer, but we know *what* it defers.

The pun is designed to defer the appearance of that 'what' for as long as is possible – 'A thousand and one nights of literary analysis lie before, a Scheherazade to keep an emperor awake beyond his intentions',[20] Hartman informs us, conjuring up an image of a radically extended paratelic state – but there is a sense in which this 'freeplay' is subject to the law of diminishing returns. Hartman's reference to the 'intriguingly, wearyingly allusive' quality of Derrida's style[21] neatly encapsulates the problem we face with this kind of critical writing. It is initially intriguing to follow the pun's adventures, but ultimately very wearying as those adventures grind on and on. Hartman would see this remorselessness as a crucial part of the process – as Derrida insists, 'This is to be continued' – but it runs the risk of turning deconstructive criticism into a relatively joyless activity, where the accent is on the perpetual slog of the guerrilla campaign rather than the messianic promise of the beyond. 'It is not the devices themselves but the interminable character of the analysis they impose that may tire us into an antagonism', Hartman admits,[22] and the limitations of the pun come sharply into focus. Not only is the pun coded and bounded, it cannot transfer us into the post-aesthetic realm that is the only real justification for the deconstructive enterprise to be continued. As wielded by someone like Hartman the pun merely brings us, despairingly enough, face to face with eternal recurrence. So we do not have the value-freedom Hartman wants, but find ourselves instead still in pursuit of the ideal, with neither reflex spontaneity nor active control achieving the desired break-through. Being antifoundationalist, deconstructionists are disposed towards spreading doubt and confusion in the enemy camp, and what better way of doing so than through the tactical deployment of a literary figure that creates the illusion of indeterminate reference and unfixed meaning. Literary artists have long been aware of the subversive power of the pun; there is, for example, the work of such Elizabethan and Jacobean dramatists as Jonson and Shakespeare, where the pun is adroitly used to mock the pretensions and undermine the status of authority figures.[23] English-language philosophers and critics, however, have tended in the main to shy away from language in its more obviously figurative mode, cultivating instead the 'judiciousness' of style remarked on by Hartman: 'Grave it certainly is, and didactic, so that the formalist or playful thinker who does not justify his enterprise by appealing to theory or science is not considered worthwhile.'[24] 'Playful' deconstruction insists on the rhetorical debts of this 'judiciousness', exploring the various ways in which philosophy (and its related critical discourses) 'reveals, negotiates or represses its own inescapable predicament as written language'.[25] We are all rhetoricians whether we are aware of it or not according to such a reading, and rhetoric is not, rhetoric cannot be, foundational.

The pun is at the forefront of this 'rhetorical turn', and it becomes crucial to the deconstructionist enterprise that it brings no commitments in its wake if it is to perform the necessary work of 'revenge' against logocentrist restrictions and limitations. Indeterminacy alone will not suffice. Hartman has argued that 'the word carries with it a certain absence or indeterminacy of meaning',[26] but more than a 'certain' absence must be found in the pun: it must also include a complete, and ontologically unalterable, separation from all possible systems of value. Paratelic states demand that the pun be an unvalorised entity in order for those states to distance themselves from the bound world of logic, where commitment reigns. But the most that probably can be claimed (and even here the claim would be hotly contested by most psychologists of humour) is that the pun is relatively *underdetermined* (that is, there is a degree of input from the unconscious). The desire for innocence of intent in this anti-logocentrist campaign simply cannot be sustained, except as a rhetorical ploy. Consigning Hartman's claims to the domain of rhetoric, while it brings out the polemical nature of the exercise, undermines their effectiveness quite severely. The need was for an escape from logic into a hermetically sealed realm where logic could not penetrate: the world of reflex which would avoid all those awkward epistemological commitments that invariably seem to lead back to foundations. Final judgement would have to be that as a method of bypassing foundations, punning in its Hartman conception will not work. It is not a value-free activity, even if its degree of epistemological determination remains open to debate.

The pun does, however, generate lots of noise, which is just what the developer of ideas wants in order to keep the arbiters of taste on edge. Arbiters of taste have very set ideas as to how discourses should conduct themselves, and 'playfulness' does not come into their definition of the critical. Hartman's answer would be that 'No question the ground is slippery, when words are grounded on words. The slippage is all around us, and the principle of stabilization not very conspicuous.'[27] Slippage of this nature does not prove the case for radical indeterminacy, but in Hartman's view it licenses the critical discourse to use techniques more usually associated with the freedom and playfulness of creative writing. 'The screw of language can always be turned further', by Derrida and his deconstructionist followers no less than by Mallarmé and his ilk.[28] However, in this context, it is interesting to note Hartman's discrimination between the 'deconstructive' and the 'literary' pun: 'Herein, of course, one difference with Joyce, who shocks and delights, rather than teaches. Every pun, in Derrida, is philosophically accountable.' What we have in Derrida is 'systematic play . . . *Serio ludere.*'[29] This may well be to underrate the philosophical implications of Joyce's linguistic exercises, but it also directs us back to the darkly nihilistic, and to the socialist mind politically dubious, side of deconstruction: to the pun as eternal recurrence in the service of an unachievable, by definition, campaign. Hartman speaks at one moment of the 'elegant opacity' of Derrida's style, at another of its being 'elegantly humorless'.[30] The humourlessness is the more worrying of the two descriptions, and leaves us with an image of deconstruction as a form of linguistic terrorism designed to grind its opponents down rather mercilessly. The prime number 'analysis' in *The Truth in Painting* springs to mind in this context. Humourless punning sounds as if it has left aesthetics well behind, and possibly humanity too. The noise at such points seems simply for its own sake.

Is it Joycean or Derridean punning that we find in *Saving the Text*? I have been treating this text as a representative piece of deconstructive criticism, an example of where the drive to go beyond aesthetics tends, but Hartman can be found resisting the deconstructionist label, as in his prefatory remarks to *Deconstruction and Criticism*:

> the critics amicably if not quite convincingly held together by the covers of this book differ considerably in their approach to literature and literary theory. . . . Derrida, de Man, and Miller are certainly boa-deconstructors, merciless and consequent. . . . But Bloom and Hartman are barely deconstructionists. They even write against it on occasion. . . . For them the ethos of literature is not dissociable from its pathos, whereas for deconstructionist criticism literature is precisely that use of language which can purge pathos, which can show that it too is figurative, ironic or aesthetic.[31]

Hartman seems to want to keep a critical distance between himself and deconstruction at this point, but whether that distance is still there in *Saving the Text* is open to question: there is frank admiration expressed in that text for Derrida's desire to purge pathos, and Hartman aligns himself with the project, slipping 'from metaphor to metaphor'[32] in what certainly looks like the approved deconstructionist fashion. If nothing else, the sheer *labour* of deconstruction – je m'ec to Kant – shines through in *Saving the Text*. Here Hartman is a serious player in the business of catching. Resonating rather than responding is clearly what is taking place in *Saving the Text*, and it might be queried whether there is a hidden political agenda at work in the process. One might begin to wonder if resonance is a form of *protection*: the invulnerability tactic at work again. The pun does not just defer meaning and presence, it also defers *critique*. Deconstruction can be a very one-sided, dialogue-destroying affair: caving in, boxing in, grinding, fragmenting and dislocating all conspire to prevent opposition, and there is an obvious political message to be drawn from such a series of manoeuvres. Perhaps, as Charles Levin has suggested, 'Derridean deconstruction is another gambit in the old philosophical game of deferring the danger of the world.'[33] Slipping from metaphor to metaphor then becomes a political act, and the strong signifier a way of suppressing dissent.

Hartman is not the whole story as far as deconstructive strategies go, and it could be argued that rather too much weight is being put by me on his practice in *Saving the Text*. Some commentators question the status of 'American' deconstruction anyway: 'having received multiple and conflictual interpretations', Christie McDonald complains, deconstruction 'took on a life of its own in the United States which no longer "belonged" to the man Jacques Derrida or to his writings'.[34] This could be interpreted as yet another move to 'protect' Derrida, from critique ('saving the deconstruction'?), but in many ways it is more interesting and illuminating to see what goes on in his name than what he is doing himself. The resonating has to continue, and the noisier it becomes – and I take *Saving the Text* to be a *very* noisy piece of writing – then the better a picture we can build up of what the projected world of post-aesthetic active interpretation actually would look like when the critic no longer 'represses his own artistic impulses'. Hartman gives it as good a try as anyone trapped in the world of sublunary deconstruction could be expected to do. If not the beyond, it is still closer to it than the controlled, and quite un-noisy, prose of such apologists for the new order as Christopher Norris and Richard Rorty. The latter can echo Hartman's criticism of arbiters of taste by arguing that 'straightforward, unselfconscious, transparent prose [is] precisely the kind of prose no self-creating ironist wants to write,'[35] but, as Jonathan Ree has rightly pointed out, 'Rorty makes no attempt to imitate the kind of prose he praises . . . he writes with an efficient and solicitous clarity.'[36] *Saving the Text*, however, finds Hartman practising what he (and before him Derrida) preaches: noisy prose that catches interminably at words. The pun may be too much of this world of values to defer that world's danger indefinitely – politics will out, I am arguing – but *Saving the Text* remains a fascinating exercise in the rhetoric of deconstruction. The final verdict of this particular confrontation, however, would have to be that the exercise can generate only a series of gestures to be undermined progressively by their own rhetoric.

$\cdot 7 \cdot$ 'A WAR ON TOTALITY'

Lyotard and the Politics of Postmodernism

Derrida's anti-authoritarianism tends to express itself in a fairly oblique manner. It has been argued that 'for strategic reasons' he 'has privileged Marx's writings', yet he can be very difficult to pin down politically.[1] Lyotard is considerably more open in this respect, 'fundamentally a political thinker', as Geoffrey Bennington notes, 'to the precise extent that he contests the totalisations fundamental to most ideas of politics'.[2] Lyotard's postmodern philosophy of resistance has an explicitly political edge to it, therefore, and also has very clearly defined targets in terms of its antifoundational programme. It takes the form of a rejection of the claims to authority of a series of cultural paradigms ('grand narratives' or 'metanarratives' to Lyotard). He speaks of a decline and progressive delegitimation of paradigms such as Christianity and dialectical philosophy in the late twentieth century. 'We no longer have recourse to the grand narratives', he informs us, 'we can resort neither to the dialectic of Spirit nor even to the emancipation of humanity as a validation for postmodern scientific discourse. ... In addition, the principle of consensus as a criterion of validation seems to be inadequate.'[3] Authorities such as the above have provided us with *foundations* for our knowledge, but Lyotard feels that they have also constituted a severe check on our cultural and personal development: 'In so far as they are dialectical forms of thought and practices, Christianity, Hegelianism, and "marxism" must be numbered amongst the many attempts to restore the West from psychosis to neurosis.'[4] Metaphysics is once again a political issue – 'Philosophy is the West's madness', Lyotard writes, 'and never ceases to underwrite its quests for knowledge and politics in the name of Truth and the Good'[5] – but Lyotard will take a more direct route to its destabilisation than Derrida tended to. This time around, the messianic promise trades even more obviously on the language of the epistemological break:

> The nineteenth and twentieth centuries have given us as much terror as we can take. We have paid a high enough price for the nostalgia of the whole and the one, for the reconciliation of the concept and the sensible, of the transparent and the communicable experience. Under the general demand for slackening and for appeasement, we can hear the mutterings of the desire for a return of terror, for the realization of the fantasy to seize reality. The answer is: Let us wage a war on totality; let us be witnesses to the unpresentable; let us activate the differences and save the honor of the name.[6]

Lyotard's 'war on totality', and the politics that underpins it, forms the subject of the next three chapters.

It will be a case of 'three times around' Lyotard, twice negatively, and once positively. In the next two chapters the critique will be essentially negative in tone, with *The Postmodern Condition, Just Gaming*, 'Lessons in paganism' and *The Differend* being the main targets.[7] In Chapter 9, with a view to keeping the lines open for dialogue between the postmodernist and socialist projects, a more positive approach will be sketched out. Lyotard is one of the more accessible of the radical antifoundationalists and perhaps postmodernism is the acceptable face of the movement, but that makes it all the more imperative to lay bare the politics involved if, as I am arguing, antifoundationalism is an ideologically problematical position in which a surface radicalism all too frequently flatters to deceive.

Postmodernism is not the easiest of terms to define, and it has been used to justify a multitude of practices in the arts of late ranging from the conservative to the *avant garde*.[8] For Lyotard it is essentially a question of attitude: 'I define *postmodern* as incredulity towards metanarratives. . . . The narrative function is losing its functors, its great hero, its great dangers, its great voyages, its great goal.'[9] Our incredulity is the product of our progressive realisation that 'there is no reason of history . . . there is no court in which one can adjudicate the reason of history.'[10] The realisation is not a once-and-for-all event, however, and Lyotard echoes Derrida's sense of the interminability of the antifoundationalist project; as Jameson has remarked, it is a case of Lyotard

> seeing postmodernism as a discontent with the disintegration of this or that high modernist style – a moment in the perpetual 'revolution' and innovation of high modernism, to be succeeded by a fresh burst of formal invention – in a striking formula he has characterized postmodernism, not as that which follows modernism and its particular legitimation crisis, but

rather as a cyclical moment that returns before the emergence of ever *new* modernisms in the stricter sense.[11]

The clear overtones of eternal recurrence identified here by Jameson help us to situate Lyotard within the nihilistic–Nietzschean strain in recent French thought, although he is also capable of introducing an optimistically libertarian note into what is otherwise a somewhat dark discourse:

> give the public free access to the memory and data banks. Language games would then be games of perfect information at any given moment. . . . For the stakes would be knowledge (or information, if you will), and the reserve of knowledge–language's reserve of possible utterances – is inexhaustible.[12]

(The inadequacy of such an apparently simple solution to the so-called 'knowledge crisis' will be dealt with later in this chapter.) Postmodernism is to be viewed, therefore, as being essentially an attitude towards modernism, however this latter phenomenon is conceived of within a given era.

Lyotard's antifoundationalist credentials reveal themselves in the way that he pursues the problem of legitimation of authority:

> if a metanarrative implying a philosophy of history is used to legitimate knowledge, questions are raised concerning the validity of the institutions governing the social bonds: these must be legitimated as well. Thus justice is consigned to the grand narrative in the same way as truth.[13]

Legitimation and proof are conspicuously different entities, although Lyotard is ultimately sceptical about claims to proof or truth: 'in the discourse of today's financial backers of research, the only credible goal is power. Scientists, technicians, and instruments are purchased not to find truth', he insists, 'but to augment power'.[14] Truth is a fiction not just for Lyotard, therefore, but also for those institutions which present themselves as being bound by it. Beneath the apparent objectivity lies a buried, and dominant, discourse of *realpolitik*, or 'the exercise of terror' as Lyotard describes it: ' "Adapt your aspirations to our ends – or else".'[15] Legitimation is accordingly a question of power, and Lyotard makes the telling point that, when it comes to socio-political, as opposed to philosophical, practice, 'utterances [are] expected to be just rather than true'.[16] This ethical shift to the argument takes us into the area where rhetorics operate: justice being a far less logically bound concept than truth, and more exposed to techniques of persuasion and emotional manipulation: 'we have been speaking of morality and public good. And here, I have no criteria; here we don't say, so and so is pagan – that is, we order or advise' (where 'paganism' is 'the denomination of a situation in which one judges without criteria'[17]).

The move into rhetoric is a characteristic one for the antifoundationalist to make, and it need not be seen as reprehensible. As Jeff Mason points out in his excellent study of the relationship between philosophy and rhetoric,

> It is perfectly possible to distinguish philosophy from rhetoric, but that does not mean we can conceive of either one of them without the other. They are different but bound to one another. We forget this point at our peril. . . . The battle between rhetoric and philosophy is really a battle of differing rhetorics.

(In Lyotard's neat formulation, 'The canonical phrase of Platonic poetics would be in sum: I deceive you the least possible'.)[18] Nevertheless, the antifoundationalist is still left with the problem of establishing *some* criterion against which his method and concepts can be judged, or at least measured (we can discount Lyotard's flippant aside that 'I have a criterion (the absence of criteria) to classify various sorts of discourse here and there' in this context[19]). In the absence of truth-value certainties all strategies are apparently equal, which makes the need for a legitimating principle imperative if a philosopher is to maintain any credibility with his audience. Derrida gave us *différance* or the trace; Hartman the pun as a reflex mechanism; Lyotard gives us 'narrativity', the narrative drive assumed to lie at the heart of all sequences of human affairs, including political and institutional systems:

> what do scientists do when they appear on television or are interviewed in the newspapers after making a 'discovery'? They recount an epic of knowledge that is in fact wholly unepic. They play by the rules of the narrative game.[20]

The narrative game is all around us: 'Theory is a form of narration without the transitivity', Lyotard proclaims, and 'we have always already been told something . . . we have always already been spoken.'[21]

Narrativity has its problems, as Lyotard readily admits, and he is biased towards a certain restricted version of it, although essentially in favour of its role in the construction of knowledge. The virtue of narrative is that it just *is*, being in effect its own justification:

> I have said that narrative knowledge does not give priority to the question of its own legitimation and that it certifies itself in the pragmatics of its own transmission without having recourse to argumentation and proof. This is why its incomprehension of the problems of scientific discourse is accompanied by a certain tolerance: it approaches such discourse primarily as a variant in the family of narrative cultures.[22]

Self-justification of this order has a self-evidential ring to it, yet it is by no means clear why we should accept narrative as some kind of honorary, or disguised, ground for knowledge – because that is how it is really functioning in *The Postmodern Condition*. Like Derridean erasure it claims to cancel out metaphysical commitments – and with them, all problems about foundations – but it could be argued that it is in reality more a case of bracketing, which temporarily suspends but never totally eliminates the commitments in question. Allow Lyotard to call life, or any other sequence you care to name, a narrative, and he will draw you along with him from that point onwards, because you have tacitly accepted the bracketing of alternative explanations: a carefully engineered radical lack of prejudice in Lyotard's favour. As deconstructive practice amply demonstrates, all the tricks of rhetoric and literary criticism can be summoned into action at this point, and the structure of argument can begin to take on an appearance of authority. If life is a narrative then it must have a language, and if it has a language then it can be deconstructed. In Lyotard's view narrative is acceptable, whereas metanarrative is not. Metanarrative is foundational and thus to be avoided. We are therefore to try to ensure that life's narrative, the individual, is set free from life's metanarrative, the systems that control the individual. Once they are defined and applied, the terms play off each other with ease, forcing reality to conform to their requirements.

The question at issue is not really whether narrative or metanarrative is preferable, but whether these terms have any relevance – or reference – within the socio-political sphere. Cancelling out, or *claiming* to cancel out, the metaphysics, does not in fact give you that relevance. It is revealing that Lyotard is essentially tolerant towards the idea of short-term contracts: 'the temporary contract is in practice supplanting permanent institutions in the professional, emotional, sexual, cultural, family, and international domains, as well as in political affairs.'[23] This is precisely the kind of tactical approach to process, in its deferral of permanence and reliance on pragmatics, that we would expect the phenomenologically radical antifoundationalist to adopt. It conjures up the spectre of, at best, aimlessness, and, at worst, opportunism.

Narrative none the less provides Lyotard with a basic antifoundationalist requirement, a starting-point which is not in the stricter philosophical sense a ground, and which accordingly does not commit one to a metaphysics of presence:

> If you are the narrator, the narratee or the narrated of a story in which you are implicated, you become dependent upon that story. And we are in fact always under some influence or other; we have always already been told something, and we have always already been spoken.[24]

Taking temporal succession as an unproblematical given (no origin, no end, process only), and adding some measure of order (how much, and under whose aegis, being a matter of some concern for Lyotard, as we shall see), we arrive at narrative: a historically underdetermined form with all the attractions that underdetermination has for the antifoundationalist, who does not want to be trapped in the infinite regress game of 'what is the ground of the ground of the ground. . .?' Metanarrative becomes the enemy, the foundation which is perceived to limit individual creativity: to orient research, to fix results, to determine behaviour.

The assumed struggle between narrative and metanarrative lies at the heart of Lyotard's antifoundational project, and, as he points out in *The Postmodern Condition*, both are deeply implicated in the knowledge crisis. Metanarrative is taken to usurp for itself the legitimating power of narrative in general, which means that a given metanarrative takes over control of knowledge: and at that point knowledge becomes a political issue. 'Knowledge is and will be produced in order to be sold', Lyotard points out, 'it is, and will be consumed in order to be valorized in a new production', and 'knowledge has become the principal force of production over the last few decades.' Knowledge is therefore inescapably inscribed in political struggle, and the perspective is global:

> Knowledge in the form of an informational commodity indispensable to productive power is already, and will continue to be, a major – perhaps *the* major – stake in the worldwide competition for power. It is conceivable that the nation-states will one day fight for control of information, just as they battled in the past for control over territory, and afterwards for control of access to and exploitation of raw materials and cheap labor.[25]

The legitimation of that knowledge becomes a crucial issue, and those who control the metanarrative are deemed to control knowledge. Since there is no necessary connection between narrative credibility and political virtue this can become a major problem, and to his credit Lyotard is very much exercised by the issue of who controls narrative. Effectively he wants narrative power to be held by individuals and not by systems, and his plea for an opening up of the data banks is an index of his concern, although it might be seen as somewhat naïve. Extension of the franchise has not led to the collapse of élitist political structures and most likely neither would open access to the data banks: that would depend on who controlled certain other narratives, most notably the economic one. Lyotard's belief that individual opposition to the system, or 'agonistics' as he calls it, will help to keep the controllers of narrative honest is touching, but sounds as if it will have more effect on the individual than the system. On occasion something more radical than agonistics is required, such as an alternative metanarrative. Feminism provides one such recent example of the virtues of the latter in changing perceptions.[26]

Lyotard is, however, much more interested in the individual than in the collectivity. 'There is a multiplicity of small narratives', he tells us,[27] and he wants to privilege these at the expense of 'grand narratives' such as Marxism, which cannot tolerate multiplicity. 'The little narrative remains the quintessential form of imaginative invention', he argues,[28] treating it as a subversive tactic in the war against the totalitarianism of metanarrative. Lyotard speaks approvingly of the delegitimation of grand narrative, and delegitimation pushes us in the direction of the open-ended narrative, where individuals can fill in the details as they go along, using whatever pragmatics seems appropriate to the situation at hand, without being committed to any predetermined pattern or conclusion such as grand narrative inevitably enforces. There is 'an absence of unity, an absence of totality', Lyotard claims, therefore

> the idea that I think we need today in order to make decisions in political matters cannot be the idea of the totality, or of the unity, of the body. It can only be the idea of a multiplicity or of a diversity.[29]

We remove the teleological constraints of grand narrative, in other words, in order to leave room for individual initiative. If we are to decontrol narrative, however, we need to be a bit more specific about the nature, most particularly the affective nature, of what it is we are decontrolling. To do so we have to return to the basis of Lyotard's analogy – literary narrative.

That narrative works on a level of pleasure has been a commonplace amongst literary theorists from Plato onwards. Whether this is to be construed as a good or a bad thing, and whether it should be encouraged or discouraged, have been more contentious matters. Moralists – Plato, neoclassical aestheticians, Marxists such as Brecht and Lukács – have emphasised the didactic role of literature in terms of their own specific ideological programmes. This explicit moral dimension would no doubt be classed as metanarrative by Lyotard and accordingly dispensed with by him. We might just ask, however, what we are left with if the moral of the tale disappears. Open-endedness from which no value judgements can be extracted to help guide future action or future response? This is no less ideologically bound a programme in its privileging of pleasure over moral responsibility. Its objective is to maximise the 'freedom' (that is, absence of external constraint) of the individual, whose pleasure-oriented personal narrative is held to transcend in importance the collective narrative, for Lyotard metanarrative, of his or her fellows.

Decontrol of metanarrative amounts to an attempt to negate the didactic dimension of literature, and thus reduce drastically the possibility of it constituting a source of politically applicable value judgements. *Laissez-faire* aesthetics releases the individual but at an ideological cost.

For all the pretension of their rhetoric ('Let us wage a war on totality') antifoundationalists almost invariably seem to end up arguing on this small-scale, individualistic basis. Reducing human history to the individual experience in this manner is seductively subversive; but is it as anti-authoritarian as it is made out to be? Or is it instead a new or more insidious form of social control which works to destabilise political action at source? Tending your own little narrative, agonistically or otherwise, looks very much like a conservative tactic to keep change to a manageable minimum within the confines of a comfortable *status quo*. A possible positive reading of the little narrative approach is suggested by Vincent Descombes:

> the fundamental issue becomes that of nihilism. Is the collapse of all beliefs a liberation or a disaster?. . . Lyotard considers it reactionary or reactive to protest against the state of the world, against 'capitalism', if we like. There should be no question of reproaching capitalism for its cynicism and cruelty; on the contrary, that tendency should be stoked. Capitalism *liquidates* everything that mankind has held to be most noble and holy; such a liquidation must be rendered 'still more liquid'. . . . Here is how the programme of active nihilism (which has on the whole been received as scandalous) may be understood: that which is noble and holy ceases to be so as soon as it is believed in not from naivety, but out of calculation.[30]

This is a dangerous road to travel, however, and most socialists will find themselves wondering at what point the aggressive pursuit of little narratives becomes collusion with capitalism rather than revolution.[31] Lyotard is perfectly capable, as we shall see in Chapter 8, of being highly critical of capitalism, but he is clearly also drawn to its protean quality and the scope that it offers for a certain kind of individual initiative. What Bennington has called 'Lyotard's increasing inability to identify with the discourse of Marxism' might well have acted as a spur to him to explore the revolutionary potential of its ideological opposite, but he is on a knife edge here between succouring and subverting power structures.[32]

Nevertheless, Lyotard would seem to feel that conscious use of agonistics and pragmatics serves to limit contemporary power structures, and he fits into a recognisably antifoundationalist tradition in this respect. Baudrillard's 'speculation to the death'[33] and Derrida's guerrilla-like conception of deconstruction's objective (Western metaphysics as 'an old cloth that must interminably be undone') are other prominent examples of this subversive attitude to dominant power structures, most notably the authoritarianism that is felt to be embedded in language. Lyotard's nihilism is arguably less extreme than is the case with either of the above, although it is still highly adversarial and language is one of its main targets:

> to speak is to fight, in the sense of playing, and speech acts fall within the domain of a general agonistics. This does not necessarily mean that one plays in order to win. A move can be made for the sheer pleasure of its invention: what else is involved in that labor of language harassment undertaken by popular speech and by literature? Great joy is had in the endless invention of turns of phrase, or words and meanings, the process behind the evolution of language on the level of *parole*. But undoubtedly even this pleasure depends on a feeling of success won at the expense of an adversary – at least one adversary, and a formidable one: the accepted language, or connotation.[34]

The introduction of an aesthetic dimension suggests a desire to separate the individual from the world of action and ideological commitments which compromises his or her innocent, game-playing self. Were Lyotard so easily caught out playing the apolitical card his work would probably not merit much sustained attention; but he *does* keep the political dimension in mind – 'I do not believe myself to be a philosopher, in the proper sense of the term, but a "politician"'[35] – and there is a persistent sense of tension in his work between political and apolitical imperatives which illustrates the sense of insecurity within the antifoundationalist position in general. The point of the fight, for Lyotard, is not just aesthetic, it is also consciously disruptive:

> it is important to increase displacement in the games, and even to disorient it, in such a way as to make an unexpected 'move' (a new statement). What is needed if we are to understand social relations in this manner, on whatever scale we choose, is not only a theory of communication, but a theory of games which accepts agonistics as a founding principle.[36]

Lyotard consistently stresses this relationship between agonistic tactics and 'new' states of affairs. Postmodern science is 'producing not the known, but the unknown'; we have 'a desire for the unknown'; game theory 'is useful in the same sense that any sophisticated theory is useful, namely as a generator of ideas'.[37] Presumably the powers-that-be are an obstacle to our breakthrough to the territory of unknown ideas, in the same sense that logocentricity is conceived of by Derrida as an obstacle to entry into the world of signs without truth, fault or origin.

Put like this the postmodernist enterprise sounds all very exciting and it would seem reactionary to raise objections to it: who would want to be against ideas, new statements or the unknown? But we might justifiably ask what we are supposed to do when we reach the promised land: go forth again presumably, singly, agonistically, actively nihilistically. The progression would appear to be from modernism to postmodernism to modernism to . . . infinity? Yet again the ahistoricist nature of the exercise comes to the fore. Those going forward have no past and are continually in the business of rejecting the present in an interminable process of cancelling and erasure. While the rhetoric can sound dramatic – 'let us be witnesses to the unpresentable; let us activate the differences' – it can also sound rather empty. The issue of rhetoric is crucial. In an antifoundationalist world rhetoric must become an increasingly import-ant aspect of philosophical discourse. Commentators like Norris have asserted that philosophy is little else than a series of more-or-less inspired fictions, and thus to be regarded as open to techniques of literary analysis: 'Philosophy – including the rational self-evidence of scientific thought – is always bound up with linguistic structures which crucially influence and complicate its logical workings.'[38] This is the 'revenge of literary theory', and in pointing out how narrativity encroaches on philosophical discourse as a legitimation device more than is usually acknowledged, Lyotard provides some of the impetus for its develop-ment. There is, for example, his analysis of Platonic dialogue, where 'the legitimation effort . . . gives ammunition to narrative by virtue of its own form: each of the dialogues takes the form of a narrative of a scientific discussion.' Platonic dialogue trades on the legitimating power of narrative, thus setting up its own particular 'knowledge crisis':

> The fact is that the Platonic discourse that inaugurates science is not scientific, precisely to the extent that it attempts to legitimate science. Scientific knowledge cannot know and make known that it is the true knowledge without resorting to the other, narrative, kind of knowledge, which from its point of view is no knowledge at all. Without such recourse it would be in the position of presupposing its own validity and would be stooping to what it condemns: begging the question, proceeding on prejudice. But does it not fall into the same trap by using narrative as its authority?[39]

There is immediately a 'knowledge crisis' when narrative comes on the scene because narrative is self-legitimating:

> Narratives, as we have seen, determine criteria of competence and/or illustrate how they are to be applied. They thus define what has the right to be said and done in the culture in question, and since they are themselves a part of that culture, they are legitimated by the simple fact that they do what they do.[40]

Narrative would seem to be at the end of the line as far as knowledge is concerned, with questions of truth eventually being transformed into questions of presentation, questions of logic into questions of rhetoric. Nor is Plato an isolated phenomenon in this respect. 'As resolute a philosophy as that of Descartes', Lyotard points out, 'can only demonstrate the legitimacy of science through what Valéry called the story of mind'.[41] Narrative keeps reasserting itself.

This is the radical side of antifoundationalism, and it has a certain surface attractiveness. We are all post-philosophers now, would appear to be the message, all politicians, all rhetoricians. Philosophy's pretensions to truth have been demonstrated to be untenable, another blow has been struck against received authority. If Plato, the arch-opponent of narrative aesthetics, can be betrayed by his own philosophical practice, then who can argue the case for anti-rhetorical rationality with much conviction any more?[42] Ignore the grand narratives (societies, systems, theories), the argument goes, and concentrate instead on the little narratives (selves):

> 'Why little stories?'
> 'Because they are short, because they are not extracts from some great history, and because they are difficult to fit into any great history. Remember the problems the Marxist narrative, to name but one, had with the student episode. How could that be fitted into a web of relations of production and class struggle?'
> '. . . history consists of a swarm of narratives, narratives that are passed on, made up, listened to and acted out; the people does not exist as a subject; it is a mass of thousands of little stories that are at once futile and serious, that are sometimes attracted together to form bigger stories, and which sometimes disintegrate into drifting elements.'[43]

The 'swarm of narratives' announces the collapse of grand narrative authority and of foundations. The post-philosophical project turns to tactics and strategy to realise its objectives. Tactics and strategy, however, assume the necessity of persuasion, and that means rhetoric. The question that inevitably arises at this point is: what are the conditions under which a given rhetoric gains plausibility?

Rhetoric can hardly be viewed as neutral: it is always in the service of an ideological position. To be a rhetorician, to engage in the task of analysing others' rhetorical practices, declared by them or otherwise, is to position your audience in a certain way. Success in this game depends very largely on an ability to manipulate the emotions, and its measure will be the size of the nuisance-value you can create in your field of activity: which is to say that market forces apply. Derrida counts as a considerable success under these terms of reference. His influence can be seen at work throughout a range of contemporary French cultural debates (as Lucien Goldmann has remarked, 'Derrida has a catalytic function' in this sphere[44]), and when it comes to American academic life there have been some spectacular victories to note: 'the fact is that deconstruction effectively displaced other intellectual programs in the minds and much of the work of the literary avant-garde', as one commentator has put it.[45] We could say that Derrida's antifoundational crusade has grown in credibility as it grows in numbers of supporters, like the Yale School, willing and able to inflict nuisance-value on the intellectual establishment. Antifoundationalism works hard at overturning traditional authority, but it substitutes another kind of authority in its stead: the authority which emanates from personal charisma. To answer the question posed above, it is under the conditions of charisma, exercised in the instance of deconstruction through the élitist technique of linguistic ingenuity, that rhetoric comes to attain plausibility. Not everyone will misuse rhetoric, but some will, some always do. It was to avoid such an outcome that foundationalism was devised. The spectre that it set out to exorcise was the spectre of clever, and possibly unscrupulous, language-game theorists (the sophists are always with us) exploiting the innocent and unwary.

Foundationalism works, therefore, to limit the abuse of language power. The risk we run when we ditch it unceremoniously is that we expose all the world's vulnerable little narratives, not so much to a tyrannical grand narrative, as to the verbally fluent, charisma-based narrative. Narratives of the latter sort will tend to want to deflect individuals ('the swarm') from connecting with those narratives rooted in a belief in collective action and a desire for radical socio-economic change. Lyotard is certainly in favour of change but his approach to it is very gradualist, in an anarchistic kind of way:

> The only way that networks of uncertain and ephemeral stories can gnaw away at the great institutionalized narrative apparatuses is by increasing the number of skirmishes that take place on the sidelines. That's what women who have had abortions, prisoners, conscripts, prostitutes, students and peasants have been doing in your country over the last decade or so. You make up little stories, or even segments of little stories, listen to them, transmit them and act them out when the time is right. . . . And use the opposite argument, and the right to be an entrepreneur, when it is a matter of checkmating some dangerous state monopoly: set up pirate radio stations, invent unorthodox teaching methods (as at dear old Vincennes), try to unionize soldiers or prostitutes . . .[46]

Individual skirmishing is no real match for the charismatic narrative. Power-games are all too often dominated by those who shout the loudest or talk the fastest, and they thrive when foundations collapse. Reducing philosophy to a form of fiction effectively removes some of the most important safeguards against abuses of power. Foundations, taking the notion in a fairly broad sense, can be justified on pragmatic grounds too.

To be fair, Lyotard is no advocate of rhetorical excess, and he is acutely aware that epistemological problems are very often solved by a fairly brutal application of *realpolitik*. Identifying what he calls 'an equation between wealth, efficiency, and truth', he goes on to argue, with considerable justification, that it is generally a case nowadays of

> No money, no proof – and that means no verification of statements and no truth. The games of scientific language become the games of the rich, in which whoever is wealthiest has the best chance of being right. . . . Scientists, technicians, and instruments are purchased not to find truth, but to augment power.

Lyotard is at his most perceptive at points like this, and he pursues, in exemplary antifoundationalist fashion, the misuse of power that results when institutions monopolise the legitimation privilege: 'Research sectors that are unable to argue that they contribute even indirectly to the optimization of the system's performance are abandoned by the flow of capital and doomed to senescence.'[47] Similar abuse is found in the political domain:

> The Party-state unrelentingly forces its citizens to tell, hear and act out nothing but its own scenario. The scenario may well change. The important point is that the Party-state is coercive; what it coerces people to do is less important.[48]

Lyotard is also perceptive about the utilitarianism prevalent in so many of our institutions (a trend that he traces back to the pervasive influence of cybernetics), where function has come to be considered the all-important factor:

> The question (overt or implied) now asked by the professionalist student, the State, or institutions of higher education is no longer 'Is it true?' but 'What use is it?' In the context of the mercantilization of knowledge, more often than not this question is equivalent to: 'Is it saleable?' And in the context of power-growth: 'Is it efficient?' Having competence in a performance-oriented skill does indeed seem saleable in the conditions described above, and it is efficient by definition. What no longer makes the grade is competence as defined by other criteria true/false, just/unjust, etc.[49]

Few left-wing theorists would dispute such a reading of recent cultural history in which the autonomy of higher education has been seriously eroded.

Lyotard has the virtue, which most recent antifoundationalists do not, that he is open to the political dimension of his theories. Having said that, it must also be said that the solutions he offers are pretty weak. Be agonistic in your philosophical discourse and you will be striking a blow against both the imperialist state and the multinationals, because you will be denying authoritarian principles of legitimation. Avoid grounds, they are probably an illusion anyway, and put your faith in narrativity. Treat all sequences as narratives and their legitimation procedures will reveal themselves to you. Follow the little narratives because the grand ones deceive you, and are no more than consensually accepted fictions anyway. Wrest control of legitimation from the powers-that-be, since 'the language game of legitimation is not state-political, but philosophical.' It is a basically libertarian programme that is being expounded, and its rhetoric is firmly directed at the individual:

> Destroy narrative monopolies, both as exclusive themes (of parties) and as exclusive pragmatics (exclusive to parties and markets). Take away the privileges the narrator has granted himself. Prove that there is as much power – and not less power – in listening, if you are a narratee, and in acting, if you are the narrated (and let the fools believe that you are singing the praises of servitude when you do so).[50]

'Destroy', 'take', 'prove', this is a dramatically presented programme of libertarian action, but it brings many awkward questions in its wake. Is it really possible for the isolated individual to get into a position to destroy narrative monopolies? Is it so easy to make the state pay attention to the efforts of isolated individuals? Who is fooling whom if the individual becomes a capitalist entrepreneur for subversive purposes? It remains to be seen whether such skirmishing on the margins will of itself be enough to dismantle a grand narrative, but it seems a rather romantic notion to espouse.

Libertarianism, of a greater or lesser kind, appears to be an active ingredient in the work of the leading French antifoundationalists. We have already seen Derrida in action against philosophical totalitarianism, restlessly seeking the opening in the totality which 'liberates time and genesis'; Baudrillard writes approvingly of a free market of signs and meaning, 'in which all classes eventually acquire the power to participate'.[51] As with Lyotard's championship of the cause of the little narrative and call for a war on totality, individual freedom seems to be the major motivating factor on display. All of these utopian visions assume foundationalism's collapse, but perhaps the collapse is more assumed than real: perhaps all that antifoundationalism has achieved is to make us aware, if regrettably so given the authoritarian overtones involved, of foundationalism's virtues. Even Hume reaches something of an accommodation with those virtues. His radical scepticism calls into doubt the regularity of all sequences in the physical world, or at the very least our ability to *prove* the necessary presence of such regularity through the medium of sense-experience. There is nothing to legitimate future action, in other words, since there is no guarantee of continuity, and so Hume introduces 'custom' as the enabling mechanism that will allow us to continue discourse in the face of the essential contingency of things. Having reached the kind of dead end that radical sceptics find so hard to avoid, he backtracks, in pragmatic fashion, into the world of action:

> Without the influence of custom, we should be entirely ignorant of every matter of fact beyond what is immediately present to the memory and the senses. We should never know how to adjust means to ends, or to employ our natural powers in the production of any effect. There would be an end at once of all action, as well as of the chief part of speculation.[52]

Hume's solution points the way the socially conscious (taking the term in its broadest sense of wanting to maintain discourse with others) sceptic has to move. The sceptic who is *not* socially conscious, whose concern is to accelerate the fragmentation of collective discourse and to problematise the shared criteria on which it is based, may proceed to embrace contingency with enthusiasm ('Contingency: that's the word which was looking for me', as Derrida declares[53]), thus raising the spectre of a possible collapse into private, and hence inaccessible, language games. Rorty makes the assumption that all the participants in his 'conversational' philosophy will understand each other, but that is a very large assumption to make in this kind of an antifoundational world.[54]

The attitude adopted towards contingency will constitute an index of the nuisance-value that an antifoundationalist will have for the philosophical establishment. The current revival of interest in rhetoric indicates the direction in which the search for discourse-preserving substitutes for foundations is moving. 'Indeed', Fish has argued, 'another word for anti-foundationalism *is* rhetoric, and one could say without exaggeration that modern anti-foundationalism is old sophism writ analytic.'[55] It is rhetoric that lies behind Lyotard's narrativity, Baudrillard's 'speculation' and Derrida's anti-logocentrist word-play. Rhetoric is a mode at once more flexible and more insidious, ideologically speaking, than 'custom'. It can lead ultimately to a very self-regarding individualism which at its worst is as élitist as anything that twentieth-century critique has to offer. Derrida, at his linguistically densest, Hartman and the Yale School at their most punningly ingenious, Baudrillard at his most cryptic, are less likely to start a revolution than to draw attention to their sheer marginality in the cultural debate. Practices such as erasure begin to look like forms of self-imposed exile from the business of adjusting means to ends. We might all agree that the poststructuralist turn is a valuable, and maybe even a necessary, one for philosophy to take, without thereby also agreeing that all discourse is merely a game in which linguistic dexterity is the individual's greatest – perhaps the individual's *only* – ambition. The latent nihilism of the proceedings announces itself at such points. Lyotard perhaps escapes the worst of this censure, but even this acceptable face of antifoundationalism is capable of taking refuge in cloudy rhetoric when the argument needs to be brought to a conclusion, as in the case of 'What is Postmodernism?': 'The answer is: Let us wage a war on totality; let us be witnesses to the unpresentable; let us activate the differences and save the honor of the name.' This 'answer' can mean anything or nothing. Whose totality? (anything can be a totality if you want it to be, just as anything can be a narrative). Which differences? Whose honour? Whose name? Is not witnessing a rather passive activity for a radical to be undertaking? What are those in charge of the erstwhile totality *doing* while 'we' are witnessing the unpresentable? When rhetoric takes over from proof it tends to look much like this, and unpacking the rhetoric leaves us with only unfulfilled, and for all practical purposes probably unfulfillable, desires. Philosophy has been collapsed into fiction ('Is there a real difference between a theory and a fiction?', Lyotard queries[56]), and the fiction found wanting. Reading against the grain, the answer to the question 'What is the politics of postmodernism?' would be: nihilistic skirmishing on the sidelines, self-imposed exile from collective discourse, the solipsism of tending one's own little narrative.

If we treat antifoundationalism as a form of radical scepticism then we can see why rhetoric has been called upon to plug the gap filled by custom in Hume. Without rhetorically based strategies we would be left with silence, and silence in the world of political action effectively equals acquiescence. Rhetoric helps the poststructuralist and postmodernist to resist acquiescence with the philosophical *status quo*, but it also serves to reinforce the ahistoricist cast to antifoundationalism, locking it into an eternal present with no reference to past states of affairs. Rhetoric encourages you to keep pushing forward into the unknown as an article of faith, erasing the debate behind you as you go (the 'historical amnesia' disapproved of by Jameson). Ahistoricism does not so much negate the problems of history, however, as leave someone else in control of them.[57] Lyotard attempts to counter this ahistoricist drift to postmodernist theory with a confrontational agonistics, giving a seemingly dialectical character to the rhetoric-led antifoundationalist enterprise;[58] yet the scale remains restricted, with the little narrative of the individual (how we get to 'us' in the closing remarks of 'What is Postmodernism?' is by no means obvious) taking precedence over the grand narrative of society. The stance is libertarian and it can be described as anti-authoritarian in intent, but not perhaps anti-authoritarian in any hegemony-threatening sense. Good intentions and messianic pronouncements are just not enough to destabilise the authoritarians in the long term.

Antifoundationalism is fundamentally suspicious of the use of meta-levels in any discourse. While there is a certain justification for this suspicion it can be taken too far and have unacceptable consequences for the anti-authoritarian thinker in the process. If meta-levels are going to be equated with authority then it seems inevitable that the radical will have to be opposed to them, especially if the radical is committed to the idea of a paradigm shift. History is littered with examples of theory-bound, foundation-bound, institutions which suppressed dissent – that is, anything that called dominant theory or foundation seriously into question[59] – and radicals are justified in referring to this history of intellectual suppression as a defence of their agonistic practice. What modern antifoundationalism often appears to be demanding, however, is not so much a paradigm shift as a permanent attitude of scepticism to any and all paradigms: 'Let us wage a war on totality.' Paradigms and meta-levels are deemed to be bad things by definition under this reading, and their practical utility in specific socio-political circumstances is being denied in favour of some kind of anarchistically inclined permanent revolution.[60] Lyotard, for example, will allow a 'multiplicity of finite meta-arguments' just as long as they are 'subject to eventual cancellation'. Yet surely it is not so much a case of meta-levels being bad by definition, as by their ideological function. It depends, in other words, on your relative positioning in the ideological debate. Ultimately we can judge a given theoretical position only by its likely effects, and the radical-sceptical one, with its disdain for means–ends policies, is most likely to result in exile from the discourse on power. Lyotard's agonistics is more viable than most strategies in this area, being directed against specific cultural abuses (the knowledge crisis, the imposition of cybernetics-inspired functionalism on intellectual enquiry, the power of the multinationals). But it remains essentially self-defeating in the way that it drives towards the abstract – 'Let us wage a war on totality' – while simultaneously denying individuals access to those metanarratives that would enable them to maximise the effect of their anti-authoritarian actions in collective endeavour. Lyotard wants action to remain on the individual level and he wants it to resist the interpretative reflex: 'It is necessary to posit the existence of a power that destabilizes the capacity for explanation.'[61] The brief glimpse of dialectics that we are afforded here is soon swallowed up in an eternal recurrence of socially unaccountable anti-interpretation. Individualism of action plus abstraction of goals is not the best recipe for social change, especially when it comes accompanied by a radical scepticism which makes a virtue out of contradiction for its own sake with scant regard for local conditions or overall aims.

$\cdot 8 \cdot$ 'THE SIGN OF AN INCOMMENSURABILITY'

The Differend and Genres of Discourse

Two main problems arise out of Lyotard's work, the problem of judgement and the problem of incommensurability. I want to turn now in this second time around Lyotard to his most sustained attempt to address these problems, *The Differend: Phrases in dispute*. Bennington has pointed out that Lyotard sometimes gives the impression 'that all the work preceding *Le Différend* is more or less radically mistaken, and that the new book cancels and supersedes all the earlier books', but emphasises that 'this question of judgement, with its aesthetico-political dimensions, will remain through the apparent later repudiation of the major manifest themes of these earlier works.'[1] The text is an acknowledgement of the difficulties to be faced in an antifoundational universe:

> As distinguished from a litigation, a differend [*différend*] would be a case of conflict between (at least) two parties, that cannot be equitably resolved for lack of a rule of judgement applicable to both arguments. One side's legitimacy does not imply the other's lack of legitimacy. However, applying a single rule of judgement to both in order to settle their differend as though it were merely a litigation would wrong (at least) one of them (and both of them if neither side admits this rule). . . . A wrong results from the fact that the rules of the genre of discourse by which one judges are not those of the judged genre or genres of discourse.[2]

The picture that emerges from the study is of a highly fragmented universe of discourse where 'genres are incommensurable', since 'each has its own interests', and there is no ultimate genre to appeal to in the event of any conflict between genres: 'The principle of an absolute victory of one genre over the others has no sense.'[3] Incommensurability is a wedge driven right into the heart of foundationalism in the way that it destroys the possibility of transcendent authority:

> Authority is not deduced. Attempts at legitimating authority lead to vicious circles. . . . The aporia of a deduction of authority, or the aporia of sovereignty, is the sign that the phrase of authorization cannot result from a phrase stemming from a different regimen. It is the sign of an incommensurability between the normative phrase and all others.[4]

This raises the question as to whether there can be any authority to appeal to *within* genres, and Lyotard implies that there can be: 'between two narratives belonging to the same genre, one can be judged stronger than the other if it comes nearer the goal of narratives: to link onto the occurrence as such by signifying it and by referring to it.' This is perilously close to a criterion of value judgement for someone who has appeared to shy away from such an entity – 'if I am asked by what criteria do I judge, I will have no answer to give' – and it is worth exploring what commitments it brings in its wake. Lyotard's example at this juncture argues that the 'Christian narrative vanquished the other narratives in Rome because by introducing the love of occurrence into narratives and narrations of narratives, it designated what is at stake in the genre itself.' What is at stake proves to be love, 'as the principal operator of exemplary narratives and diegeses', and it is derived from 'a commandment of universal attraction, *Love one another*, addressed to all heroes, all narrators, and all narratees'. The Christian narrative exemplifies this commandment better than its rivals, Lyotard claims, and thus is able to link on to other narratives and encompass them within its own: 'all of the events already told in the narratives of infidels and unbelievers can be re-told as so many signs portentous of the new commandment (the synoptic tables of the two Testaments).'[5]

Several problems arise with an analysis of this sort. 'What is at stake' is clearly the authority to which we are supposed to appeal, and that makes it sound like an essence, at which point we immediately enter into problems with metaphysical commitments. In the absence of any exhaustive analysis of the concept of love in the other narratives in question, it must remain unclear exactly why the Christian version of love is deemed by Lyotard to approximate more closely to the ideal. Might it not be argued that what we are faced with in this particular historical example is incommensurability? (Incommensurability applies between genres, I admit, but the boundary between narrative and genre in Lyotard is by no means as clear as it might be.) Who decides what is at stake and whether it has been adequately realised? The winners? In retrospect it is easy to see, in brute socio-historical terms, which was the stronger narrative in the Roman case chosen by Lyotard, but would that be apparent *now* in a conflict within a given genre? When you try to pin them down, signifying, referring and designating what is at stake in a genre are extremely vague criteria for interpretation. Antifoundationalism has a tendency to lead us into just such interpretive culs-de-sac as this.

The real problem of judgement lies between genres, however, and Lyotard insists that it is our duty 'to bear witness to the differend';[6] that is, not to opt for the foundationalist route out of incommensurability, tempting though that choice may be. This latter manoeuvre is the besetting sin of intellectuals: 'An intellectual', Lyotard argues, 'is someone who helps forget differends, by advocating a given genre, whichever one it may be (including the ecstasy of sacrifice), for the sake of political hegemony.' Philosophers, on the other hand, are on the side of the angels, in the business of 'detecting differends and in finding the (impossible) idiom for phrasing them'.[7] This is philosophy as a resistance to foundations and it has something of the guerrilla quality that we have come to associate with Derrida. The goal of postmodernist philosophy is to unsettle us and prevent us from succumbing to the lure of totality in all its many guises: 'Are "we" not telling, whether bitterly or gladly, the great narrative of the end of great narratives? For thought to remain modern, doesn't it suffice that it think in terms of the end of some history?'[8] The end of history becomes just one more genre peddled by intellectuals for their own self-interested purposes, and it is to be countered by the development of what Lyotard calls a 'philosophical politics apart from the politics of "intellectuals" and of politicians' (the 'increasing inability to identify with the discourse of Marxism' is clearly visible behind such bitter asides as this[9]). Rather conveniently for Lyotard's project, politics, in his formulation of it anyway, 'is not *a* genre', though 'it bears witness to the nothingness which opens up with each occurring phrase and on the occasion of which the differend between genres of discourse is born.'[10] Philosophical politics, then, is to be seen as a flexible response to new states of affairs, a response not in thrall to outmoded grand narratives such as dialectics, which orient research and fix results: 'As for the philosophy of history, about which there can be no question in a critical thought, it is an illusion born from the appearance that signs are exempla or schemata.'[11] The differend works against such a radical excess of prejudice (Marx is described by Lyotard as being a 'prisoner of the logic of result'); it is 'reborn from the very resolution of supposed litigations. It summons humans to situate themselves in unknown phrase universes, even if they don't have the feeling that something has to be phrased. (For this is a necessity and not an obligation).'[12] 'Unknown phrase universes' demand skirmishing on the sidelines, the refusal on the part of the individual to play the grand narrative game: 'We want a politics based upon narratives, which are social elements, and not upon knowledge.'[13] Judgement at such points becomes tactical in terms of the little narrative taking place, rather than having to be submitted to any logic of result. 'You can't make a political "program" with it', Lyotard remarks of such judgement, but you can, in one of his favourite phrases, 'bear witness to it'.[14]

Whether bearing witness to the differend, incommensurability and unknown phrase universes will destabilise entrenched grand narratives remains an unresolved question, but the antifoundational import of *The Differend*'s argument is clear. The objective throughout is to undermine what Lyotard refers to as the 'infallible third party' argument of foundationalist discourse:

> This dilemma is the one that assails all philosophies based on showing. . . . They generally elude the dilemma through recourse to the testimony of some infallible third party, to whom what is hidden from the current 'addressee' of the ostensive phrase is supposedly absolutely (constantly) revealed. There is little difference in this regard between the God of the Cartesians and the pre-predicative cogito of the phenomenologists. Both groups admit an entity who is in a state of 'cosmic exile'.[15]

There is no such third party to the little narrative: differends and incommensurabilities problematise its very possibility. Legitimating authority, such as it is in Lyotard, remains locked within genres, where it obeys the dictates of 'political' rather than metaphysical necessity. Skirmishing is legitimated negatively by the fact that there is no supreme genre:

> The idea that a supreme genre encompassing everything that's at stake could supply a supreme answer to the key-questions of the various genres founders upon Russell's aporia. Either this genre is part of the set of genres, and what is at stake in it is but one among others, and therefore its answer is not supreme. Or else, it is not part of the set of genres, and it does not therefore encompass all that is at stake, since it excepts what is at stake itself.[16]

Lyotard is caught by the same logic, of course, and it is highly questionable whether he resolves it satisfactorily by the 'politics is not a genre' move. Rather in the manner of erasure or 'tonk' this is just too convenient a move for a blind eye to be turned to it, and by Lyotard's own admission it has the effect of rendering politics outside what is at stake anyway. Calling politics the realm of bearing witness to what is at stake takes us no further forward as to how to resolve debates *concerning* what is at stake.

Lyotard rather too easily glosses over this problem, as in the following exchange from 'Lessons in paganism':

'If you abandon the theoretical model, you abandon the democratic model, and you throw the door wide open to tyranny.'

'No, to paganism. What we need is a politics which is both godless and just.'[17]

Paganism requires consent, however, and it is by no means clear that such consent is generally forthcoming ('you must live a very sheltered life indeed if you suppose that the big industry and big social movements associated with modernity are a thing of the past', as Ree tartly remarks[18]). Nor is it clear what justice actually is. Lyotard remarks that

There are no criteria because the idea of criteria comes from the discourse of truth and supposes a referent or a 'reality' and, by dint of this, it does not belong to the discourse of justice. This is very important. It must be understood that if one wants criteria in the discourse of justice one is tolerating de facto the encroachment of the discourse of justice by the discourse of truth.

Yet again this kind of move seems just too convenient, and Lyotard's insistence on the 'determinate singularity' of all discourses looks like nothing so much as a way of avoiding the issue of what is at stake.[19] It also remains to be seen whether demarcating truth off from other discourses is an effective break against the development of tyranny. It assumes that there will be enough goodwill present within discourses to allow the 'multiplicity of little narratives' to thrive – and that is precisely what is at stake. The differend seems to have brought us full circle back to a recognition, however reluctantly arrived at, of foundationalism's virtues.

The first two times around Lyotard have revealed several questionable moves in the prosecution of the war on totality. The more his arguments are pressed the more they seem to take refuge in rather empty rhetoric, the 'bearing witness' ploy which never reduces to anything very concrete in terms of individual action. There has to be a real fear that this 'outline of a politics that would respect both the desire for justice and the desire for the unknown' would leave the individual very exposed were it ever put into practical action.[20] Lyotard's concern for the individual is highly laudable, as is his dislike of authoritarian systems, but despite the political perspective his work is still heavily inscribed with the ideologically suspect motives which mark modern, and most particularly

French, antifoundationalism. We are not yet beyond aesthetics, hard though Lyotard tries to provide us with a route to that desired state.

·9· 'I HAVE A DREAM OF AN INTELLECTUAL'

'Svelteness' and the War on Totality

Our first two times around Lyotard from a left-wing perspective seem to lead rather inexorably to his categorisation as a neo-conservative thinker: a champion of the individual but a disbeliever in the efficacy of theory-led collective action: 'Majority does not mean large number', he asserts emotively, 'it means great fear.'[1] The case against him has been succinctly summed up by Sarup:

> Politically it is clear that thinkers like Lyotard and Foucault are neo-conservatives. They take away the dynamic which liberal social thought has traditionally relied upon. They offer us no theoretical reason to move in one social direction rather than another. On the whole post-structuralists think of rationality as a limiting framework. They are against what they call the imperialism of reason. Lyotard's intellectual trajectory has brought him to a position where he now wants to abstain from anything that is connected with the 'metanarrative of emancipation'.[2]

The problem of Foucault is not one that I wish to follow up here, although I will be returning to him briefly in a moment; but I do want to consider whether, this third time around Lyotard, we can salvage anything of the postmodernist project for socialism. Perhaps *despite* the conservatism, if we let the charge stand, there are lessons for the socialist 'metanarrative of emancipation' in Lyotard. (Lyotard's not unreasonable argument against metanarratives of emancipation is that 'neither economic nor political liberalism, nor the various Marxisms, emerge from the sanguinary last two centuries free from the suspicion of crimes against mankind'.[3]) As promised, I will be taking a more positive line on Lyotard this, third, time around, and it is a line that leads back to the individual: to the concept of 'svelteness', a guerrilla-like attitude of flexible and creative response by the individual to late capitalism's many and insistent pressures:

> it is work in the nineteenth-century sense that must be done away with, and by other means than unemployment. Stendhal was already saying this at the beginning of the nineteenth century: the ideal is no longer physical strength as it was for the man of antiquity; it is suppleness, speed, the ability to metamorphose (go to a ball in the evening and fight a war at dawn). Svelteness, awakening, a Zen and Italian term.[4]

'Svelteness' might just be the means of an accommodation being reached between postmodernist and socialist theory. There are dialectical over-tones to svelteness – it might be seen as a more creative version of antithesis, antithesis for the postmodern world perhaps – and it will be read back into the texts by Lyotard that we have already examined in Chapters 7 and 8 in order to maximise their subversive potential.

Returning to Foucault briefly, his vision of 'the intellectual' can help us to understand the desire that lies behind svelteness:

> I have a dream of an intellectual who destroys self-evidences and universalities, who locates and points out in the inertias and constraints of the present the weak points, the openings, the lines of stress; who constantly displaces himself, not knowing exactly where he'll be nor what he'll think tomorrow, because he is too attentive to the present.

Bennington argues that 'Lyotard would no doubt think that this account still gives too great a privilege to the intellectual, or fails to recognize that the description destroys its object',[5] but I feel that we can nevertheless find common cause between the Foucaultian anti-univer-salist intellectual and the Lyotardean svelte individual. Svelteness is a state of mind, a condition of readiness to confront and displace metanarratives as they relentlessly try to impose their will on vulnerable individuals. It requires the individual – thinker, aesthete and warrior all in one, in what sounds like an idealised version of the urban guerrilla of Marxist mythology[6] – to be a permanently vigilant antithesis to cultural pressure of the late capitalist variety. There is the attentiveness to the present, the will to resist universalities and the call for eternal re-creation of the self in this image that recalls Foucault's 'dream'. Both are engaged in a war on totality. It is the dream of going beyond aesthetics, of escaping from the constraints of systems, logic and value judgement. The svelte individual, the one who has rejected the claims of any and all metanarratives, is not so bound, and is to be encouraged to engage in the kind of resistance campaigns mapped out in *The Postmodern Condition* and 'Lessons in paganism'. I want to return to those two works now, reading the svelte individual back into them to see how much this might alter our previously negative perspective on the postmodernist project.

It is easy to pick holes in ideas like 'skirmishing on the sidelines', with their suggestion of an uncoordinated gradualist approach to change, but it has to be acknowledged that sometimes they work. In the examples given in 'Lessons in paganism', women who have had abortions over the last few decades *have* helped to alter the climate of public opinion about the act, such that the law has been modified to some extent in most Western countries; private entrepreneurs in the media (pirate radio, for example) *have* helped to loosen up the practices of state monopoly broadcasting institutions; alternative teaching methods have led many educational institutions at least to *examine* the teaching process and the power relationships implicit within it; the unionisation of prostitutes has drawn attention to the fact that sex is in fact a highly discriminatory form of *work*.[7] 'You make up little stories, or even segments of little stories, listen to them, transmit them and act them out when the time is right'; this is the kind of ferment that is always going on under the surface of society amongst the disaffected and the marginalised, and it may well be the most effective means of protest their situation allows. One might take their actions as evidence of grand narrative failure on their behalf. The less grandiose way of describing Lyotard's 'war on totality' is as protest politics. Issue-led politics of this kind has never been very popular on the European left, which is generally more concerned to impose and implement change from above, but again one has to look at each situation on its own merits. Svelte skirmishing, reacting to circumstances in terms of individual need rather than administrative convenience, can be courageous, as well as revolutionary in its own way. Little narratives cannot always wait on grand narratives to take effect (the promised millennium is a very poor consolation for immediate individual distress), or to adjust to rapidly changing conditions. Clearly, the ideal is for there to be dialectical interaction between little narratives and grand narratives: both are required in a healthy society. To be truly successful, grand narrative must work at individual level without coercion, and also provide scope for individual initiative; but the tone of impatience to be noted in both 'Lessons in paganism' and *The Postmodern Condition* suggests that, in Lyotard's opinion, this is not always so, and that something drastic and dramatic has to be done when grand narrative fails the individual. Svelteness is the suitably dramatic response sketched out. Rhetorical gesture it may be, but it is directed against a very real grand narrative problem: what happens when grand narrative legitimation procedures and individual desire go out of synchrony? Increasingly, as Bennington notes, that will be the focus of Lyotard's philosophical enquiry: '*how to judge* what is here called the "critical function" of what is here called "desire"'.[8] 'There is a natural finality in desire', Lyotard claims, 'or in the persistence of being what one is',[9] which signals quite clearly where his sympathies will lie in any choice to be made between desire and grand narrative legitimation: the svelteness of desire escapes questions of foundation, in Lyotard's opinion.

What Bennington has referred to as 'the broad and simplifying categories characteristic of *The Postmodern Condition*'[10] make better sense when viewed as a guide to protest politics by the svelte individual. In fact, in its crudeness and directness of approach – so lacking in what Jonathan Ree has referred to as 'that streak of hesitancy which is such an important (and amiable) part of traditional philosophical institutions'[11] – lies much of the work's appeal. This is a book of practical political philosophy. What the individual is reacting to in this case is the wholesale, and potentially dehumanising, commercialisation and computerisation of individual existence in postindustrial society. This is a situation in which the multinational corporations have 'reached the point of imperiling the stability of the State', thus putting the individual even more at risk of exploitation and marginalisation (corporations being even less answerable to the individual than are states).[12] Further marginalisation is likely to occur because of a perceived crisis within capitalism:

> The crisis of over-capitalisation that the world economy has been suffering since 1974 and will suffer for sometime to come invalidates the presupposition of the discursive genre of post-Keynesian political economy, namely that a harmonious regulation of needs and the means to satisfy them in work and in capital, with a view to the greatest enjoyment of goods and services for all – that this regulation is possible, and on the way to being achieved.[13]

This is fertile ground for the svelte individual, caught between increasingly ineffectual political grand narratives (often more concerned at 'saving the phenomena' of the theory than with the plight of the individual) and socially divisive, as well as socially selective, economic decline that works to destroy the integrity of the individual by means of unemployment or underemployment. Lyotard's call to open up the data banks to the scrutiny of the general public is designed to prevent computerisation from becoming 'the "dream" instrument for controlling and regulating the market system, extended to include knowledge itself and governed exclusively by the performativity principle'. Something unpredictable, such as svelteness promises, is required to break this dangerous cycle of social control which, Lyotard not unrealistically prophesies, 'would inevitably involve the use of terror'.[14] It is the unpredictability of svelteness that Lyotard is relying upon to break up narrative monopolies, and it is that unpredictability which poses such problems for rationalist-oriented social theories of the Marxist kind. Areas of conflict here are many and varied. The individual can all too often appear to be an anarchistically inclined entity to the prevailing political system, no matter how liberation-conscious the latter may consider itself to be. Similarly, the system, whether corporate capitalism or corporate state, can present an authoritarian and oppressive face on occasion to even the most well-disposed and socially minded of individuals. Lyotard has homed in on an area of considerable difficulty for grand narrative social theorists: the nature of the balance between individual and system. In most cases the system has a distinct advantage. Svelteness is designed to counteract the *realpolitik* that traditionally lurks behind grand narrative politics.

Svelteness lies at the heart of Lyotard's theory of agonistics. He emphasises 'the agonistic aspect of society' in which individual ' "moves" necessarily provoke "countermoves" ', and the more disorienting the move the better: 'Reactional countermoves are no more than pro-grammed effects in the opponent's strategy; they play into his hands and thus have no effect on the balance of power.'[15] It is unpredictability that Lyotard wants, because as long as that unpredictability is on the horizon grand narrative power relationships can never be put into operation: and, he notes, 'what is striking is that someone always comes along to disturb the order of "reason".'[16] The unpredictability of the unexpected move, the new statement, the unconditioned response, has a specific political role to play in preventing authority from ever becoming entrenched. What is needed to prevent abuse of power is 'not only a theory of communication, but a theory of games which accepts agonistics as a founding principle'.[17] Svelteness then becomes a case of countering institutional moves and countermoves (themselves relatively predictable) by unexpectedly disorienting individual moves and countermoves. The objective is to displace the boundaries of institutions, to keep unpredictability permanently on the horizon by means of svelte action:

> Does the university have a place for language experiments (poetics)? Can you tell stories in a cabinet meeting? Advocate a cause in the barracks? The answers are clear: yes, if the university opens creative workshops; yes, if the cabinet works with prospective scenarios.[18]

What is being advocated is a piecemeal, gradualist approach to social change unlikely to appeal to those in thrall to imperialist grand narratives, but it does have the powerful effect of bringing dialectics right down to personal level: the agonistically minded individual then becomes a living antithesis to authoritarianism. Put in Lyotard's small-scale context of operations, agonistics is far less remote from the individual's concerns than dialectics can often appear to be. Perhaps the only question that needs to be asked is if such programmes of action have to be exclusive of a grand narrative? Lyotard seems to assume they must be, but the difference between an agonistics of emancipation and a metanarrative of emancipation may not be as unbridgeable as he thinks. It is not impossible to theorise a grand narrative which can encompass, and even actively encourage, little-narrative unpredictability: that can happen, for example, in the arts – a point to which I will return. Grand narrative is not necessarily entirely blind to the importance of the symbolic acts in which little narratives specialise.[19]

A more pressing question arises as to whether there is an implicit metanarrative at work in Lyotard's social theory. That casually dropped-in phrase 'founding principle' clearly needs closer examination. When is a founding principle not foundational? Presumably when the theory it sanctions proves to have the desired effects, the 'pragmatics' of which Lyotard so regularly speaks; but that is merely circular reasoning of the kind that is easily dealt with by the 'usual superficial criticism' school – or even pragmatic antifoundationalists of the Fish variety. 'Why are post-structuralists so frightened of the universal?', Sarup wonders, and 'why is Lyotard telling us yet another grand narrative at the end of grand narrative?'[20] The problem is compounded when Lyotard argues that, as regards scientific pragmatics, 'it is now dissension that must be emphasized. Consensus is a horizon that is never reached. . . . It is necessary to posit the existence of a power that destabilizes the capacity for explanation.'[21] If dissension is necessary then it is beginning to sound suspiciously universal and logocentric. Bennington has tried to defend Lyotard against such a charge by claiming that

> the impression that book [*The Postmodern Condition*] may have created, namely that dissensus was a telos proposed in opposition to the telos of consensus defended by Habermas, was mistaken. What idea could we possibly have of a pure dissensus? Dissensus implies conflict, and *pure* conflict is unthinkable.

This is ingenious but it does not entirely solve the problem. Pure or not, dissensus is being used as a founding principle in this instance and that raises the spectre of the absolute. Bennington argues that *The Differend* is to be read as 'an attempt to refine on the "dissensus" of *The Postmodern Condition*, away from any teleological or narrative invest-ment',[22] but this is to endow something like grand narrative status on *The Differend* within Lyotard's oeuvre, which seems like a dubious move to make (and in Derrida's terms of reference one verging on ultrastructuralism). At such points Lyotard looks to be caught up in the same cycle of the history of metaphysics and the destruction of the history of metaphysics as Derrida, and we are left with the manifest paradox that agonistics, the projected scourge of foundational philosophy, can get under way only by trading on the benefits of foundationalism. Svelteness is not as metaphysically innocent as it might like to appear.

Lyotard will want to play the incommensurability card at such a juncture, and we might now consider whether this can help to retrieve his theory of agonistics to any significant extent. Agonistics takes place within a discourse, and discourses have two main properties for Lyotard: they need no foundation, and they are incommensurable.

> The paganism elaborated in the Instructions in question is more akin to an Idea in Kant's sense. This paganism is not demonstrated; it is not derived; it cannot be articulated or deduced. It is simply the Idea of a Society, that is, ultimately, of a set of diverse pragmatics (a set that is neither totalizable nor countable, actually). The specific feature of this set would be that the different language games that are caught up in this pagan universe are incommunicable to each other. They cannot be synthesized into a unifying metadiscourse. . . . This social universe is formed by a plurality of games without any one of them being able to claim that it can say all the others.[23]

This is familiar enough antifoundationalist territory – no logocentre, no genre of all genres to act as a break on our metaphysically radical discourse. The argument that seems to be developing is that if a discourse needs no foundation for its *existence*, then no foundation is necessary either for anything that takes place within it. Pragmatics have agreed rules but these rules can be changed, indeed agonistics can be the way of bringing about such changes by radical moves and countermoves. There is no need to *justify* discourse, Lyotard is, quite rightly, arguing, therefore no need to justify its pragmatics or agonistics. Such things simply persist. Justification, such as it is, is local and tactical within a discourse, which, by definition, cannot communicate with, nor in any way encroach upon, the pragmatics of any other discourse: 'if one wants criteria in the discourse of justice one is tolerating de facto the encroachment of the discourse of justice by the discourse of truth.'[24] This separation of discourses enables Lyotard to make prescriptive statements – in effect, he is saying 'one ought to be agonistic', 'one ought to be svelte' – and then to claim that he is under no obligation to demonstrate the truth of these statements because prescription and truth inhabit different, incommensurable, discourses. At that point, pragmatics takes over:

> These rules prescribe what must be done so that a denotative statement, or

an interrogative one, or a prescriptive one, etc., is received as such and recognized as 'good' in accordance with the criteria of the game to which it belongs.[25]

Late twentieth-century science, or 'postmodern science' as Lyotard prefers to call it, provides him with a considerable source of examples of both incommensurability and the virtues of agonistics. He is drawn, predictably enough, to catastrophe theory and chaos theory:

> All that exist are 'islands of determinism.' Catastrophic antagonism is literally the rule. . . . Postmodern science – by concerning itself with such things as undecidables, the limits of precise control, conflicts characterized by incomplete information, '*fracta*', catastrophes, and pragmatic paradoxes – is theorizing its own evolution as discontinuous, catastrophic, nonrectifiable, and paradoxical. It is changing the meaning of the word *knowledge*, while expressing how such a change can take place. It is producing not the known, but the unknown.[26]

Producing not the known but the unknown is the goal of agonistics and svelteness, which can take their cue from the basically antagonistic character of natural systems. At the heart of nature lies conflict. Postmodern science is taken to justify agonistic–svelte behaviour, although it should be pointed out that such grounding of one theory on another leaves the grounded theory in a very vulnerable position. Scientific theories in modern times tend to have very short life-spans, and chaos–catastrophe may prove to be no exception. Post-postmodern science may look very different to postmodern, thus depriving Lyotard of much of the force of his theories. Catastrophic antagonism is literally the rule only as long as the theory holds. If it is still defended *after* that point, then we have a case of saving the phenomena on our hands, and a consequent loss of credibility for the postmodernist position.

For the time being, however, postmodern science does provide a model for svelteness and agonistic behaviour. We might characterise it as a programme as follows: take nothing on trust; keep the limits of your theories under pressure; generate displacement and paradox: in other words, use little narratives, the more wayward the better, as a weapon in the war against grand narratives. 'The intelligentsia's function should not be to tell the truth and save the world, but to will the power to play out, listen to and tell stories'.[27] Lyotard's intellectual edges towards Foucault's 'dream' with such pronouncements. Further than that, it is the playing out, listening and telling of *incommensurable* stories which do not attempt to encroach on each other's pragmatics, stories which respect each other's right to exist:

> don't forget that when I draw your attention to a few minor political

matters and issues in contemporary history, I am merely telling you a story, unfolding a little story of my own. As a preliminary lesson, I would suggest that, rather than asking if that story is more or less true than any other, you should simply note that it exists, that it is the product of an almost invincible power to tell stories that we all share to a greater or lesser extent. ... When I tell my story, I am not acting as a mouthpiece for some universal history. And I make no claim to being a professional theorist, or to be saving the world by reminding it of a lost meaning.[28]

'You should simply note that it exists' ('neither comment, nor underscore, nor extract'), although you are at liberty to respond with a narrative of your own in the agonistic game of move and countermove; and if your narrative proves to be at variance with your opponent's, then both of you must just 'bear witness to the differend'. If such prescriptives lack the 'dynamic' referred to by Sarup, they also lack the pressurising tactics (for Lyotard, 'terrorism') that is all too common a feature of grand narrative discourse. The 'argument from authority' is signally missing. Another way of reading 'incommensurability' is as respect for individual narratives, and that might be seen as one of the more appealing characteristics of Lyotard's postmodern project; although there is always the nagging doubt in the back of one's mind that this assumes more goodwill than may actually exist in the world. 'You throw the door wide open to tyranny. ... No to paganism' is still a highly optimistic conclusion to draw; regrettably enough, most of us would see tyranny as the far more likely prospect in the aftermath of theory's abandonment.

Questions might also be raised about the foundational appearance of the quasi-Kantian 'Idea of Society' that legitimates pragmatics, agonistics and svelteness. This undemonstratable, underivable, unarticulatable and undeducible entity has something of the character of the Derridean trace as well ('always already there'), but we are justified in asking whether it has disguised commitments. On closer inspection it would seem that it does. It is not *simply* the 'Idea of a society' but the idea of a certain *kind* of society, one with 'diverse pragmatics' which are already defined as 'incommunicable'. Paganism, rather conveniently, includes exactly what Lyotard's theory of society requires. We are sliding back towards founding principles and all their attendant problems. Paganism sounds like a telos, it seems to function like a telos, but of course it cannot *be* a telos, or Lyotard's antifoundational enterprise collapses. In the same way that he moves rather quickly from the sheer *existence* of narrative (which needs no philosophical legitimation), to preference for a certain *kind* of narrative (which *does* need such legitimation), Lyotard slides from society to his ideal society. It is in that gap that his antifoundationalist project is at its most suspect. Even as he moves through it at speed the foundationalist dilemma is taking shape again.

If we allow him the move, Lyotard is capable of sounding anything like a neo-conservative. The attack on capitalism in 'The sign of history' being a case in point:

> Since Marx, we have learned that what presents itself as unity for the phrases of the postmodern Babel, as something that is capable of verifying them, at least in experience subject to concepts and direct presentation – we have learned that this is the impostor-subject and blindly calculating rationality called Capital, especially when it lays hold of phrases themselves in order to commercialize them and make surplus-value out of them in the new condition of the *Gemeinwesen* called 'computerized society'. . . we can easily find what we need to judge the pretension of Capital's phrase to validate all phrases according to its criterion of performativity, and the imposture which puts that phrase in the place of the critical judge – to judge this pretension and this imposture, to criticize them and to re-establish the rights of the critical tribunal.[29]

These are impeccably radical sentiments and they hardly merit the label 'neo-conservative'. When svelteness, agonistics and pragmatics are directed towards *this* goal, then they can be supported wholeheartedly from the left. The doubts start to return only when we ask whether the differend of itself will be enough to hold that critical tribunal together. Or if the incommensurable little narratives of the 'we' above can ever have enough cohesiveness to bring down a grand narrative. Nevertheless, for all his post-Marxist posturing, Lyotard retains some residues of his Marxist past.[30]

If residues remain, they stop well short of acceptance of grand narrative in any form, and svelteness will be the appropriate attitude to adopt to keep it at bay. Our choice is polarised by Lyotard: either grand narrative or little narrative, either submission or svelteness. But again one might speculate as to whether there cannot be dialectical interaction, whether the one kind of narrative necessarily precludes the existence of the other. The arts suggest otherwise on this latter point. Little narratives can flourish there within larger theories or programmes: a surrealist painting can express the ideals of the movement; a jazz musician can find room for improvisation and individual creativity within a musical theory that in some ways is highly prescriptive; an author or playwright is not necessarily limited creatively by writing didactic works to express a political or social theory. Multiplicity is entirely possible within a theoretical framework in such cases. Lyotard might argue that we are talking about discourses rather than metanarratives here and that the analogy therefore does not hold, but the relation of individual practitioner to discourse looks very like that of little narrative to grand narrative. The problem surely lies in the rigidity of the grand narrative –

and the solution in its flexibility. Rather than cutting the individual free from all systems of explanation and modes of collective action, we might better work to build in greater flexibility to our grand narratives: to build in something like svelteness with its overtones of healthy scepticism towards abuse of authority. Marxism, to take a case in point, can be interpreted in a wide variety of ways. One often feels that Lyotard dwells on the worst possible case of the grand narratives he does not like, without acknowledging that more positive readings are possible. Baby invariably seems to go with bathwater.

The strength of Lyotard's polemic is that it does concentrate attention on the vulnerable and frequently neglected little narrative, and he has a point that this has been subjected to some indefensible treatment over the 'sanguinary last two centuries'. The polemic is often very good indeed, and Lyotard's scepticism often well justified. Whether he is also justified in the extent of his iconoclasm is more debatable. It is easy enough to pick holes in foundationalism, much more difficult to articulate a position of your own without smuggling in foundational assumptions by the back door. Lyotard is frequently guilty of this latter sin, and the final verdict would have to be that his rhetoric is better than his logic. It is true that there are analytical precedents for Lyotard's use of incommensurability (see the work of Kuhn and his followers[31]) and paradox and aporia (in the case of a contradiction within a logical proof, assume what you want[32]), but they rarely draw such an extreme conclusion as Lyotard does – namely that we can scrap foundationalism once these entities come on to the scene. When it comes to antifoundationalism I would still argue that a surface radicalism all too frequently flatters to deceive, but Lyotard's surface is not without its lessons for the left nevertheless.

·10· 'THE TEXT MUST SCOFF AT MEANING'

Baudrillard and the Politics of Simulation and Hyperreality

Many of the themes encountered in the work of Derrida and Lyotard also appear in Jean Baudrillard, whose provocative and iconoclastic theories about the interpretive process are very much in the antifoundationalist line of development. In this chapter I will be confronting Baudrillard's theories of history, reality and aesthetics, in order to demonstrate a particularly extreme version of the anti-judgemental imperative: a version which might best be called post-aesthetic. There is a distinctly apocalyptic cast to Baudrillard's thought, and he consistently wants to go beyond the realm of value judgement:

> For the problem of the disappearance of music is the same as that of the disappearance of history: it will not disappear *for want of* music, it will disappear for having exceeded that limit point, vanishing point, it will disappear in the perfection of its materiality, in its own special effect (beyond which there is no longer any aesthetic judgement or aesthetic pleasure, it is ecstasy of musicality and its end). It is exactly the same with history. Here too we have exceeded that limit where, by the sophistication of events and information, history as such ceases to exist.[1]

Beyond aesthetic judgement and aesthetic pleasure, in true antifoundationalist fashion, 'the text must obliterate all reference ... the text must scoff at meaning.'[2] Using a range of texts, mainly from later in his career when his post-aestheticism is at its most developed, I will be considering whether Baudrillard's theories of simulation and hyperreality can be turned to tactical account by a materialist philosophy, or whether they are merely sterile and negative when it comes to planning political action. Eventually I will be looking in closer detail at that quintessentially post-aesthetic text, *America*.

It is possible to take Baudrillard too seriously. This is not hard-edged philosophical argument most of the time, but deliberately provocative (on occasion even playful) remarks from the far reaches of the anti-foundationalist enterprise. 'Only signs without referents, empty, sense-less, absurd and elliptical signs, absorb us', we are informed, as the Derridean world of signs without truth, fault or origin is simply assumed to be the world that we already inhabit.[3] Baudrillard offers even less in the way of proof for his often outrageous statements than do Derrida or Lyotard ('patience and immersion in the particular do not seem to be his particular virtues', as Douglas Kellner somewhat tartly observes), and he presents us with a strange dream-like realm where 'reality no longer has the time to take on the appearance of reality . . . reality is nothing other than its own simulation.'[4] This is McLuhanism for the millennium – except that, as Baudrillard warns us, 'the year 2000 will perhaps not take place'[5] – and it does not bear any great weight of philosophical analysis (for all that one commentator can speak of 'the metaphysical pain of Baudrillard', and another of there being a 'bitter Nietzschean edge' to his work[6]). Clearly, we shall need to engage with the concepts of simulation and simulacra, hyperreality and the end of history to some extent, but the major reason for including Baudrillard in a study of this nature is to discover where post-aesthetics takes criticism. To confront Baudrillard is to confront the post-aesthetic mentality in full flight from meaning: 'One does not escape meaning by dissociation, disconnection or deterritorialization. One escapes meaning by replacing it with a more radical simulacrum, a still more conventional order.'[7] The attitudes struck are more interesting than the arguments usually are, and Baudrillard gives out some very clear signals in *America* of how we are supposed to behave in a post-aesthetic world: 'The only question in this journey is: how far can we go in the extermination of meaning, how far can we go in the non-referential desert form without cracking up and, of course, still keep alive the esoteric charm of disappearance?'[8] The extermination of meaning sounds like a highly political activity in which to be engaged – extermination for whom, by whom, and by whose authority? – and it will be that aspect of Baudrillard's project in which I shall be most interested. It is what Baudrillard *represents*, his role as an icon of post-aestheticism, that primarily will be under investigation, rather than his manifest failings as a theorist for what Norris has called 'the new irrationalism'.[9] Norris is only one of many hostile comment-ators to berate Baudrillard for his 'numerous non-sequiturs' and 'philosophical muddles', and even Baudrillard's supporters acknowledge his failings in this regard, although with a little effort these can be turned into necessary structural elements of a postmodern sensibility: 'If Baudrillard's *theoretical blindspot* is his failure as a systematic (scientific) theorist because of his privileging of the poetic imagination', Arthur Kroker writes, 'this may be because his writing is an artistic strategy in which words are probes into the immanent logic of *panic* science – words that need to work hysterically in order to *exceed* the desperate logic of hyperrealism.'[10] Baudrillard is to be prized, therefore, for his *refusal* to play the theoretical game, and we can see quite clearly the direction that post-aesthetic discourse wants to take us in. We turn our attention now to what Baudrillard's journey reveals.

Simulation takes us beyond foundations, it is 'the generation by models of a real without origin or reality: a hyperreal', and 'with it goes all of metaphysics. No more mirror of being and appearances, of the real and its concept.'[11] At a stroke we are cut free by Baudrillard from the world of epistemological commitments and delivered into the value-free realm beyond judgement. Neither are we to regard this event as in any way threatening:

> We leave history to enter simulation. . . . This is by no means a despairing hypothesis, unless we regard simulation as a higher form of alienation – which I certainly do not. It is precisely in history that we are alienated, and if we leave history we also leave alienation.[12]

This is at the very least an ingenious way of approaching the problem of alienation, and Baudrillard will display something of that post-alienated sensibility in *America* and *Cool Memories* ('there is a charm and a particular freedom about letting just anything come along'[13]). This is not just post-aesthetic it is also post-Marxist, and it is not difficult to see why Baudrillard has received such a hostile reception on the left. (Remarks like 'There are things one can no longer talk about or cannot yet talk about again. Their ghosts have not yet been stabilized. Marxism?' hardly help matters either.[14]) According to Marxist theory, alienation is a problem to be worked on and overcome *in* history, and not something to be dismissed casually, as it is here by Baudrillard. The possibility of social change is being denied in Baudrillard, with history inexorably accelerating towards its end – 'It will come to a standstill, and fade out like light and time on the edge of an infinitely dense mass . . .' – all the while carrying an apparently helpless mankind with it: 'everything happens as if we were continuing to manufacture history, whereas in accumulating signs of the social, signs of the political, signs of progress and change, we only *contribute to the end of history*.'[15] The poetic very much has the upper hand over the theoretical at such points, although it is clear that if Baudrillard is right then there is not much scope for the theoretical imperative or the exercise of value judgement. It is as if the post-aesthetic had already overtaken us:

We are no longer in the society of spectacle which the situationists talked about, nor in the specific types of alienation and repression which this implied. The medium itself is no longer identifiable as such, and the merging of the medium and the message (McLuhan) is the first great formula of this new age. There is no longer any medium in the literal sense: it is now intangible, diffuse and diffracted in the real, and it can no longer even be said that the latter is distorted by it.[16]

We have almost transcended active interpretation in such a state. All that is left to do is to record our impressions in the detached manner of post-aestheticism: 'Nostalgia born of the immensity of the Texan hills and the sierras of New Mexico: gliding down the freeway, smash hits on the Chrysler stereo, heat wave.'[17] We are asked to celebrate 'the power of a meaningless signifier' in our discourse, of 'language when it no longer has anything to say'.[18]

Images of dissolution are characteristic of Baudrillard, for whom 'simulation threatens the difference between "true" and "false", between "real" and "imaginary"'; history 'implodes in the here and now'; and we are continually witnessing 'the collapse of reality into hyperrealism'.[19] Foundations of discourse cannot exist in such a disorienting universe where reality cannot be distinguished from its models, and Baudrillard sees a political significance in simulation: 'it always suggests, over and above its object, that *law and order themselves might really be nothing more than a simulation.*'[20] If his theory of simulation is correct then the ground of political authority is destroyed. In the presence of uncertainty as to whether it is in itself reality or appearance, whether it is *confronting* reality or appearance, another metanarrative simply dissolves. Baudrillard cultivates such uncertainty for political effect, although this can lead him into some questionable analyses, as it does with gender politics and feminism in *Seduction*.

Seduction is presented as a way of undermining systems and meaning, and it is claimed to be a specifically feminine trait; the 'strength of the feminine is that of seduction'.[21] Power and authority is not to be confronted or challenged but, instead, seduced, and when it is seduced it loses its pretension to be a guardian of the truth: 'The masculine . . . possesses unfailing powers of discrimination and absolute criteria for pronouncing the truth. The masculine is certain, the feminine is insoluble.'[22] Seduction is seen as a force that prevents truth and authority from ever becoming properly established, a permanently available an-tithesis that, like Lyotardean narrative, needs no justification, but just simply exists and persists:

> seduction need not be demonstrated, nor justified – it is there all at once,
> in the reversal of all the alleged depth of the real, of all psychology,

anatomy, truth, or power. It knows (this is its secret) that *there is no anatomy*, no psychology, that all signs are reversible.[23]

A political programme is building up here, which is deploying seduction against systems rather in the way that Lyotard deployed svelteness against capitalism. Seduction, like svelteness, turns politics into a game – although with the serious aim of denying politics its traditional authoritative role in human affairs – and it assumes the same sense of unpredictability and flexibility at individual level. It is a case of individual guile against brute system, and the system is incapable of second-guessing the individual when it is confronted by 'femininity as a principle of uncertainty'.[24] Introducing uncertainty into this particular power game emphasises the antifoundational nature of the exercise, and we are asked to note

> The capacity immanent to seduction to deny things the truth and turn it into a game, the pure play of appearances, and thereby foil all systems of power and meaning with a mere turn of the hand. The ability to turn appearances in on themselves, to play on the body's appearances, rather than with the depths of desire. Now all appearances are reversible . . . only at the level of appearances are systems fragile and vulnerable . . . meaning is vulnerable only to enchantment . . . why become stuck undermining foundations, when a *light* manipulation of appearances will do.[25]

Seduction trades on simulation, accelerates the process of simulation, and since 'simulation too is insoluble'[26] it undermines the claims of masculinity (the symbol for entrenched power and authority in this extended metaphor) to be in any effective control over its area of discourse. With that control, which amounts to the traditional ability to solve the phenomena, go the pretensions of foundationalism. Seduction is an attitude of mind that can be extended to all systems: 'In the last analysis there is nothing to prevent things from being seduced like beings – one simply has to find the game's rules.'[27] When it is moved out into a wider context in this way the concept takes on something of 'the bitter Nietzschean edge' referred to by Kroker, becoming 'a defiant seduction, a dual, antagonistic seduction with the stakes maximized, including those that are secret'.[28] This is seduction taken past its 'ritual' and 'aesthetic' phases (agonistic and ironic in character, respectively), into its 'political' phase, 'whereby seduction becomes the informal form of politics, the scaled-down framework for an elusive politics devoted to the endless reproduction of a form without content'.[29]

The 'bitter Nietzschean edge' can be pushed even further into what sounds like yet another guerrilla campaign to be conducted within language:

In truth there is nothing left to ground ourselves on. All that is left is theoretical violence. Speculation to the death, whose only method is the radicalization of all hypotheses. Even the code and the symbolic are terms of simulation – it must be possible somehow to retire them, one by one, from discourse.[30]

The sense of detachment that characterizes the post-aesthetic reflections of *America* and *Cool Memories*, should not be allowed, however, to distract us from the highly politically motivated antifoundational campaign that engenders them. The playfulness of those two texts is reached by means of some *very* serious play indeed:

Such is the fatality of every system devoted through its own logic to total perfection, and thus total defectiveness, to absolute infallibility and thus incorrigible extinction: all bound energies aim for their own demise. This is why the only strategy is *catastrophic*, and not in the least dialectical. Things have to be pushed to the limit, where everything is naturally inverted and collapses. At the peak of value, ambivalence intensifies; and at the height of their coherence, the redoubled signs of the code are haunted by the abyss of reversal. The play of simulation must therefore be taken further than the system permits.[31]

We note the same intense dislike of imperialist and totalitarian systems that we saw at work in Derrida and Lyotard, and the same impetuous drive towards a value-free realm of signs. Post-aesthetics is born in a catastrophic and violent break with authority, and it describes a world where 'art is dead, not only because its critical transcendence is gone, but because reality itself, entirely impregnated by an aesthetic which is inseparable from its own structure, has been confused with its own image'.[32] The world of signs without truth, fault or origin has been reached. Baudrillard can now simultaneously make pronouncements and protect himself from any challenge to those pronouncements, in yet another version of the 'invulnerable discourse' ploy deprecated by Wood's 'sceptical friend': 'I am no longer in a position to "reflect" anything. I can only push hypotheses to the limit, remove them from their critical zone of reference, make them go beyond the point of no-return.'[33] It is the kind of disclaimer that we have come to expect, and also to treat with suspicion, from the antifoundationalist.

We have come to suspect it for the usual superficial reasons. It is hard to see how, if reality *has* become confused with its image, we could step outside the process to signal the fact: at points like this the words 'image' and 'reality' cease to mean much anyway. Or how, if media really *were* as intangible, diffuse and diffracted in the real as Baudrillard claims they are, we could know anything about that fact either. If Baudrillard is 'no longer in a position to reflect anything', how can he tell that 'it is reality today that is hyperrealist'?[34] 'We will never know what anything was before its disappearance in the completion of its model', Baudrillard blithely informs us, 'such is the era of simulation';[35] but if we do not, and cannot, know, did it ever exist at all except in Baudrillard's fevered imaginings? These are, in effect, *poetic* rather than theoretical statements, designed to make us reflect critically on the nature of our culture, our use and abuse of media and technology, and so on; but to say that is already to lessen the force of the remarks, to put quotation marks around them, to turn them into relatively harmless metaphors. Baudrillard, for whom 'the cool universe of digitality has absorbed the world of metaphor and metonymy',[36] clearly wants his remarks to have a higher status than the merely metaphorical. Nevertheless, we do seem to have yet another case of postmodernist discourse on our hands where the rhetoric is far better than the logic. Claims to go beyond value judgement have a nasty habit of undermining themselves. No matter how strenuously his defenders try to deflect such a charge, it always ends up sounding like special pleading on his behalf:

> If Baudrillard's *aesthetic blindspot* is his refusal of a theory of value, that is because Baudrillard has drunk deeply of Nietzsche's insight that 'value' is the dynamic discourse of nihilism, and to speak of the 'recovery of the question of value' is only to assent to the language of deprivation.[37]

It is hard to think what could *not* be justified using such a line of analysis as Kroker's above, and we can also query the weight being laid on Nietzsche's 'insight'. Is it by any chance being treated as a 'ground' for Baudrillard's practice? If it is not, then why should we accept the refusal? If it is, then Kroker and Baudrillard have to start negotiating the minefield of metaphysical commitments which 'drunk deeply' and 'insight' are trying desperately to hide from us. Neither prospect is a particularly comfortable one for the antifoundationalist to face. Once again we have to confront the political significance of 'a position which precludes the validity of any criticism'.[38]

Even from within postmodernism, Baudrillard's rhetoric can be called into question. In Lyotard's terms of reference, as we have seen, the end of history is little better than a metanarrative: 'Are "we" not telling, whether bitterly or gladly, the great narrative of the end of great narratives? For thought to remain modern, doesn't it suffice that it think in terms of the end of some history?' As Bennington points out, 'despite claims to the contrary, Baudrillard still operates a critique, founded, as any critique must be for Lyotard, on the uncriticized postulation of a lost referent.'[39] Baudrillard not infrequently evinces a sense of nostalgia for that lost referent:

This is why today the 'little music' of history also escapes us: it disappears in the excessive reference (which functions as 'deterrence', as dissuasion) it vanishes in the microscopy, in the instantaneousness of information, it too is seized by the uncertainty principle. At the very heart of information, it is the event, it is history which is haunted by its disappearance. . . . By definition, this 'vanishing point' is unlocatable, this point before which there *was* history, there was music, there was a meaning to events, to the social, to sexuality.[40]

This nostalgia for an unrecoverable world where there once was history and meaning (simply a case of nostalgia for a lost metanarrative in Lyotard's view) surfaces strongly in *America*, where it is seen in metaphorical terms as the collision between European and American cultural values:

We are still at the centre, but at the centre of the Old World. They who were a marginal transcendence of that Old World are today its new eccentric centre . . . From the day when that eccentric modernity was born in all its glory on the other side of the Atlantic, Europe begin to disappear.

Nor is there any doubt where Baudrillard's sympathies ultimately tend: 'the resounding truths, the realities of genuinely great moment today are to be found along the Pacific seaboard or in Manhattan.'[41] There is a frank recognition of unrecoverability and a commitment to the new world of hyperreality and non-referentiality, but we might say that, for all his insistence that he does not reflect anything, Baudrillard's post-aesthetics is subtly inscribed with a sense of foundationalism's significance. Metaphor is not innocent here either.

Another area where Baudrillardean metaphor manifestly is not innocent is *Seduction*, and it would be indefensible not to consider what commitments are being displayed in this context in breach of the author's studied pose of non-reflectiveness. Seduction is not without its virtues as an antithesis to power, being 'stronger than power because it is reversible and mortal, while power, like value, seeks to be irreversible, cumulative and immortal'.[42] It is the remorseless identification of seduction with the feminine, with a particular *vision* of the feminine as an uncertainty principle, that calls for critical comment. Baudrillard would no doubt want to hide behind his metaphor, but he does suggest someone still in thrall to a largely discredited metanarrative at this point (patriarchy), and it is not surprising that feminists have taken him to task over what Kate Soper, calling Baudrillard's bluff, describes as his 'rhetorical blandishment redolent with nostalgia for the good old days when men ruled and women cajoled'. Soper homes in on the cultural stereotypes that underpin seduction's supposedly radical postmodernity, arguing that while 'it is true that it is not officially as an ideologue of patriarchal culture that Baudrillard offers this Rousseauian advice', it is

> interesting, all the same, that it remains out of place for woman directly to contest the father's authority, and that our cultural duty requires us still to have recourse to the subtler arts of cajolery: to beguile the phallus round. By such means, so Baudrillard tempts us to think, woman will readily contrive to wrap the symbolic order around her charming little finger.[43]

This is, quite rightly, to take the metaphor absolutely seriously, and I would say that Soper has revealed a deep vein of neo-conservatism within the Baudrillardean project that clashes quite dramatically with his expressed desire to take all of us beyond the realm of value judgement. Rhetoric is not so easily drained of all significance as Baudrillard would seem to believe. If there is theoretical violence at work in *Seduction*, then it is of an unacceptably selective kind, more likely to reinforce than to shake the discourse of patriarchy. Once again, there is a sense of nostalgia for lost referents to be noted, that may make us want to question the author's revolutionary credentials. Politics keeps returning to haunt postmodernism's pretensions, with gender politics very much in the forefront. Rather surprisingly, the end of history does not seem to include the end of gender stereotyping: that is one 'vanishing point' of authority that theory has yet to exceed.

'Vanishing points' and cultural stereotypes are in an interesting state of tension in Baudrillard's most sustained exercise in the post-aesthetic mode, *America*, to which I now turn in more detail. In this highly symbolic journey from the old world of Europe, the world of 'the art of thinking, of analysing things and reflecting on them', of 'historical subtlety and conceptual imagination', to postmodern America, a society so hyperreal that 'no one is capable of analysing it', the stated objective is to break through the act of interpretation:

> We'd need the whole film of the trip in real time, including the unbearable heat and the music. We'd have to replay it all from end to end at home in a darkened room . . . live it all again on the video at home in real time.[44]

To replay the whole trip would be to have reached the vanishing point of criticism: the whole experience presented and re-presented resolutely minus underscoring, commenting or extracting of any kind. That is not what we receive in *America*, the book format militates against such indulgence, but the ideal state towards which post-aesthetics aspires becomes clear: recording, not analysing or interpreting, pure presentation and re-presentation, not *explication de texte*. The postmodern critic is there to register, preferably without judgement, although a judgement has of course already been made in deciding what to confront and what to register. What follows in *America* is a series of impressions, pared down of critical judgement as much as its author can manage it. I say as much as he can manage, because there is always that lurking sense of nostalgia for the lost referents of history and meaning to be allowed for, throughout this journey celebrating non-referentiality and the extermination of meaning.

America alternates between deserts and cities, and in each case Baudrillard strives to submerge the self in the random unfolding of events. 'Driving is a spectacular form of amnesia. Everything is to be discovered, everything to be obliterated', he tells us, which might sum up the post-aesthetic stance: svelte-like receptivity to a now which is always already an unrecapturable not-now. The theoretical violence in this instance is directed against one's individual past, which is to be jettisoned in favour of 'a trip without any objective', best undertaken in desert heat where 'the acceleration of molecules ... contributes to a barely perceptible evaporation of meaning.'[45] The desert becomes the ultimate vanishing point of referents where the self dissolves: 'No desire: the desert', in Baudrillard's neatly turned aphorism. True to his Situationist roots, Baudrillard turns America into a vast, dislocating spectacle ('every special effect can be found here', he notes approvingly of New York City), where everything he sees only confirms his belief in the death of aesthetics:

> We fanatics of aesthetics and meaning, of culture, of flavour and seduction, we who see only what is profoundly moral as beautiful and for whom only the heroic distinction between nature and culture is exciting, we who are unfailingly attached to the wonders of critical sense and transcendence find it a mental shock and a unique release to discover the fascination of nonsense and of this vertiginous disconnection, as sovereign in the cities as in the deserts. To discover that one can exult in the liquidation of all culture and rejoice in the consecration of indifference.[46]

Baudrillard exposes himself to American culture in order to destroy his vestigial critical sense, his *Europeanness*, in the new world's profusion of disconnected signs. Unlike Europe, nothing ever quite adds up to a pattern in America, everything is in a state of disorienting ferment where signs appear to have no past, and the only possible reaction is to record the ceaseless creation and destruction of a hyperreal society. Inversion of reality is the norm in this setting: 'it is Disneyland that is authentic here! The cinema and TV are America's reality!'[47] In a society where a soup-can can become art, where art and industry now exchange signs, anything might be regarded in an aesthetic light:[48] 'Modern demolition is truly wonderful. As a spectacle it is the opposite of a rocket launch.

The twenty-storey block remains perfectly vertical as it slides towards the centre of the earth. ... What a marvellous modern art form this is.'[49]

What Baudrillard finds in America is a society that appears to lack any sense of meaning or reason for its existence: a text that has obliterated all reference, that rudely scoffs at meaning. It has speeded up, perhaps brutalised, existence, particularly in the cities, to the point where it has gone beyond human rationality. New York, a city of anti-architecture 'without considerations of setting, well-being, or ideal ecology', represents this absence of meaning in its starkest post-aesthetic form:

> Why do people live in New York? There is no relationship between them. Except for an inner electricity which results from the simple fact of their being crowded together. A magical sensation of contiguity and attraction for an artificial centrality. This is what makes it a self-attracting universe, which there is no reason to leave. There is no human reason to be here, except for the sheer ecstasy of being crowded together.[50]

There is a lack of the universal in such a city, a lack of any possibility of there *being* a universal. New York simply *is*. We just observe and record it, we do not judge it – there is no point to such an exercise. Sheer existence has become an end in itself, stopping well short of the point where significance and meaning, in the European logocentric sense, can be read in:

> I DID IT!
> The slogan of a new form of advertising activity, of autistic performance, a pure and empty form, a challenge to one's own self that has replaced the Promethean ecstasy of competition, effort and success. ... I ran the New York marathon: 'I did it!' ... The marathon is a form of demonstrative suicide, suicide as advertising: it is running to show you are capable of getting every last drop of energy out of yourself, to prove it ... to prove what? That you are capable of finishing.[51]

This is individual existence as simulation, its only value being what Baudrillard refers to elsewhere as 'the value of a finality without purpose'.[52] There is a sense in which his Europeanness is intruding at this point, and there is a mildly disapproving note evident. 'Do we continually have to prove to ourselves that we exist?' he goes on to ask shortly afterwards, with all the implicit self-confidence of the post-Cartesian European intellectual scoffing at others' search for meaning. But there is clearly also a fascination with the pure and empty form of this 'new fanaticism for a faceless performance' (the marathon even moves Baudrillard 'to tears').[53] What else is *America*, after all, but a proclamation of 'I did it!' about a journey having only 'the value of a finality without purpose'?

Baudrillard has a keen eye for images of self-absorption in finalities without purpose. There is 'breakdancing', for example, that 'feat of acrobatic gymnastics', where the participants 'seem to be digging a hole for themselves within their own bodies, from which to stare out in the ironic, indolent pose of the dead'.[54] There is the academic at his computer, caught in 'an endless feed-back loop with the machine'.[55] There is jogging:

> You stop a horse that is bolting. You do not stop a jogger who is jogging. Foaming at the mouth, his mind riveted on the inner countdown to the moment when he will achieve a higher plane of consciousness, he is not to be stopped. If you stopped him to ask the time, he would bite your head off.[56]

Add a walkman-headset to the jogger, and the image of non-reflective, postmodern solipsism is complete. Complete enough to spark off a collision between vanishing points and European nostalgia for lost referents in the author:

> Not to be aware of the natural light of California, nor even of a mountain fire that has been driven ten miles out to sea by the hot wind, and is enveloping offshore oil platforms in its smoke, to see nothing of this and obstinately to carry on running by a sort of lymphatic flagellation till sacrificial exhaustion is reached, that is truly a sign from the beyond.[57]

The commitment to lost referents, to the 'real' world as it were, seems to be in the ascendancy in this passage, until we reach that 'sign from the beyond'. 'Beyond' is the ultimate objective of the postmodern project, and here in the image of the headset-equipped jogger is someone for whom the end of history has become a present reality. There is no sense of alienation here – as Baudrillard claims there cannot be come the end of history, because 'if we leave history we also leave alienation' – and despite our 'nostalgia ... for that good old drama of subject and object',[58] this is where the logic of Baudrillardean postmodernism must eventually take us. We vanish into the world of post-aesthetics, where authority's power over the individual simply dissolves: 'This entire society, including its active, productive part – everyone – is running straight ahead, because they have lost the formula for stopping.'[59] The formula in question is the logocentre, or grand narrative, or foundations, whatever acts as a break on the extermination of meaning and the instant obliteration of the past. European nostalgia may recur on occasion but it is clear that, in philosophical and cultural terms, *America* is an endorsement of the virtues of 'running straight ahead'. In that state the vestigial critical sense of the European intellectual evaporates, as does the logocentrist drama of subject and object. It is the 'unique release' Baudrillard seeks, into liquidation and indifference.

America in general, New York in particular, is what emerges from theoretical violence and speculation to the death, and it holds a compelling fascination for Baudrillard:

> It is a world completely rotten with wealth, power, senility, indifference, puritanism and mental hygiene, poverty and waste, technological futility and aimless violence, and yet I cannot help but feel it has about it something of the dawning of the universe. Perhaps because the entire world continues to dream of New York, even as New York dominates and exploits it.[60]

Politically, this sounds somewhat less than appealing – aimless violence seems a high price to pay for the release from history and alienation – but to Baudrillard it has the quality of a 'ravishing hyperrealism', and he calls on us, in millenarian fashion, to 'enter America as fiction' on the grounds that 'America is something that is beyond us all . . .'.[61] Violence, the physical rather than the theoretical kind, is never far below the surface of this journey – 'America has never been short of violence', Baudrillard admits – but the author develops another of his celebrated blindspots about it whenever it comes to declaring his allegiance to this postmodern ideal: 'Yes, California (and America with it) is the mirror of *our* decadence, but *it* is not decadent at all. It is hyperreal in its vitality, it has all the energy of the simulacrum.'[62] Aimless violence is clearly an aspect of all this positive-sounding vitality and energy, but it is carefully kept out of the equation at this point – otherwise the desirable trait of non-decadence could not be claimed. Or are we to assume that in a post-aesthetic world, where, by definition, all actions are aimless, violence too must lie beyond judgement? This is very worrying, and might make us wonder at the wisdom of contributing actively to bring about the end of history. Is aimless violence what awaits us at the end of the line in Derrida's world of signs without truth, fault or origin? Or in Lyotard's pagan utopia of little narratives? We need to ask ourselves just what it is that we are running straight ahead into, brave new world or anarchy. 'The cool universe of digitality has absorbed the world of metaphor and metonymy' – and also, perhaps, of human value.

In this respect, Baudrillard's cultivation of indifference is worrying too. 'We in Europe are stuck in the old rut of worshipping difference', it is claimed, which 'leaves us with a great handicap when it comes to radical modernity, which is founded on the absence of difference'.[63] The most formidable expression of this indifference, a veritable 'orgy' of it in Baudrillard's words, is to be found in America's rampant consumerism –

'practical liberation whether we like it or not, whether or not we deplore its wastefulness and obscenity'. But exploitation of resource, wastage of resource, cannot be neutral actions, not in a world split into North and South. Indifference to exploitation and wastage is ultimately indifference to *humanity*, and the postmodern can soon come to seem the most ideologically loaded of cultural projects. 'Politics *frees itself* in the spectacle, in the all-out advertising effect', we are told,[64] but only if you are inside that spectacle, that effect. It may be the most trivial of observations to make, but it is nevertheless one worth making: leaving aside the question of whether everyone shares Baudrillard's desire and *wants* to go to America, not everyone *can* go to America (economic migrants are not exactly being encouraged these days). We enter the hyperreal and go beyond judgement at someone else's expense, politically speaking.

The runner becomes a perfect icon of postmodern sensibility, oblivious to his surroundings, running purposelessly straight ahead, dangerous when disturbed. He has gone beyond registering the sense of mystery that the European intellectual can still detect in American culture; he has gone past the vanishing points of subjectivity, judgement and collective action. Baudrillard stands poised before those same vanishing points, only too ready, it would seem, to emulate the jogger and lose himself in the 'mystery of a society which seeks to give itself neither meaning nor an identity, which indulges neither in transcendence nor in aesthetics', where even the architecture has about it 'something non-speculative, primitive, and savage'.[65] America begins to sound like the state of nature with technology added on, and those are ideal conditions for the dissolution of the subject. Baudrillard's journey takes on something of the character of a religious quest, a desire to immerse the self in the sheer mystery of being, a desire to *humble* the self perhaps. It is no accident that the desert is such an insistent presence in the text. It is a symbol of dehumanisation, of the purity and emptiness that lie beyond rational existence, and Baudrillard's response to it is quasi-spiritual in tone:

America always gives me a feeling of real asceticism. Culture, politics – and sexuality too – are seen exclusively in terms of the desert, which here assumes the status of a primal scene. Everything disappears before that desert vision. Even the body, by an ensuing effect of undernourishment, takes on a transparent form, a lightness near to complete disappearance. Everything around me suffers this same desertification. But this radical experimentation is the only thing that enables me to get through and produces that astral quality I have not found anywhere else.[66]

The dismantling of selfhood has been a traditional concern of religion, both Eastern and Western, and everything about the language in this passage suggests a similar desire on Baudrillard's part. Desertification takes us to the outer edge of the poststructuralist campaign against the subject. Further than this one cannot go within philosophy. When desertification enters the project, logic stops and faith takes over, and it is indeed by act of faith that America has to be accepted: 'If you are prepared to accept the consequences of your dreams – not just the political and sentimental ones, but the theoretical and cultural ones as well – then you must still regard America today with the same naïve enthusiasm as the generations that discovered the New World.'[67] Naïve enthusiasm is rarely the province of the European intellectual, it must be said, and when its practical expression becomes the jogger and the breakdancer (those potent symbols of advanced desertification of the self and scoffing at meaning) then it seems to signal no less than the death of politics. Once again it has to be asked, at whose expense is this death prosecuted? 'Life is cinema', Baudrillard glibly asserts – but who is operating the equipment?[68]

America is, to say the least, a bleak landscape for socialist theory. The postmodern registers here as a brute force that just has to be accepted. It is a point beyond resistance where there is no right of appeal, no right to do anything but rush blindly on to the end of history. It is a state of aimlessness as far as the individual subject is concerned, that holds out no more attractive prospect than finality without a purpose. In this technocratic nightmare, where the ethics of the state of nature meets the dehumanising power of technology, the individual is at maximum risk from brute systems. The politics of post-aesthetics does not inspire much confidence on dissection, and as Richard Harland has remarked, 'Baudrillard's later writings seem to be closing doors rather than opening them.'[69] Yet for all its post-Marxist posturing and brave new postmodern world gloss, *America* can be a very traditional work in its way. There is, as Kellner points out, a distinctly *fin-de-siècle* air about it.[70] The world-weary European intellectual wanders through an alien landscape, parading his *ennui* for all to see, looking to shed his, and Europe's, cultural past in the coming millennium, rubbishing reason and the entire Enlightenment project as he progresses. There is also a highly traditional air of spiritual autobiography about Baudrillard's quest. Baudrillard's pilgrim seeks salvation from the ills of this world, from the constraints of reason and consciousness, and he finds it in desertification: in other words, in submission to a higher power.[71] The politics here do not seem to be too promising either. The *fin-de-siècle* feeling is, if anything, stronger still in *Cool Memories*, where even the loose thematics of *America* are missing. We are left with scattered fragments of discourse and gnomic utterances, delivered in a rather melancholic tone from the very edge of the postmodern consciousness and its project of scoffing at meaning and referentiality: 'What was final and causal has become aleatory. etc., etc.' Dialogue about foundations simply disappears into that dismissive 'etc., etc.' (classic 'invulnerable discourse' tactics), and it is now a case of 'letting just anything come along, with the grace – or ennui – of a later destiny'.[72] Politics has stopped, aesthetics has stopped, and we have reached point zero for interpretation. The flight from meaning is complete.

·11· CONCLUSION

Limits, Beyonds and Surface Radicalism

We began this series of confrontations with Derrida at the limit of philosophy, and have progressed to Baudrillard, seemingly well past that limit, 'letting just anything come along'. Foucault's 'dream' has been realised, we might say, but it seems to have lost its subversive potential somewhere along the way and disempowerment set in. Derrida's self-effacing trace has turned into the self-effacing, and self-abasing, intellectual. Active interpretation, by way of active nihilism and speculation to the death, has collapsed into critical stasis. We need to start asking whether this stasis is the logical end of the poststructuralist–postmodernist project, the apotheosis of the 'libertarian pessimism' that Eagleton sees as the project's hallmark.[1] The logic of Baudrillard's position is certainly impeccable: if value judgement has been superseded, if the end of history really is upon us, then why bother to act at all? Beyond aesthetics lies, perhaps, not liberation but stagnation. Antifoundationalism seemed to promise so much more than that. Is Baudrillard then to be our guide as to where an anti-aesthetics inevitably must lead? To a post-aesthetic desert? Or to what Norris has dubbed 'a kind of systematically inverted Platonism: a fixed determination to conceive no idea of what life might be like outside the cave'?[2]

It is stretching a point, and no doubt highly logocentrist into the bargain, to damn Derrida and Lyotard through Baudrillard, but the latter thinker nevertheless has considerable symbolic significance for a study of the anti-judgemental imperative. While both Derrida and Lyotard are crucially aware of having to fight foundationalism, and its assumed authoritarianism, from within (where, as Derrida somewhat despairingly admits, our 'every transgressive gesture reencloses us'[3]), Baudrillard simply acts as if the battle had already been won. It is as if he has just casually walked across the line dividing theory from practice. The low theoretical content of his work can be taken as an index of his belief that we are simply beyond the problem that theory had been addressing. Following the logic of radical antifoundationalism to its bitter end, Baudrillard maroons us in a world of aimless violence, critical stasis and the irretrievable breakdown of collective action ('The number of people here who think alone, sing alone, and eat and talk alone in the streets is mind-boggling'[4]). We are delivered into the state of nature plus technology, with all its attendant dangers for the isolated subject. Where Baudrillard sees a brave new postmodern world and a welcome release from a dead tradition, I would see the dark side of the antifoundationalist dream, the nightmare vision conjured up by Israel Scheffler of a world populated by 'isolated monads, within each of which belief forms without systematic constraints'.[5] I want to continue to argue that there are things to be retained for any liberation-conscious philosophy from the projects of Derrida and Lyotard, but Baudrillard might stand as a highly instructive warning to us of what the antifoundationalist line of development can be made to sanction in the name of liberation. Awaiting the isolated individual is, in Baudrillard's vision, a rather terrible political bleakness. Antifoundationalism as a pressure group within philosophy is one thing, antifoundationalism as a mode of existence is quite another. Calling *America* a poetic rather than a theoretical text cannot disguise the fact that it is an *expression* of a theoretical position, and that the position in question is in political terms of reference élitist. The death of discourse represents the death of dissent. Baudrillard notes the presence of some of the sadder specimens of vagrant humanity in New York's streets – and he has the leisure to do so – but in real terms he has nothing to offer these victims of a system that he regards as personally liberating.[6] New York City is symbolic of a discourse that has broken down, which is precisely the state that poststructuralism and postmodernism are forever striving to engineer, but as pictured by Baudrillard it seems to be as productive of personal alienation as personal liberation.

The logic of this study has been to suggest that as tactical movements within philosophy and culture theory, deconstruction and postmodernism have a lot to offer, but that the politics involved in their operation are often highly questionable: at times impossibly utopian, and at other times dangerously naïve about how to confront entrenched power structures. Svelteness and seduction work only on the smallest of scales. Anti-aesthetics as practised by Derrida, Lyotard and their followers is ultimately self-defeating since it problematises their own judgements no less than those of their opponents, and it needs to be subsumed under a more practically oriented political philosophy if it is ever to realise its subversive potential. That is the topic to which I now finally turn, to see if the lines of communication can be kept open between the worlds of deconstruction/postmodernism and the left.

The strong point, politically speaking, of the Derridean and Lyotardean projects is the challenge to authoritarianism, especially *intellectual* authoritarianism. Derrida's assault on ultrastructuralism in 'Force and signification' remains exemplary in this respect: a brilliantly sustained critique (again, I would defend the use of the word in this particular context) on the way that teleology can infiltrate, and circumscribe, the critical process. Ultrastructuralism's radical excess of prejudice is, as Derrida quite rightly points out, against the best interests of criticism, which very soon declines into a mechanical exercise severely lacking in creative input under such a regimen. Encouraging philosophers and critics to keep their theoretical commitments under stress, to strive all the time towards the limit of theory, is an entirely laudable enterprise and one of the most positive aspects of Derrida's libertarian pessimism. The sceptical spirit of philosophical enquiry demands no less. Lyotard's attack on imperialist grand narrative has similar virtues. The critical faculty has a habit of disappearing in the face of the accumulated power of such narratives, to be replaced by the all-too-human tendency to save the theory, no matter what the evidence to the contrary may be. The long, lingering death of Soviet communism provides an object lesson in this regard. In pointing out how we often let theories dominate us (less a case of naïve enthusiasm on the individual's part than of a strained doctrinalism), both Derrida and Lyotard are performing a valuable cultural service. It becomes questionable only when the transition is made from theories (which can be analysed according to their individual merits and demerits, as in the case of ultrastructuralism or Marxism) to theory, and the theoretical imperative, *in general*. At that point the pessimism takes over from the libertarianism, and it is a pessimism that can easily spill over into the political domain, as I would argue is ultimately the case with Baudrillard, where it registers as an attitude of passive acceptance to the power of the hyperreal. The transition paves the way for the collapse of discourse, or at best for a collapse into a babble of incommensurable discourses, and it is hard to see how this can be to the individual's advantage since it has such an isolating effect.

We start with a challenge to authority and hierarchy: we end with the problematisation of communication. It is in the ensuing shift where the problems with the project become manifest. The individual is abandoned into solipsism and alienation in a fairly cavalier fashion hardly calculated to promote confidence in the theory's politics, and the self-defeating cycle of the antifoundationalist argument sets in with a vengeance: you cannot communicate the incommunicability of communication, you cannot discourse on the end of discourse, or send messages back from beyond the event horizon of the end of history. Communication may well be imperfect – although it is difficult to see how even *that* could be proved – but that does not mean that some accommodation, rough and ready though it may be, cannot and will not be reached. Clearly, that happens with Derrida and Lyotard, or there would be no fuss over their theorising (or anti-theorising). It is all a matter of emphasis in this area. Poststructuralism and postmodernism choose to emphasise where communication seems to break down (the blink that closes the eye); their opponents, where communication seems to work (the interval between the blinks, if the eye closes it must also open). A decision – and it is a decision with political implications in terms of how you want to situate your audience, how you want it to react – has been made before the event. Derrida's aptly named 'blind tactics' choose to emphasise the blinks, and how we are isolated from each other and any meaningful control over discourse, but that is not the whole story. What Jeff Mason calls Derrida's 'hot tropical philosophy' can be only partial, a philosophy of the outside, and 'outsiders do not exist with no inside to be outside of' (just as Derrida can place himself on the margins of discourse only if there is a centre to be marginal to).[7]

These are the usual superficial criticisms being rehearsed yet one more time, and they can always be made to apply to anyone who takes the antifoundationalist route; but they do not prove the validity of the foundationalist position. Neither is it possible simply to go back to foundationalism, however it is expressed, as if radical antifounda-tionalism had never happened. Too much has occurred in the interim for an uncomplicated foundationalism to reassert itself with any sense of conviction: the law of identity has been put under too much stress, the rhetorical debts of philosophical discourse have been too tellingly outlined (Platonic dialogue, the Cartesian 'story of mind', etc.[8]). The foundationalist claim to be in possession of unproblematical, self-evidential verification procedures runs into difficulty at a certain point – the point at which the blink occurs, for example. Lyotard scores a subtle hit when he chooses to speak of 'legitimation' rather than 'verification'. What is at stake in the foundationalism debate is in fact *power*. Who has the power to say what will count as acceptable thought, utterance and direction for action? Who has the power to control entrance to the discourse and the prestige that inevitably accompanies membership? To claim a foundation is to claim the right to dictate the character of the opposition, and that is a position of considerable power to occupy. It is precisely that power that is being challenged by radical antifounda-tionalists, and it can be said in their defence that they are not the only ones to play the invulnerable discourse game. It is perhaps no surprise that they have been driven to that expedient in reprisal. Indeed, if one had to construct a defence of radical antifoundationalist practice, it would be that nothing less than shock tactics, including stealing the rights to invulnerability, is likely to have much effect on the discourses being called into question. The inside will not listen to the outside, or the centre to the margins, unless forced to do so.

Considerable claims might be made for the value of shock tactics within discourses. Scepticism has always traded on its shock value within philosophy (what else could one call raising the spectre of causeless effects or effectless causes in Hume's case?), using it as a means of preventing the discourse from lapsing into mere dogma, of making 'self-important people', in Whiteley's nicely observed phrase, feel 'still more uncomfortable'. This is an altogether necessary part of the philosophical enterprise, and one that has to be re-created by each generation of philosophers in its own 'thorough and pervasive' form. Seen in this way, radical antifoundationalism is the abrasive outside that keeps the inside from relaxing into the comfort of assumed invulnerability. Whether blind or not, the tactics can claim a considerable amount of success on this score. It is that quality of abrasiveness that ought to appeal to the left, which has every historical reason to fear the lapse into dogma and the assumption of invulnerability. Stalinism remains a large and embarrassing stain on the twentieth-century socialist project. The anti-authoritarian side of poststructuralism and postmodernism is certainly worth preserving, and suggests at the least the need for a loosening up of criteria of judgement on the left, for a constant exploration of the limits of theory no matter what the nuisance caused. Feminism continues to make these demands on socialism, as do poststructuralism and postmodernism. All three movements have taught socialists to search for hidden assumptions in their own theories, and also to pay greater attention to the effects of the application of a theory than to the purity of its principles. Those are entirely necessary lessons to be learned, or re-learned, on the left. One might also say that all three theories have usefully re-directed the left's attention to the individual, who is all too easily lost in the shuffle of collective action. The answer to the subjugation of the individual to the collective is clearly not the submergence of the individual in the hyperreal, that would be merely to exchange domination for limbo; but a space for negotiation has nevertheless been opened up by the impact of these outsider theories, for that most delicate of issues on the left, individual liberation.

This is to argue for continuing dialogue with deconstruction and postmodernism, for all that reading against the grain reveals the presence of the suspect qualities so endemic to outsider theories. The sense in which these theories resist absorption and domestication is the sense in which they have most value, functioning as the outside that keeps the inside under necessary stress and tension. The liberating power of an anti-aesthetics has to be acknowledged, even if it sometimes leads in directions that are clearly hostile to socialism (*America*), and even if the politics engendered by the problematisation of judgement can appear on occasion dangerously naïve. Eagleton takes Lyotard to task on the latter score, remarking that it is hard to see how *The Postmodern Condition*'s blurring of the distinction between truth-value and rhetorical seductiveness could not 'authorize the narratives of Nazism, provided they are grippingly enough recounted', and noting witheringly that Lyotard would force us to conclude that 'There is no such thing as political knowledge, whatever the African National Congress may think it is up to.'[9] Postmodernism leaves itself wide open to such attacks from the left, but in Lyotard's defence it has to be said that in many ways *The Postmodern Condition* has proved to be a very prophetic work. A certain interpretation of the grand narrative of Marxism did subsequently lose credibility in Eastern Europe, and did subsequently collapse. We cannot conclude from this, as Lyotardean postmodernism unmistakably invites us to, that any *possible* interpretation of this particular grand narrative would lack credibility, or that any version whatsoever of socialism must of necessity at some point implode under the weight of its assumed internal contradictions. That is the characteristically questionable move from particular theory to general theoretical imperative that marks the broad-brush approach of *The Postmodern Condition*. But Lyotard was prophetically enough signalling how the authority of the theory in general might not survive a mass realisation of its radical disjunction from current practice. On the minus side, it is by no means clear that anything like Lyotard's desired state of paganism has emerged in the aftermath of this grand narrative collapse. Some rather older grand narratives like nationalism, religious fundamentalism, proto-fascism and anti-semitism seem to have reappeared instead.[10] Lyotard is overly optimistic about the likely outcome of a power vacuum such as has occurred in Eastern Europe in the early 1990s (although as I write the situation is still very fluid in this area).

Derrida is not so much politically naïve, perhaps, as politically evasive, but then deconstruction is an evasive theory, self-cancelling and hard to turn to political account (with the ever-present qualification as regards feminism that if one is designated the subordinate term of an assumed binary opposition, then evasiveness seems as legitimate a political weapon as any). Derrida's work at the *Collège International de Philosophie* does have a political dimension, however, in its critique of philosophy *as* an institution and *in* institutions. There is a fascinating interview between Derrida and Geoff Bennington which addresses this side of the former's work, and succeeds in bringing out that intriguing mixture of suggestiveness and evasiveness that renders Derrida so politically problematical to the left. Stressing the politically suggestive side of deconstruction (by way of quotation from an old GREPH seminar paper of Derrida's), Bennington puts it to Derrida that '*the time has now come to deliver the politics*'. Derrida reacts sharply with a flurry of self-cancellations:

> I will insist that there is no such thing as a deconstructive *enterprise* – the idea of a *project* is incompatible with deconstruction . . . 'The time has come': what does that mean? Of course I was not *delivering* – I think I've never delivered anything – I was not delivering the politics of deconstruction . . . I don't think that 'the time has come' for anything.

Derrida also seems to take refuge in institutional philosophy, and, by extension, its foundations of discourse:

> I never said a word against philosophy. I insisted on the contrary that philosophy was not dead and that the closure of philosophy was not the death of philosophy. . . . And even if you deconstruct philosophy or if you want to think of the limits of philosophy, of the special kind of limits of philosophy, you have not only to philosophise in a general and a historical way but to be trained in the history of philosophy and to go on learning and teaching philosophy. That's why I am true to philosophy.[11]

This is a far cry from all the millenarian talk of 'beyonds' with which deconstructive writing is punctuated (beyond aesthetics, humanism, good and evil, the pleasure principle), and if Derrida is really advocating nothing more radical than *thinking* the limits of philosophy in his various meditations on language and metaphysics, then the academic establishment has nothing very much to worry about from this quarter. The discourse goes on, its historical integrity intact, its institutional base essentially untouched. Derrida's *Collège* is just one more member, albeit an eccentric one, of the philosophical power structure. Perhaps we could resurrect the accusation of neo-conservativism at this point. Norris gives us the ammunition to do so when he refers to a Derrida who 'repeatedly insists on the need to keep faith with this "vigil" of enlightenment'.[12] Perhaps on the other hand there are yet more lessons for the left, particularly the more dogmatic left, in Derrida's sentiments above. There are benefits to be gained from thinking the limits of foundationalism, in terms of directing our attention to the problematical interface of theory-power and individual desire. As a way of keeping a theory in that productive state of tension which defers a lapse into dogmatism, there is much to be said for the antifoundationalist imperative. Deconstruction simply takes its place in the history of philosophical scepticism on this reading, with foundationalism and antifoundationalism marking each other's limits. Stanley Fish notwithstanding, such a theoretical opposition does have ideological consequences.

When we make the transition from abstract philosophy to concrete politics, a transition that a socialist philosophy positively encourages, foundationalism and purity of theory cease to mean much anyway. Rhetoric inescapably comes to play an increasingly important part in the process by which theory becomes practice, and in that sense practice is consistently pushing us beyond logic into narrative. Grand narratives will be accepted or rejected on the basis of their perceived effects rather than on their philosophical purity, feminism and Eastern Europe providing interesting case studies of the act of rejection. More thinking about the limits might prevent such collapses by inhibiting the drive towards dogmatism that is inscribed within theory.[13] Poststructuralism and postmodernism demand that we think those limits constantly and they have a liberationist impact in this regard. The anti-authoritarianism of the theories is both genuine and a response to a genuine problem. Perhaps the pessimism can even be seen in a positive light as a refusal by such theorists to cut themselves off from the arena of debate: a convoluted political gesture, I agree, but a political gesture all the same.

The effect of treating deconstruction as mere thinking about theoretical limits is to reduce its subversive potential, as well as to cast doubt on its frequently expressed desire for the beyond, thus rendering Derrida a much more conventional figure in recent intellectual history. This is to reiterate the charge of surface radicalism, and Derrida's insistence that he is in fact 'true to philosophy' might be read as yet another plea from within purist-minded philosophy to leave everything as it is and to defer the danger of the world. Again, it has to be said that antifoundationalism seemed to promise so much more than this – and had been thought to do so by deconstruction's more enthusiastic apologists.[14] What price the revenge of literary theory if one is, after all, to be true to philosophy? One might express similar disappointment over Lyotard's *rapprochement* with Kant in *Just Gaming* and *The Differend*, which, for all his qualification of the Kantian project ('Kantian themes ... deployed to very un-Kantian ends' in Norris's shrewd assessment), looks suspiciously like a regressive move in the sense of a return to a pre-Marxist and pre-Hegelian (and therefore non-grand narrative) dialectic: a case of going back to an altogether safer area of debate.[15]

Baudrillard's intellectual self-abasement in the face of American culture is in stark contrast to such apparent lapses into recuperationism, and appears the more radical gesture, if misguidedly so. It is as if Derrida and Lyotard themselves were tacitly acknowledging that they have been promising more radicalism than they either can, or even really want to, deliver. Indeed, Derrida is claiming to have nothing at all to deliver. 'Deconstruction is a situation' not a project, he insists, and as such it does not undermine institutions: 'everything which is living today lives through deconstruction, especially the academy.' This is hardly the stuff of political radicalism, and in that respect we will have to make do with Derrida's comment about the situation that deconstruction is deemed to leave in its wake: 'it's not a new order but it's a permanent process of disordering order.'[16] The spectre of eternal recurrence returns. We do not in fact go beyond, we merely use the beyond as a threat to create a maximum sense of disorder within existing theory's sense of order. We may be in the presence of not-quite-philosophy, but it is manifestly not-quite-*philosophy* rather than not-quite-something-else. The form that the disordering proceeds to take, however, is still calculated to arouse alarm and resentment in the establishment: radicalism is in the eye of the beholder, and deconstruction's nuisance-value remains high. Post-modernism's nuisance-value remains high too, particularly on the left, and the tactical deployment of 'beyonds' in both theories has forced some anguished re-examination of philosophy's limits. Rhetorical success at least can be claimed, and although that may sound like damning with faint praise, the high value put on rhetoric by both theories would argue otherwise. In this latest engagement in the age-old conflict between rhetoric and philosophy, the message is that rhetoric should not be expelled from the philosophical commonwealth but regarded instead as an absolutely necessary internal irritant to philosophical method, and, from that perspective, the wilder the rhetoric the better. It is the awkward Derrida, rather than Norris's proto-establishment figure, who has a virtue for philosophical debate.

If these present confrontations have suggested that there are useful lessons for the left to be found in deconstruction and postmodernism, and that these theories are to be regarded as a necessary source of tension within foundational and institutional philosophy, such factors should not be allowed to disguise the fact that the underlying politics, whether acknowledged as such or not by the theorists in question, are often highly suspect. A certain kind of subject lives on in the pages of deconstruction and postmodernism, in defiance of the obituaries put out by several generations of French cultural theorists and philosophers, but it is a subject whose work is cut out for her. She can become lost, and politically immobilised, in the maze that is deconstruction, in the infinitely repetitive deferrals and erasures of thought and action that the theory celebrates. She can become reduced to skirmishing on the sidelines with grand narrative in a Lyotardean universe, svelte but isolated, trusting in the ultimate arrival of a paganism that requires a self-denying ordinance on the part of power structures if it is to have any realistic hope of success. She can be forced into the ideologically regressive mode of seduction of authority in Baudrillard, or offered the poisoned chalice of self-abasement before the all-conquering power of the hyperreal. Isolation and alienation seem to beckon on all sides. Having gone through all these processes, having been seduced by the many tantalising glimpses offered of what lies beyond authority and constraint in their myriad forms, she can then be confronted by an apparent affirmation of institutionalism: 'I never said a word against philosophy . . . That's why I am true to philosophy.' It is hard not to conclude that, ultimately, a surface radicalism does indeed flatter to deceive. An anti-aesthetics which delivered would be self-defeating, but this is an anti-aesthetics which does not even deliver.

Perhaps we are expecting too much of these theories, taking their rhetoric at face value rather than as an invitation to re-examine the limits and procedures of one's own theory. Perhaps we are looking for a sense of consistency unrealistic in theories so dedicated to the pursuit of aporia. Paradoxically enough for theories which go to such lengths to reject *explication de texte*, it all comes down to interpretation in the end. Just as Derrida has pointed out that Nietzsche and Heidegger are susceptible to conflicting political interpretations, so too is the work of Derrida, Lyotard and, no doubt, Baudrillard.[17] There is a right and a left deconstruction, in other words, and a right and a left postmodernism. In that sense, the theories themselves have not escaped judgement, no matter how much they may have played the invulnerable discourse card. That is a paradox, and it seems appropriate to end our confrontation with these theories on such a note, bearing in mind that paradox, for all its frustrations, can be one of the most fruitful of states for truly enquiring philosophers to find themselves in.

Notes

Chapter 1

1. Jacques Derrida, *Positions*, trans. Alan Bass (1981), p. 6; *idem, Margins of Philosophy*, trans. Alan Bass (1982), p. xxiii.
2. Jean-François Lyotard and Jean-Loup Thébaud, *Just Gaming*, trans. Wlad Godzich (1985), p. 15.
3. Jacques Derrida, *Signeponge/Signsponge*, trans. Richard Rand (1984), p. 30.
4. Henry Staten, *Wittgenstein and Derrida* (1984), p. 159.
5. See *ibid.* for a discussion of the connections between these two philosophers. John Llewelyn also explores similarities between Derrida and Wittgenstein in *Derrida on the Threshold of Sense* (1986), although he disputes the idea that the latter is really an antifoundationalist: 'Despite a widespread interpretation of his later work, Wittgenstein is never against foundations. He is against a philosophical picture of what they are' (*ibid.*, p. 102).
6. Jacques Derrida, *Writing and Difference*, trans. Alan Bass (1978), p. 292; *idem, The Post Card: From Socrates to Freud and beyond*, trans. Alan Bass (1987), p. 187.
7. Jean-François Lyotard, *The Postmodern Condition: A report on knowledge*, trans. Geoffrey Bennington and Brian Massumi (1984), p. 82.
8. Peter Dews can be exempted from such a criticism. See Chapter 1, 'Jacques Derrida: The transcendental and difference', of his excellent *Logics of Disintegration: Post-structuralist thought and the claims of critical theory* (1987), for an interesting contextualisation of Derrida within modern hermeneutics: 'it can be argued that some of what are taken to be novel Derridean arguments are in fact less original than they seem, when seen against the background of the hermeneutic tradition' (*ibid.*, p. 1).
9. Jean-François Lyotard, 'Unpublished conversations with René Guiffrey', trans. Geoffrey Bennington, in Geoffrey Bennington, *Lyotard: Writing the event* (1988), pp. 104–5.
10. *The Post Card*, p. 344.
11. Staten, *Wittgenstein and Derrida*, p. 156; Newton Garver, Introduction to

Jacques Derrida, *Speech and Phenomena and Other Essays on Husserl's Theory of Signs*, trans. David B. Allinson (1973), p. xxviii.

12. Robert Magliola seeks to establish common ground between Derrida and Hume in *Derrida on the Mend* (1984). See, for example, the discussion on self-identity, pp. 23–4. Llewelyn, however, is more sceptical: 'Derrida resists the suggestion that he is ... a renovated Hume, supposing Hume was a philosophical sceptic, which Derrida doubts' (*Derrida on the Threshold of Sense*, p. 102).

13. Not least in American academic circles, where antifoundationalism has been much in vogue of late. See, for example, the work of Richard Rorty, particularly *Philosophy and the Mirror of Nature* (1980), *Consequences of Pragmatism* (1982) and *Contingency, Irony and Solidarity* (1989).

14. Derrida himself has expressed sympathy with Marxism on occasion: 'I would reaffirm that there is some possible articulation between an open marxism and what I am interested in ... Marxism presents itself, has presented itself from the beginning with Marx, as an open theory which was continually to transform itself' (James Kearns and Ken Newton, 'An interview with Jacques Derrida', *Literary Review*, 14 (1980), pp. 21–2). For an exploration of the links between Derrida and Marx, see Michael Ryan, *Marxism and Deconstruction: A critical articulation* (1982): 'Derrida is not a marxist philosopher, nor is deconstruction a marxist philosophy. This does not mean, however, that deconstruction does not have radical political implications and uses' (*ibid.*, p. 9).

Chapter 2

1. Jacques Derrida, 'Letter to a Japanese friend', in David Wood and Robert Bernasconi (eds.), *Derrida and Différance* (1988), pp. 1–5 (p. 3); Christopher Norris, *What's Wrong with Postmodernism?* (1990), p. 67.

2. *Positions*, p. 24. 'Epistemological break' has been glossed as 'the leap from the pre-scientific world of ideas to the scientific world; this leap involves a radical break with the whole pattern and frame of reference of the pre-scientific (ideological) notions, and the construction of a new pattern' ('Glossary' to Louis Althusser and Etienne Balibar, *Reading Capital*, trans. Ben Brewster (1970), p. 310). The break assumes an incommensurability between the respective patterns and frames of reference – precisely what many commentators hold obtains between deconstruction and analytical philosophy.

3. 'And must we not return and run down that other lane out before us, down that long, terrible lane – must we not return eternally?' (Friedrich Nietzsche, *Thus Spake Zarathustra*, trans. R. J. Hollingdale (1969), p. 179). Textuality is a state of interminability for Derrida: 'beyond the philosophical text there is not a blank, virgin, empty margin, but another text' (*Margins of Philosophy*, p. xxiii).

4. Sartre conceived of the human condition as a relentless series of choices to be made by the individual. There is 'a constantly renewed obligation to remake the *Self*, since 'at each instant we are thrust into the world and engaged there' (Jean-Paul Sartre, *Being and Nothingness*, trans. Hazel E. Barnes (1958), pp. 35, 37).

5. *The Postmodern Condition*, p. 10.

6. *Ibid.*, p. 16.
7. *Writing and Difference*, p. 3.
8. *Ibid.*, p. 11.
9. *Ibid.*, p. 292.
10. Jonathan Culler, *Structuralist Poetics: Structuralism, linguistics and the study of literature* (1975), p. 248.
11. *Writing and Difference*, pp. 4–5.
12. 'There is no such thing as a "metaphysical-concept." There is no such thing as a "metaphysical-name." The "metaphysical" is a certain determination or direction taken by a sequence or "chain." It cannot as such be opposed by a concept but rather by a process of textual labour and a different sort of articulation' (Jacques Derrida, *Dissemination*, trans. Barbara Johnson (1981), p. 6). Llewelyn notes an improvisatory quality about Derrida's terms; *différance*, for example, is to be treated as 'a product of *bricolage*, improvisation, more than of engineering', and although such terms function as 'universal operators', their 'generality is so generous that it cannot be contained within a universal concept' (*Derrida on the Threshold of Sense*, pp. 41, 11). This sounds suspiciously like having one's cake and eating it to me.
13. *Positions*, p. 43.
14. *Speech and Phenomena*, pp. 130, 131, 137.
15. *Derrida on the Mend*, p. 87.
16. *Ibid.*, p. 57.
17. Geoffrey Hartman, *Saving the Text: Literature/Derrida/philosophy* (1981), p. 22.
18. *Ibid.*, p. 51.
19. Edmund Husserl, *Phenomenology and the Crisis of Philosophy*, trans. Quentin Lauer (1965), p. 146.
20. *Speech and Phenomena*, p. 135.
21. *Phenomenology and the Crisis of Philosophy*, pp. 146, 147. 'Prejudice' is to be understood here in the sense of preconception, or pre-judging. The desirability of such a suspension of prejudice has been questioned, most notably by Gadamer, for whom the term has entirely positive connotations: 'Prejudices are not necessarily unjustified and erroneous, so that they inevitably distort the truth. In fact, the historicity of our existence entails that prejudices, in the literal sense of the word, constitute the initial directedness of our whole ability to experience. Prejudices are biases of our openness to the world. They are simply conditions whereby we experience something – whereby what we encounter says something to us' (Hans-Georg Gadamer, *Philosophical Hermeneutics*, trans. David E. Linge (1976), p. 9).
22. Howard Gardner, *The Quest for Mind: Piaget, Lévi-Strauss and the structuralist movement* (1972), p. 43.
23. Introduction to Edmund Husserl, *The Idea of Phenomenology*, trans. William P. Alston and George Nakhnikian (1964), p. xxi.
24. Edo Pivčević, *Husserl and Phenomenology* (1970), p. 71.
25. *Structuralist Poetics*, p. 246.
26. *Ibid.*, p. 249. Dews is much more critical, arguing that Derrida's commitment to *différance* leaves him 'unable to explain how the experience of meaning is able to occur at all' (*Logics of Disintegration*, p. 98).
27. Introduction to Harold Bloom *et al.*, *Deconstruction and Criticism* (1979), p. vii.

28. *Ibid.*, p. viii.
29. Ferdinand de Saussure, *Course in General Linguistics*, eds. Charles Bally, Albert Sechehaye and Albert Reidlinger, trans. Wade Baskin (1960), p. 67.
30. *Ibid.*, p. 69.
31. Roland Barthes, *Image-Music-Text*, trans. Stephen Heath (1977), p. 39.
32. *Course in General Linguistics*, p. 131.
33. *Ibid.*, p. 133.
34. *Ibid.*, p. 123.
35. 'Besides this, there is another connexion of ideas wholly owing to *chance or custom*. Ideas that in themselves are not at all of kin come to be so united in men's minds that it is very hard to separate them; they always keep in company, and the one no sooner at any time comes into the understanding but its associate appears with it; and if they are more than two which are thus united, the whole gang always inseparable, show themselves together' (John Locke, *An Essay Concerning Human Understanding*, ed. A. D. Woozley (1964), pp. 250–1).
36. *Writing and Difference*, p. 5.
37. Christopher Norris, *The Deconstructive Turn: Essays in the rhetoric of philosophy* (1983), p. 2.
38. Staten, *Wittgenstein and Derrida*, p. 91.
39. *The Deconstructive Turn*, p. 12.
40. Madan Sarup, *An Introductory Guide to Post-structuralism and Postmodernism* (1988), p. 58. Llewelyn gives a slightly less defensive version of the predicament when he argues that deconstruction 'is a treatment by homoeopathy ... since it employs – and, one is tempted to say, is parasitic upon – the poison from the system it treats' (*Derrida on the Threshold of Sense*, p. 39); but this is to beg the question again about whether the system *is* poisoned, no less than about the virtue of homoeopathic remedies.
41. 'I am citing, but as always rearranging a little. Guess the number of false citations in my publications . . .' (*The Post Card*, p. 89).
42. Vincent B. Leitch, *Deconstructive Criticism: An advanced introduction* (1983), p. 246.
43. Geoffrey Hartman, 'Tea and totality: The demand of theory on critical style', in Gregory S. Jay and David L. Miller (eds.), *After Strange Texts* (1985), pp. 29–45 (p. 32).
44. *Saving the Text*, p. 24.
45. M. H. Abrams, 'Literary criticism in America: Some new directions', in M. H. Abrams and James Ackerman, *Theories of Criticism: Essays in literature and art* (1984), pp. 9–30 (p. 29).
46. *After Strange Texts*, p. 39.
47. Jacques Derrida, 'Living on:Border lines', trans. James Hulbert, in Bloom *et al.*, *Deconstruction and Criticism*, pp. 75–176 (p. 152).
48. Samuel Weber, 'Afterwords: Literature – just making it', trans. Brian Massumi, in Lyotard and Thébaud, *Just Gaming*, pp. 101–20 (p. 103).
49. *The Postmodern Condition*, p. 60.
50. *Ibid.*, p. xxiv.
51. *What's Wrong with Postmodernism?*, p. 38.
52. *Ibid.*, pp. 49, 50.
53. *Ibid.*, p. 70; David Wood, 'Following Derrida', in John Sallis (ed.), *Deconstruction and Philosophy: The texts of Jacques Derrida* (1987),

pp. 143–60 (p. 158); Jacques Derrida, 'Afterword: toward an ethic of discussion', in *Limited Inc*, 2nd edn (1988), p. 146.
54. *What's Wrong with Postmodernism?*, p. 56.
55. See particularly Pierre Macherey, *A Theory of Literary Production*, trans. Geoffrey Wall (1978).
56. 'Yet I doubt that Derrida can be domesticated. We have not seen it all before' (*Derrida on the Threshold of Sense*, Preface, p. xi).

Chapter 3

1. René Descartes, *Philosophical Writings*, trans. Elizabeth Anscombe and Peter Thomas Geach (1970), p. 9.
2. *Ibid.*, p. 61.
3. *Ibid.*, p. 32.
4. *Ibid.*, p. 67.
5. *Ibid.*, p. 90.
6. C. H. Whiteley, 'Epistemological strategies', *Mind*, 78 (1969), pp. 25–34 (p. 26).
7. For a survey of the debate in the twentieth century, see Willis Doney (ed.), *Descartes: A collection of critical essays* (1967) and Michael Hooker (ed.), *Descartes: Critical and interpretive essays* (1978).
8. 'Epistemological strategies', p. 26.
9. David Hume, *A Treatise of Human Nature*, ed. D. G. C. Macnabb (1962), pp. 39, 313.
10. See *ibid.*, Appendix A, pp. 341–6.
11. *Ibid.*, pp. 216–17.
12. 'Epistemological strategies', p. 26. The confirmation principle is defined as follows: 'A principle of this kind is confirmed when it is found that by assuming it, by inferring in accordance with it, we can arrive at true beliefs, verified by observation, which we could not have arrived at without assuming the principle. The correct strategy is therefore to investigate what verifiable truths are attainable by the use of each of these principles and not attainable without them' (p. 32).
13. 'The following essay is written in the conviction that *anarchism*, while perhaps not the most attractive *political* philosophy, is certainly excellent medicine for *epistemology*, and for the *philosophy* of science . . . it will become clear that there is only *one* principle that can be defended under *all* circumstances and in *all* stages of human development. It is the principle: *anything goes*' (Paul Feyerabend, *Against Method: Outline of an anarchist theory of knowledge* (1978), pp. 17, 28).
14. *Treatise*, pp. 301, 302.
15. *Speech and Phenomena*, pp. 64–5.
16. *Writing and Difference*, p. 292.
17. 'For him [Hegel], truth means system; it means, moreoever, a unique and complete system' (*A Dictionary of Philosophy*, 2nd edn, ed. Jennifer Speake (1983), p. 139). As Derrida notes, Hegelianism is often regarded 'as the ultimate reassembling of metaphysics' (*Margins of Philosophy*, p. 80).
18. G. W. F. Hegel, *Phenomenology of Spirit*, trans. A. V. Miller (1977), pp. 408, 409, 124–5.
19. Introduction to *ibid.*, p. vi.

20. Chaos theoreticians, interestingly enough, make the opposite assumption of certainty within uncertainty (see James Gleick, *Chaos: Making a new science* (1987)). In Lyotard's words, 'all that exist are "islands of determinism"' (*The Postmodern Condition*, p. 59). For a discussion of the relationship between Derridean *différance* and Hegelian 'difference', see John Llewelyn, 'A point of almost absolute proximity to Hegel', in Sallis, *Deconstruction and Philosophy*, pp. 87–95. Llewelyn argues that 'What is of interest to us here is this "up to a certain point" of Derrida's writing, the way its path passes through a point of almost absolute proximity to Hegel and explains why he says that he is doing no more than a repeated rehearsal of Hegel's lines' (p. 92).

21. 'It must be observed at the outset, that the phenomenon we investigate – Universal History – belongs to the realm of *Spirit*. The term "World," includes both physical and psychical Nature. Physical Nature also plays its part in the World's History, and attention will have to be paid to the fundamental natural relations thus involved. But Spirit, and the course of its development, is our substantial object' (G. W. F. Hegel, *The Philosophy of History*, trans. J. Sibree (1956), p. 16). The reference to 'fundamental natural relations', subordinated though they are to 'Spirit', points towards Marx.

22. Karl Marx and Friedrich Engels, *The Communist Manifesto*, trans. Samuel Moore, ed. Frederic L. Bender (1988), pp. 55, 75.

23. Friedrich Engels, *Anti-Dühring* (*Herr Eugen Dühring's revolution in science*) (1976), pp. 153, 182.

24. Adam Schaff, 'Marxist dialectics and the principle of contradiction', *Journal of Philosophy*, 57 (1960), pp. 241–50 (p. 242).

25. There are of course multi-valued formal logics, such as those spawned by intuitionist mathematics, which challenge classical logic (intuitionism takes issue with the law of the excluded middle, for example); but the extent to which such logics really escape classical constraints has been much disputed.

26. Friedrich Nietzsche, *The Will to Power*, trans. Walter Kaufmann and R. J. Hollingdale (1967), p. 267. For an excellently detailed analysis of eternal recurrence, see Bernd Magnus, *Nietzsche's Existential Imperative* (1978); for perspectivism, see Alexander Nehamas, *Nietzsche: Life as literature* (1985).

27. *Phenomenology and the Crisis of Philosophy*, p. 147.

28. Martin Heidegger, *Being and Time*, trans. John Macquarrie and Edward Robinson (1962), pp. 174, 175.

29. *Being and Nothingness*, pp. 186, 28. For a discussion of possible Sartrean influences on Derrida, see Christina M. Howells, 'Derrida and Sartre: Hegel's death knell', in Hugh J. Silverman (ed.), *Continental Philosophy II: Derrida and deconstruction* (1989), pp. 169–81.

30. Ludwig Wittgenstein, *Philosophical Investigations*, trans. G. E. M. Anscombe (1968), p. 20.

31. David Pears, *Wittgenstein* (1971), p. 168.

32. *Wittgenstein and Derrida*, p. 87.

33. *Consequences of Pragmatism*, p. xix.

34. *Contingency, Irony, and Solidarity*, pp. 52, 51.

35. Stanley Fish, *Doing What Comes Naturally: Change, rhetoric, and the practice of theory in literary and legal studies* (1989), pp. 347, 348, 353, 355. For a fuller exposition of the 'theory has no consequences' argument,

see *idem, Is There a Text in This Class?: The authority of interpretive communities* (1980).
36. *What's Wrong with Postmodernism?*, p. 141.

Chapter 4

1. Christopher Norris, *Derrida* (1987), pp. 79, 113; *The Deconstructive Turn*, p. 7.
2. Lorna Sage, review of Jacques Derrida, *Dissemination*, in the *Observer*, 10 January 1982. Derrida's meditations on 'I have forgotten my umbrella', an isolated phrase in quotation marks in Nietzsche's unpublished manuscripts, represents some sort of extreme test of the philosophical establishment's tolerance of the pursuit of whimsy (see Jacques Derrida, *Spurs: Nietzsche's styles*, trans. Barbara Harlow (1979), pp. 123–43).
3. *Speech and Phenomena*, p. 51.
4. *Positions*, pp. 28–9.
5. Jacques Derrida, *The Ear of the Other: Otobiography, transference, translation: Texts and discussions with Jacques Derrida*, trans. Peggy Kamuf, ed. Christie McDonald (1986), p. 141.
6. *The Post Card*, p. 508.
7. *Signsponge*, p. 104.
8. *Ear of the Other*, p. 147.
9. *Deconstruction and Criticism*, pp. 84, 83–4. Note: square brackets in original.
10. *The Post Card*, p. 304. There are echoes of chaos theory to be noted yet again; in this case of fractal geometry and Mandelbrot sets: 'But Mandelbrot found that as the scale of measurement becomes smaller, the measured length of a coastline rises without limit, bays and peninsulas revealing ever smaller subbays and subpeninsulas – at least down to atomic scales, where the process does finally come to an end. Perhaps ... The picture was beginning to come into focus now. His [Mandelbrot's] studies of irregular patterns in natural processes and his exploration of infinitely complex shapes had an intellectual intersection: a quality of *self-similarity*. Above all, fractal meant self-similar. Self-similarity is symmetry across scale. It implies recursion, pattern inside pattern. ... Mandelbrot likes to quote Jonathan Swift: "So, Nat'ralists observe, a Flea/Hath smaller Fleas that on him prey,/ And these have smaller Fleas to bite 'em,/ And so proceed ad infinitum"' (Gleick, *Chaos*, pp. 96, 103).
11. *Writing and Difference*, p. 3.
12. *Ibid.*, p. 5.
13. *Ibid.*, p. 11.
14. *Ibid.*, p. 15.
15. *Ibid.*, p. 6.
16. *Ibid.*, p. 17. For Derrida's most sustained meditation on the non-innocence of metaphor ('its bottomless overdeterminability') see 'White mythology', in *Margins of Philosophy*, pp. 207–71 (p. 243).
17. *Writing and Difference*, p. 11.
18. Claude Lévi-Strauss, *The Raw and the Cooked: Introduction to a science of mythology, I*, trans. John and Doreen Weightman (1969), p. 147.
19. *Writing and Difference*, p. 6.

20. *Ibid.*, p. 279.
21. *Image-Music-Text*, p. 80. Square brackets in original. Barthes is not always the orthodox structuralist, but even when proclaiming the virtues of 'polysemy' and 'plurivocity', he will demand that plurality of meaning be reducible to a code: 'To interpret a text is not to give it a (more or less justified, more or less free) meaning, but on the contrary to appreciate what *plural* constitutes it. Let us first posit the image of a triumphant plural, unimpoverished by any constraint of representation (of imitation). In this ideal text, the networks are many and interact, without any one of them being able to surpass the rest; this text is a galaxy of signifiers, not a structure of signifieds; it has no beginning; it is reversible; we gain access to it by several entrances, none of which can be authoritatively declared to be the main one; the codes it mobilizes extend *as far as the eye can reach*, they are indeterminable ... the systems of meaning can take over this absolutely plural text, but their number is never closed' (Roland Barthes, *S/Z*, trans. Richard Miller (1974), pp. 5–6). For all that there are poststructuralist leanings on display here – the shift in concern from signifieds to signifiers clearly signals this – meaning is still being constrained and channelled (into codes in this case), and remains within a system: even if the system under discussion is an expanding rather than a closed one. Meaning is being brought under concepts, and the action leaves Barthes some way short of a world of signs without truth, fault or origin: where meaning 'mobilizes' and systems 'take over' then there is still a structural consciousness at work, the deconstructionist would argue.
22. *Writing and Difference*, p. 18.
23. *Ibid.*, p. 28.
24. *Ibid.*, p. 20.
25. *Ibid.*, p. 25.
26. *Ibid.*, p. 27.
27. *Ibid.*, p. 6.
28. *Ibid.*, p. 19.
29. *Ibid.*, pp. 29–30.
30. David Wood, 'Style and strategy at the limits of philosophy', *The Monist*, 63 (1980), pp. 494–511 (p. 506).
31. *Derrida on the Mend*, p. 49.
32. *Writing and Difference*, p. 280.
33. *The Post Card*, pp. 408, 409.
34. *Writing and Difference*, p. 6.
35. A view attributed to the ancient Greek philosopher Cratylus, who, it has been argued, 'developed a debased form of Heracliteanism' which emended the original 'twice' to 'once'. See G. S. Kirk and J. E. Raven, *The Presocratic Philosophers* (1957), pp. 185, 197–8.
36. Christopher Norris, *The Contest of Faculties: Philosophy and theory after deconstruction* (1985), p. 18.
37. Jacques Derrida, *Of Grammatology*, trans. Gayatri Chakravorty Spivak (1976), p. 23.
38. *Ibid.*, pp. 60–1.
39. *Ibid.*, p. 60.
40. *Ibid.*, p. 66.
41. *Ibid.*, p. 67.

42. *Ibid.*, p. 44.
43. *Ibid.*, p. 10.
44. Thomas Hobbes, *Leviathan*, ed. C. B. Macpherson (1968), p. 186.
45. *Image-Music-Text*, p. 148.
46. John R. Searle, 'Reiterating the differences: A reply to Derrida', *Glyph* (1977), pp. 198–208 (p. 202). For Derrida, Searle is the most dogmatic of intentionalists: 'faced with a *Reply* so serenely dogmatic in regard to the intention and the origin of an utterance or of a signature, I wanted before all "serious" argument to suggest that the terrain is slippery and shifting, mined and undermined. And that this ground is, by essence, an underground' ('Limited Inc a b c . . .', trans. Samuel Weber, in Jacques Derrida, *Limited Inc* (1988), pp. 29–110 (p. 34)).
47. W. K. Wimsatt and M. C. Beardsley, 'The intentional fallacy', in *The Verbal Icon: Studies in the meaning of poetry* (1954), pp. 3–18.
48. Steven Knapp and Walter Benn Michaels, 'Against theory', in W. J. T. Mitchell (ed.), *Against Theory: Literary studies and the new pragmatism* (1985), pp. 11–30.
49. E. D. Hirsch, *Validity in Interpretation* (1967), p. 48.
50. *Idem, The Aims of Interpretation* (1976), p. 8.
51. *Validity in Interpretation*, pp. 47, 48.
52. *Derrida on the Threshold of Sense*, p. 59.
53. *Against Theory*, p. 30.
54. See the various papers in *ibid.*, for example.
55. *Writing and Difference*, p. 293.
56. *Ibid.*, p. 278.
57. *Ibid.*, pp. 279–80.
58. *Ibid.*, p. 293.
59. Steven Knapp and Walter Benn Michaels, 'A reply to Richard Rorty: What is pragmatism?', *Against Theory*, pp. 139–46 (p. 145).
60. *Positions*, p. 29.
61. Spivak, Introduction to *Of Grammatology*, p. xliii. For an argument that *différance* is in fact an *absolute* concept, see Dews, *Logics of Disintegration*, pp. 24, 96.
62. *Positions*, p. 26.
63. Geoffrey Hartman, *Saving the Text*, p. 46.
64. Introduction to *Of Grammatology*, p. xlv.
65. *Positions*, p. 6. Rorty, in his usual down-to-earth fashion, points out that 'Derrida cannot *argue* without turning himself into a metaphysician, one more claimant to the title of the discoverer of the primal, deepest vocabulary' (Richard Rorty, *Essays on Heidegger and Others: Philosophical papers volume 2* (1991), p. 101).
66. *Speech and Phenomena*, p. 135.
67. Introduction to *Of Grammatology*, p. lxxxi. The 'messianic promise' carries over into the work of other deconstructionists. Thus Wayne Booth notes of J. Hillis Miller that he 'finally offers us something like a religious vision'. Whereas Spivak is only embarrassed by this aspect of the deconstructive project, Booth, the staunch pluralist, is openly annoyed: 'But it is always clear that we must plunge into this wave of the future or be damned as reactionary defenders of ethnocentrism, logocentrism, and recuperation' (Wayne Booth, *Critical Understanding: The powers and limits of pluralism* (1979), pp. 216, 366–7, n. 18).

68. *Of Grammatology*, pp. 8, 10.
69. *Ibid.*, p. 5.
70. *Ibid.*, p. 14.
71. Jacques Derrida, '*Du tout*', in *The Post Card*, pp. 497–521 (p. 499). The editorial note to Major's introduction to this piece is as follows: 'Major is referring to Derrida's discussion of Lacan's misquotation of Poe's quotation of Crebillon on the last page of "Le facteur de la verité". . . . The reader is reminded that *dessein* means scheme, design, whole, *destin* means destiny, fate. (*Destin* is Lacan's misquotation of *dessein*.)'
72. Spivak complains that 'the *East* is never seriously studied or deconstructed in the Derridean text' (Introduction to *Of Grammatology*, p. lxxxii); Magliola's linkage of Buddhism and deconstruction goes some way to rectify this omission.
73. *Derrida on the Mend*, pp. 49–50.
74. *Ibid.*, pp. 53–4.
75. *Ibid.*, p. 57.
76. *Ibid.*, p. 87. Note: square brackets in original.
77. *Ibid.*, p. 127.
78. 'Tonk' was invented to poke fun at the theory of analytic validity (where inferences are held to be valid solely because of the meaning of the terms they contain). Prior argued that this had the unfortunate conclusion that, as long as we devised an appropriate logical operator, we could infer anything that we wanted – such as $2 + 2 = 5$:

    2 and 2 are 4   (P)
    Therefore, 2 and 2 are
      4 tonk 2 and 2 are 5   (Q)
    Therefore 2 and 2 are 5 (R)

[Where 'tonk' is defined as that which allows us to infer a conclusion, R, from the conjunction of two statements, P and Q]. ('The runabout inference-ticket', *Analysis*, 21 (1960), pp. 38–9.)
79. *Deconstructive Criticism*, p. 236.
80. *Derrida on the Mend*, p. 127. Note: square brackets in original.

Chapter 5

1. *Deconstruction and Criticism*, p. 152.
2. Jacques Derrida, *The Truth in Painting*, trans. Geoff Bennington and Ian McLeod (1987), p. 12.
3. From this point on I will give separate references to 'Living on' and 'Border lines'. This is purely for the reader's convenience in consulting references, rather than a value judgement as to the discreteness of the texts. Thus the current reference is 'Border lines', pp. 173–4.
4. 'Border lines', p. 82, 'Living on', p. 83.
5. *The Truth in Painting*, p. 9.
6. 'Living on', p. 85. 'Signifying frustration' is how Barbara Johnson neatly sums up Derrida's refusal 'to "get to the point"' (Introduction to *Dissemination*, p. xvi).
7. 'Border lines', pp. 145–6.
8. 'Living on', p. 103.
9. J. Hillis Miller, 'The critic as host', in Bloom *et al.*, *Deconstruction and*

Criticism, pp. 217–53 (p. 226). For a brief survey of poststructuralist readings of *The Triumph of Life*, see Chapter 4 of Michael Fischer, *Does Deconstruction Make Any Difference?: Poststructuralism and the defense of poetry in modern criticism* (1985).

10. *The Truth in Painting*, p. 269.
11. I. A. Richards, *Principles of Literary Criticism* (1960), p. 30. I have slightly modified Richards here. In fact, he suggests that the philosopher is in an even *worse* position than the aforesaid blind man.
12. 'Border lines', pp. 175, 84–5.
13. 'Living on', p. 75. Square brackets in original. For a reading of Derrida's tactics in 'Living on:Border lines', see Christopher Butler, *Interpretation, Deconstruction, and Ideology* (1984), pp. 79–82. Although initially sympathetic ('this marvellously rhetorical opening' (p. 79)), Butler is ultimately doubtful of the value of Derrida's linguistic virtuosity ('play of a rather tired kind' (p. 81)).
14. *Positions*, p. 3.
15. 'Living on', pp. 76–7.
16. *The Truth in Painting*, pp. 1–2.
17. Henri Ronse, interviewing Derrida in *Positions*, p. 5. Gregory Ulmer makes an interesting analogy between Derrida's writing style and op art, referring to his 'concern for everything marginal, supplementary, everything having to do with borders rather than centers' as 'op writing' (Gregory L. Ulmer, *Applied Grammatology: Post(e)-pedagogy from Jacques Derrida to Joseph Beuys* (1985), p. 40).
18. *The Truth in Painting*, p. 3.
19. *Positions*, pp. 22, 14.
20. *The Truth in Painting*, p. 2.
21. 'Following Derrida', p. 158. Returning to the issue of invulnerability, it is one of the ironies of deconstruction that its strategies can be used by opponents to similar effect. As Wayne Booth almost gleefully notes after an anti-Derrida diatribe, 'Needless to say, everything I write about Derrida is, like everything he writes, *sous rature*, "under erasure": cross out this footnote' (*Critical Understanding*, p. 367, n. 18).
22. Jacques Derrida, 'Geschlecht II: Heidegger's hand', trans. John P. Leavey, Jr., in Sallis, *Deconstruction and Philosophy*, pp. 161–96 (p. 184).
23. Jonathan Culler, *On Deconstruction: Theory and criticism after structuralism* (1983), p. 274.
24. 'Pass Notes' column, *The Sunday Correspondent*, magazine section, 15 April 1990, p. 53. Baker's novel *The Mezzanine* (1989) has something of the quality of teasing frustration to be found in Derrida's critical writings. It is a 135-page-long story of one man's journey up an escalator during his lunch hour, which comes complete with long, rambling footnotes to delay the slow progress of what is fairly minimal narrative action anyway. Although Baker's hero does complete the journey, we are treated to a great deal of narrative performative supplementarity on the way.
25. 'Following Derrida', pp. 146–58. Note: square brackets in original.
26. Jacques Derrida, *Edmund Husserl's 'Origin of Geometry': An introduction*, trans. John P. Leavey, Jr. (1978), p. 70n.
27. 'Living on', pp. 171–2.
28. *Ibid.*, p. 107.

29. *The Truth in Painting*, p. 175.
30. 'Living on', pp. 161, 139.
31. *The Truth in Painting*, p. 21. For Lyotard on Valerio Adami, see 'Anamnesis of the visible, or candour', trans. David Macey, in Jean-François Lyotard, *The Lyotard Reader*, ed. Andrew Benjamin (1989), pp. 220–39.
32. *The Truth in Painting*, p. 19.
33. *Ibid.*, p. 205.
34. *Ibid.*, pp. 208–9.
35. *Ibid.*, p. 262.
36. *Ibid.*, p. 263.
37. *Ibid.*, p. 257.
38. *Ibid.*, p. 377.
39. *Ibid.*, p. 155.
40. 'Following Derrida', pp. 158–9.
41. *The Truth in Painting*, pp. 198–200.
42. 'Ultimately, by interrogating an ideology, one can establish the existence of its limits because they are encountered as an impassable obstacle. . . . By means of a text it becomes possible to escape from the domain of spontaneous ideology, to escape from the false consciousness of self, of history, and of time. The text constructs a determinate image of the ideological, revealing it as an object rather than living it from within as though it were an inner conscience; the text explores ideology . . . puts it to the test of the written word' (Macherey, *A Theory of Literary Production*, p. 132).
43. *Derrida*, p. 186.
44. *The Post Card*, p. 12.
45. Norris refers to it as 'mock-epistolary' in his discussion of the text in *What's Wrong with Postmodernism?* (see pp. 56–64).
46. Manfred Frank has expressed considerable disquiet about poststructuralism's impact in Germany: 'The new French theories are taken up by many of our students like an evangel. . . . It seems to me that young Germans are here eagerly sucking back in, under the pretense of opening up to what is French and international, their own irrationalist tradition, which had been broken off after the Third Reich' (quoted in Jürgen Habermas, 'Work and Weltanschauung: The Heidegger controversy from a German perspective', trans. John McCumber, *Critical Inquiry*, 15 (1989), pp. 431–56 (p. 436)).

Chapter 6

1. *Positions*, p. 29.
2. Introduction to *Of Grammatology*, p. lxxv.
3. *Saving the Text*, p. 85.
4. 'That would be source study and *explication de texte* all over again. . . . Reading should be an *errance joyeuse* rather than the capitalization of great books by interpretive safeguards' (*ibid.*, p. 52).
5. Sigmund Freud, *Complete Psychological Works*, I–XXIV, ed. J. Strachey *et al.* (1953–74), VIII, p. 45.
6. Geoffrey Hartman, *Criticism in the Wilderness* (1980), p. 216; 'Tea and totality', p. 32.
7. *Saving the Text*, pp. 22, 18, 46.

8. *Works*, VIII, p. 45.
9. T. R. Shultz and M. B. Scott, 'The creation of verbal humour', *Canadian Journal of Psychology*, 28 (1974), pp. 421–5 (p. 424).
10. A. Rapp, 'Toward an eclectic and multilateral theory of humour and laughter', *Journal of General Psychology*, 36 (1947), pp. 207–19 (p. 211).
11. H. Giles and G. S. Oxford, 'A multidimensional theory of laughter causation', *Bulletin of the British Psychological Society*, 23 (1970), pp. 7–105 (pp. 97, 99).
12. *The Deconstructive Turn*, p. 3.
13. Norman R. F. Maier, 'A gestalt theory of humour', *British Journal of Psychology*, 2 (1932), pp. 69–74 (p. 70).
14. L. Deckers and P. Kizer, 'Humor and the incongruity hypothesis', *Journal of Psychology*, 90 (1975), pp. 215–18 (p. 216).
15. D. I. Kenny, 'The contingency of humor appreciation on the stimulus-confirmation of joke-ending expectations', *Journal of Abnormal and Social Psychology*, 51 (1955), pp. 644–8 (p. 648).
16. M. J. Apter and K. C. P. Smith, 'Humour and the theory of psychological reversals', in A. J. Chapman and H. C. Foot (eds.), *It's a Funny Thing, Humour* (1977), pp. 95–100 (pp. 95, 96, 98).
17. *Saving the Text*, p. 77.
18. The tendency for deconstructionist critics to collapse their arguments into poetry, an art form with a very free attitude toward the rules of syntax, suggests one direction for the discourse to take. Thus Magliola, a frequent exponent of the technique, ends *Derrida on the Mend* with lines from Gerard Manley Hopkins: 'Whorled wave, whelked wave, – and drift' (p. 163). Where one would go from there, however, is not at all clear. A discourse of cryptic poetic utterances, no less than one of cryptic mystic utterances, would represent little real threat to structures of power, and is no aid to dialogue either.
19. *Saving the Text*, p. 149.
20. *Ibid.*, p. 213.
21. *Ibid.*, p. 2.
22. *Ibid.*, p. 22.
23. See, for example, the treatment of the 'fantastical Spaniard', Don Adriano de Armado, by his page Moth in Shakespeare's *Love's Labour's Lost*.
24. Hartman, 'Tea and totality', p. 29.
25. Norris, *The Deconstructive Turn*, p. 12. Derrida insists that 'philosophy is played out in the play between two kinds of writing' (*Dissemination*, p. 149).
26. Bloom *et al.*, *Deconstruction and Criticism*, p. viii.
27. *Saving the Text*, p. 64.
28. *Ibid.*, p. 45.
29. *Ibid.*, p. 22.
30. *Ibid.*, pp. xxv, 22.
31. Bloom *et al.*, *Deconstruction and Criticism*, p. ix. Culler concurs with this assessment of Bloom, arguing that 'his work explicitly attempts that most nondeconstructive of tasks, the development of a psychological model for describing the genesis of poems, and he explicitly takes issue with deconstruction by insisting on the primacy of the will: the will of strong poets locked in battle with their titanic precursors' (*On Deconstruction*, p. 29).

32. *Saving the Text*, p. 24.
33. Charles Levin, 'La greffe du zèle: Derrida and the cupidity of the text', in John Fekete (ed.), *The Structural Allegory: Reconstructive encounters with the new French thought* (1984), pp. 201–27 (p. 224).
34. Christie McDonald, Preface to Derrida, *Ear of the Other*, pp. ix–x. Rodolphe Gasche is particularly dismissive of American deconstruction: 'So called deconstructive criticism . . . is but an offspring of New Criticism . . . and has done little more than apply what it takes to be a method for reading texts to the unproblematized horizon of its discipline. As a result, the genuine impact that Derrida's philosophy could have on literary criticism has not been, or at best has hardly been, noticed' (Rodolphe Gasche, *The Tain of the Mirror: Derrida and the philosophy of reflection* (1986), pp. 255–6). Derrida himself seems to have some reservations about what has been done in his name (see *Ear of the Other*, pp. 85–6).
35. *Contingency, Irony, and Solidarity*, p. 89.
36. Jonathan Ree, 'Timely meditations', *Radical Philosophy*, 55 (1990), pp. 31–9 (p. 37). Rather woundingly, Ree suggests that Rorty's un-noisy style has 'given him a not ignoble reputation as the only post-modernist anyone can understand, or the poor-person's Derrida' (*ibid.*).

Chapter 7

1. Wood, 'Following Derrida', p. 158. For an attempt, if not a particularly successful one, to force Derrida to declare his hand politically, see the interview conducted by Jean-Louis Houdebine and Guy Scarpetta in *Positions*, pp. 37–93. Derrida does make some explicitly political references (Vietnam, Paris 1968, the assassination of Martin Luther King) in the introduction to 'The ends of man' (*Margins of Philosophy*, pp. 111–36), but they are left rather undeveloped: 'I have simply found it necessary to mark, date, and make known to you the historical circumstances in which I prepared this communication. These circumstances appear to me to belong, by all rights, to the field and the problematic of our colloquium' (*ibid.*, p. 114).
2. *Writing the Event*, p. 9.
3. *The Postmodern Condition*, p. 60.
4. Jean-François Lyotard, 'Figure foreclosed', trans. David Macey, in *The Lyotard Reader*, pp. 69–110 (p. 95).
5. *Idem*, 'One of the things at stake in women's struggles', trans. Deborah J. Clarke, with Winifred Woodhull and John Mowitt, in *The Lyotard Reader*, pp. 111–21 (p. 118).
6. *Idem*, 'Answering the question: what is postmodernism?', trans. Regis Durand, Appendix to *The Postmodern Condition*, pp. 71–82 (pp. 81–2).
7. For an excellent study of Lyotard's early work (pre-*Postmodern Condition*), see Dews, *Logics of Disintegration*, Chapter 4, 'Jean-François Lyotard: from perception to desire'. For selections from Lyotard's as yet incompletely translated early works, such as *Discours, figure* and *Economie libidinale*, see Benjamin, *The Lyotard Reader* and Bennington, *Writing the Event*.
8. For a useful brief survey of the various current usages of the terms 'postmodern' and 'postmodernism', see Margaret A. Rose, 'Post-modern pastiche', *British Journal of Aesthetics*, 31 (1991), pp. 26–35. See ICA

Documents 4 and 5 (1986), for a survey of the effect of postmodernism on a range of the arts; in particular, Martin Jay, 'In the empire of the gaze', pp. 19–25, and John Wyver, 'Television and postmodernism', pp. 52–4 (television); Kenneth Frampton, 'Some reflections on postmodernism and architecture', pp. 26–9, and Demetri Porphyrios, 'Architecture and the postmodern condition', p. 30 (architecture); Michael Newman, 'Revising modernism, representing postmodernism', pp. 32–51 (visual arts); and Angela McRobbie, 'Postmodernism and popular culture', pp. 54–8 (popular culture). For analyses of postmodernism in literature, see Brian McHale, *Postmodernist Fiction* (1987) and Edmund J. Smyth (ed.), *Postmodernism and Contemporary Fiction* (1991).

9. *The Postmodern Condition*, p. xxiv.
10. *Just Gaming*, p. 73.
11. Frederic Jameson, Foreword to *The Postmodern Condition*, p. xvi. 'A work can become modern only if it is first postmodern. Postmodernism thus understood is not modernism at its end but in the nascent state, and this state is constant' (Lyotard, 'What is postmodernism?', p. 79).
12. *The Postmodern Condition*, p. 67.
13. *Ibid.*, p. xxiv.
14. *Ibid.*, p. 46.
15. *Ibid.*, p. 64.
16. *Ibid.*, pp. 32–3.
17. *Just Gaming*, pp. 18, 16.
18. Jeff Mason, *Philosophical Rhetoric: The function of indirection in philosophical writing* (1989), pp. 73, 92; Jean-François Lyotard, *The Differend: Phrases in dispute*, trans. George Van Den Abbeele (1988), p. 22.
19. *Just Gaming*, p. 18.
20. *The Postmodern Condition*, pp. 27–8. Lyotard's elastic conception of narrative looks to be a logical extension of Barthes: 'The narratives of the world are numberless . . . narrative is present in myth, legend, fable, tale, novella, epic, history, tragedy, drama, comedy, mime, painting (think of Carpaccio's *Saint Ursula*), stained glass windows, cinema, comics, news item, conversation' (*Image-Music-Text*, p. 79).
21. Jean-François Lyotard, 'Lessons in paganism', trans. David Macey, in *The Lyotard Reader*, pp. 122–54 (pp. 135, 137).
22. *The Postmodern Condition*, p. 27. For a different conception of narrative 'pragmatics' as presupposing certain shared values in society, see Jürgen Habermas, 'What is universal pragmatics?', in *Communication and the Evolution of Society*, trans. Thomas McCarthy (1979), pp. 2–3.
23. *The Postmodern Condition*, p. 66.
24. 'Lessons in paganism', p. 137.
25. *The Postmodern Condition*, pp. 4–5.
26. Lyotard views feminism less as an alternative metanarrative than as an antifoundational challenge to the metanarrative imperative: 'women are discovering something that could cause the greatest revolution in the West something that (masculine) domination has never ceased to stifle: there is no signifier.' Most feminists are more likely to see it as a case of the signifier being *misused*, or of other signifiers being suppressed by patriarchy ('One of the things at stake', p. 120). For an attempt to link feminism and postmodernism, see Craig Owens, 'The discourse of others: feminists and

postmodernists', in Hal Foster (ed.), *Postmodern Culture* (1985), pp. 57–82. Owens sees an 'intersection' between 'the feminist critique of patriarchy and the postmodernist critique of representation' (*ibid.*, p. 59).

27. *Just Gaming*, p. 59.
28. *The Postmodern Condition*, p. 60.
29. *Just Gaming*, p. 94.
30. Vincent Descombes, *Modern French Philosophy*, trans. L. Scott-Fox and J. M. Harding (1980), pp. 181–2.
31. Jameson argues for collusion: 'I believe that the emergence of postmodernism is closely related to the emergence of this new moment of late, consumer or multinational capitalism. I believe also that its formal features in many ways express the deeper logic of that particular social system' (Frederic Jameson, 'Postmodernism and consumer society', in Foster, *Postmodern Culture*, pp. 111–25).
32. *Writing the Event*, p. 47.
33. Jean Baudrillard, 'The structural law of value and the order of simulacra', in Fekete, *The Structural Allegory*, pp. 54–73 (p. 59).
34. *The Postmodern Condition*, p. 10.
35. *Just Gaming*, p. 55.
36. *The Postmodern Condition*, p. 16.
37. *Ibid.*, pp. 60, 67, 60.
38. *The Deconstructive Turn*, p. 3.
39. *The Postmodern Condition*, p. 29.
40. *Ibid.*, p. 23.
41. *Ibid.*, p. 29.
42. It would be more precise to say that Plato opposes certain *kinds* of narrative aesthetics: those of dramatic poets 'clever enough to assume any character and give imitations of anything and everything'. Such beings will be expelled from the commonwealth in favour of 'poets and story-tellers of the more austere and less attractive type' (Plato, *The Republic*, trans. Francis MacDonald Cornford (1941), p. 85).
43. 'Lessons in paganism', pp. 132–3, 134.
44. Quoted by Wallace Martin, in Introduction to Jonathan Arac, Wlad Godzich and Walbze Martin (eds.), *The Yale Critics: Deconstruction in America* (1983), p. xix.
45. Paul Bove, 'Variations on authority: some deconstructive transformations of the new criticism', in *ibid.*, pp. 3–19 (p. 6).
46. 'Lessons in paganism', pp. 132, 152.
47. *The Postmodern Condition*, pp. 45–6, 47.
48. 'Lessons in paganism', p. 131.
49. *The Postmodern Condition*, pp. 51, 33.
50. 'Lessons in paganism', p. 153.
51. *Writing and Difference*, p. 26; 'The structural law of value', p. 62.
52. David Hume, *An Enquiry Concerning Human Understanding*, ed. L. A. Selby-Bigge, rev. P. H. Nidditch (1975), p. 45.
53. *The Truth in Painting*, p. 200.
54. See *Philosophy and the Mirror of Nature*, pp. 389–94 particularly. Rorty speaks of 'the difference between treating philosophy as a voice in a conversation and treating it as a subject, a *Fach*, a field of professional inquiry' (*ibid.*, p. 391).
55. *Doing What Comes Naturally*, p. 347.
56. *Just Gaming*, p. 5.

57. In Jameson's reading, postmodernism's 'fragmentation of time into a series of perpetual presents' serves the cause of multinational capitalism, which remains in effective control: 'The informational function of the media would thus be to help us forget, to serve as the very agents and mechanisms for our historical amnesia' ('Postmodernism and consumer society', p. 125).

58. Jonathan Ree argues that Lyotard is in fact a latter-day historicist, 'reactivating the same old Hegelian historicist routines which had been so astringently faced down by the classic neostructuralists' (Jonathan Ree, 'Dedicated followers of fashion', *The Times Higher Educational Supplement*, 916, 25 May 1990, pp. 15–17 (p. 17). 'Neostructuralist' is Ree's preferred term for 'poststructuralist'.

59. Thomas Kuhn's work is an obvious source of examples of this kind. See particularly *The Copernican Revolution: Planetary astronomy in the development of Western thought* (1957) and *The Structure of Scientific Revolutions* (1976).

60. Feminism might be regarded as just such a new paradigm with specific practical utility. Lyotard remarks, quite rightly, of scientific paradigms, that 'what has definitional value today will be shelved tomorrow as accessory'; but his interest seems to be less in the utility of the current definition than in the contingency that might be inferred from past experiences of accessoriness (*The Differend*, p. 53).

61. *The Postmodern Condition*, pp. 66, 61.

Chapter 8

1. *Writing the Event*, pp. 2, 97.
2. *The Differend*, p. xi. Note: square brackets in original.
3. *Ibid.*, pp. 159, 138.
4. *Ibid.*, p. 142. There are echoes of Quine here. See the thesis of the 'indeterminacy of radical translation' as outlined in W. V. O. Quine, *Word and Object* (1960).
5. *The Differend*, pp. 159, 160.
6. *Ibid.*, p. xiii.
7. *Ibid.*, p. 142.
8. *Ibid.*, pp. 135–6.
9. *Ibid.*, p. xiii. 'Nor do we want to correct Marx, re-read him or read him in the sense in which the little Althusserians want to make us "read *Capital*": interpret it according to its "truth". We do not plan on being true, on giving the truth of Marx, we are wondering how it is with libido in Marx, and "in Marx" means in his text and his interpretations, and principally his practical interpretations. We shall treat him, rather, as a "work of art"' (Jean-François Lyotard, 'Libidinal economy', in *Writing the Event*, p. 30). This might *just* be interpreted as a plea for an 'open Marxism', but the bitterness of the tone suggests that even this loose an accommodation with dialectics may be beyond Lyotard's patience.
10. *The Differend*, pp. 139, 141.
11. *Ibid.*, p. 171.
12. *Ibid.*, pp. 172, 181.
13. 'Lessons in paganism', p. 135.
14. *The Differend*, p. 181.

15. *Ibid.*, p. 42.
16. *Ibid.*, p. 138.
17. 'Lessons in paganism', p. 135.
18. 'Dedicated followers of fashion', p. 15.
19. *Just Gaming*, p. 98; Samuel Weber, Afterword to *Just Gaming*, p. 103.
20. *The Postmodern Condition*, p. 67.

Chapter 9

1. *Just Gaming*, p. 99.
2. *An Introductory Guide*, p. 140. For an overtly Marxist analysis of Lyotard, see Alex Callinicos, *Against Postmodernism: A Marxist perspective* (1989). Hartman detects a conservative quality in Derrida as well, although his remarks conspicuously lack Sarup's pejorative tone: 'It may seem ingenious to characterize Derrida as a conservative thinker. Yet, the "Monuments of unageing intellect" are not pulled down. They are, in any case, so strong, or our desire is so engaged with them, that the deconstructive activity becomes part of their structure. No cargo cult is in view' (*Saving the Text*, p. 24). The clear suggestion is that deconstruction, rather like Wittgensteinian philosophy, leaves everything as it is. To push this line of interpretation further, it has been argued that we can view Hartman and his Yale School companions 'as iconoclasts or wily conservatives' (Wallace Martin, Introduction to Arac *et al.*, *The Yale Critics*, p. xxix). Habermas has criticised poststructuralists in general as 'Young conservatives', whose work sets out to 'justify an irreconcilable antimodernism' (Jürgen Habermas, 'Modernity – An incomplete project', trans. Seyla Ben-Babib, in Foster, *Postmodern Culture*, pp. 3–15 (p. 14)).
3. Jean-François Lyotard, 'Defining the postmodern', trans. G. Bennington, in *ICA Documents* 4 and 5, pp. 6–7 (p. 6).
4. *Idem*, 'Rules and paradoxes and svelte appendix', trans. Brian Massumi, *Cultural Critique*, 5 (1986), pp. 209–19 (p. 219). A brief personal digression is in order at this point. I first came across this material when, as a member of the editorial collective of *Radical Philosophy*, the 'Svelte appendix' section was rejected for publication in that journal in a translation by Mark S. Roberts ('Svelte discourse and the postmodern question', taken from Jean-François Lyotard, *Tombeau de l'intellectuel et autres papiers* (1984), pp. 77–87). The debate at the editorial meeting was generally quite hostile to what was described by several members as 'off the top of the head' philosophy, and seemed to me to crystallise the division as it then stood between Anglo-American and continental philosophy. Having already written a critical article on *The Postmodern Condition* for the journal ('Lyotard and the politics of antifoundationalism', *Radical Philosophy*, 44 (1986), pp. 8–13), I was spurred to write a commentary on 'Svelte discourse' ('Svelte discourse and the philosophy of caution', *Radical Philosophy*, 49 (1988), pp. 31–6), treating the collective's decision as a symbolic act in terms of the relations between the two discourses. Chapters 7, 8 and 9 of this present book take these two articles as their collective point of departure.
5. Michel Foucault, interview with Bernard-Henry Levy, *Oxford Literary Review*, 4 (1980), pp. 3–14 (p. 14); *Writing the Event*, p. 7 (even more

damningly, Bennington points out that Foucault's vision did not prevent him 'from *acting* like an intellectual in the traditional sense' (*ibid.*)).

6. Trotsky, literary critic and army commander, is an obvious role model in this context: 'Yet almost as remarkable in its way as Trotsky's military accomplishments is the fact that, as he was speeding from one front to another in his famous armoured train, he was reading recently published French novels' (Paul N. Siegel, Introduction to Leon Trotsky, *On Literature and Art* (1970), p. 7); suppleness, speed and the ability to metamorphose are well in evidence here.

7. In this latter case, see Frédérique Delacoste and Priscilla Alexander (eds.), *Sex Work: Writings by women in the sex industry* (1988).

8. *Writing the Event*, p. 97.

9. *Just Gaming*, p. 48.

10. *Writing the Event*, p. 115.

11. Jonathan Ree, 'Proletarian philosophy: a version of pastoral?', *Radical Philosophy*, 44 (1986), pp. 1–7 (p. 6). Far from being 'hesitant', Bennington detects a note of 'brutality' in Lyotard's writing (*Writing the Event*, p. 17).

12. *The Postmodern Condition*, p. 5.

13. Jean-François Lyotard, 'The sign of history', trans. G. Bennington, in *The Lyotard Reader*, pp. 393-401 (p. 393). In 'Svelte appendix' capitalism is presented as 'the problem that overshadows all the others' in today's world (p. 215).

14. *The Postmodern Condition*, p. 67.

15. *ibid.*, p. 16.

16. *ibid.*, p. 61.

17. *ibid.*, p. 16.

18. *ibid.*, p. 17.

19. Sarup argues a divorce between grand narrative and the symbolic: 'In recent years Lyotard has supported symbolic protest actions because he believes that through such actions societal veils are dropped. But. . . . Once a political act is severed from revolution and becomes symbolic, then all it does is produce a shock effect. . . . In detaching action from political goals this sort of activity becomes a self-defeating convention' (*An Introductory Guide*, p. 108).

20. *ibid.*, p. 133.

21. *The Postmodern Condition*, p. 61.

22. *Writing the Event*, pp. 140, 141.

23. *Just Gaming*, p. 58.

24. *ibid.*, p. 98.

25. *ibid.*, p. 100.

26. *The Postmodern Condition*, pp. 59, 60. Lyotard makes extensive use of the work of René Thom and Benoit Mandelbrot on pp. 58–61.

27. 'Lessons in paganism', p. 153. Rorty is fairly scathing about the notion that postmodern science legitimates something like permanent revolution, arguing that 'to say that "science aims" at piling paralogy on paralogy is like saying that "politics aims" at piling revolution on revolution. No inspection of the concerns of contemporary science or contemporary politics could show anything of the sort. The most that could be shown is that talk of the aims of either is not particularly helpful' (Richard Rorty, 'Habermas and Lyotard on modernity', in Richard J. Bernstein (ed.), *Habermas and Modernity* (1985), pp. 161–75 (p. 163)).

28. 'Lessons in paganism', pp. 125, 126.
29. 'The sign of history', p. 410.
30. Lyotard was a member of the *Socialisme ou Barbarie* group, whose 'critique of Marxism from within Marxism . . . finally touches bottom with the discovery that Marxism itself has to be rejected, not simply in terms of its specific claims, but as a general mode of theorizing' (Brian Singer, 'Introduction to Castoriadis', in Fekete, *The Structural Allegory*, pp. 3–5 (p. 3)). The critique of capitalism – 'one of the names modernity goes by' – that Lyotard offers in 'Svelte appendix', also retains a Marxist flavour (p. 215).
31. Incommensurability features largely in the Kuhn–Popper debate. See Imre Lakatos and Alan Musgrove (eds.), *Criticism and the Growth of Knowledge* (1970).
32. '*Rule of negation elimination* ("neg elim"). Every proposition *q* is a direct consequence of the pair of propositions *p* and -*p*. Thus from a pair of contradictory propositions every proposition may be regarded as following. This rule may seem odd to the reader unfamiliar with symbolic logic. He would perhaps wish to contend that we should assume that *nothing* follows from contradictory results, instead of assuming that *everything* follows. This rule, however, is probably best interpreted as meaning, "Anything is true if a contradiction is true"' (Frederic Brenton Fitch, *Symbolic Logic* (1952), p. 54).

Chapter 10

1. Jean Baudrillard, 'The year 2000 will not take place', trans. Paul Foss and Paul Patton, in E. A. Grosz, Terry Threadgold, David Kelly, Alan Cholodenko and Edward Colless (eds.), *Futur Fall: Excursions into postmodernity* (1986), pp. 18–28 (pp. 21–2).
2. Jean Baudrillard, *Cool Memories*, trans. Chris Turner (1990), p. 53.
3. *Idem*, *Seduction*, trans. Brian Singer (1990), p. 74.
4. Douglas Kellner, *Jean Baudrillard: From Marxism to postmodernism and beyond* (1989); Jean Baudrillard, *Simulations*, trans. Paul Foss, Paul Patton and Philip Beitchman (1983), p. 152; *Seduction*, p. 151. Kellner's is easily the most comprehensive introduction to Baudrillard's intellectual development currently available in English.
5. 'The year 2000', p. 25.
6. John Fekete, 'Introductory notes for a postmodern value agenda', in *idem* (ed.), *Life After Postmodernism: Essays on value and culture* (1988), pp. i–xix (p. xviii); Arthur Kroker, 'Panic value: Bacon, Colville, Baudrillard and the aesthetics of deprivation', in *ibid.*, pp. 181–93 (p. 184). For a discussion of Baudrillard's debt to Nietzsche, see Kellner, *Jean Baudrillard*, pp. 89–92.
7. *Seduction*, p. 138.
8. Jean Baudrillard, *America*, trans. Chris Turner (1988), p. 10. Despite the commitment to extermination of meaning, Baudrillard can be turned to critical account. See, for example, Tony Thwaites's analysis of Thomas Pynchon's *The Crying of Lot 49* in terms of simulacra theory (Tony Thwaites, 'Miracles: hot air and histories of the improbable', in Grosz *et al.*, *Futur Fall*, pp. 82–96).
9. *What's Wrong with Postmodernism?*, p. 179.
10. *Ibid.*, p. 24; 'Panic value', p. 183.

11. *Simulations*, pp. 2, 3.

12. 'The year 2000', p. 23.

13. *Cool Memories*, p. 3. Baudrillard is capable of making this state of passivity sound far less attractive on occasion, as when he describes the self as 'now only a pure screen, a switching center for all the networks of influence' (Jean Baudrillard, 'The ecstasy of communication', trans. John Johnston, in Foster, *Postmodern Culture*, pp. 126–33 (p. 133).

14. *Cool Memories*, p. 232.

15. 'The year 2000', pp. 21, 27.

16. *Simulations*, p. 54. For Baudrillard's debt to Situationism, see Sadie Plant, 'The situationist international: a case of spectacular neglect', *Radical Philosophy*, 55 (1990), pp. 3–10. 'The very tracks of the Situationist International can be read in the work of Jean Baudrillard, whose postulation of a "hyperreality" develops the spectacle to a point at which there is no notion of reality to which it may be opposed. . . . The absence of meaning which this entails leads Baudrillard to a position which precludes the validity of any criticism, since there are no structures, values, or purposes with which it can proceed. The spectacle is no longer an alienated inversion of reality, but its total substitution' (*ibid.*, p. 7). Another commentator refers to Baudrillard's 'burglary operation' on Situationism (Keith Reader, *Intellectuals and the Left in France Since 1968* (1987), pp. 131–2).

17. *America*, p. 1.

18. *Seduction*, pp. 74–5, 175.

19. *Simulations*, p. 5; 'The year 2000', p. 21; *Simulations*, p. 141.

20. *Simulations*, p. 38.

21. *Seduction*, p. 7.

22. *Ibid.*, p. 11.

23. *Ibid.*, p. 10.

24. *Ibid.*, p. 12.

25. *Ibid.*, pp. 8, 10.

26. *Ibid.*, p. 11.

27. *Ibid.*, p. 143.

28. *Ibid.*, p. 178.

29. *Ibid.*, p. 180.

30. 'The structural law of value', p. 59.

31. *Ibid.*, p. 58.

32. *Simulations*, pp. 151–2.

33. 'The year 2000', p. 19.

34. *Simulations*, p. 1.

35. 'The year 2000', p. 23.

36. *Simulations*, p. 152.

37. Kroker, 'Panic value', p. 183.

38. Plant, 'The situationist international', p. 7.

39. *Writing the Event*, p. 35.

40. 'The year 2000', p. 22.

41. *America*, pp. 81, 23.

42. *Seduction*, p. 46.

43. Kate Soper, 'Feminism, humanism and postmodernism', *Radical Philosophy*, 55 (1990), pp. 11–17 (p. 14). Soper goes on to suggest that if Baudrillard wanted to clear himself of the anti-feminist charge, he would need to 'show his good faith by yielding up the language of "female sacrifice" and "female

seduction". And let him ask men, too, to put a hand in the churn of cultural revolution. Or is the subversion of the Symbolic to be wholly women's work?' (*ibid.*, p. 17, n. 12). These are unanswerable sentiments, and further testimony of the problem that the metanarrative of feminism poses for poststructuralism and postmodernism. Jane Gallop also calls Baudrillard to account on seduction in Alice Jardine and Paul Smith (eds.), *Men in Feminism* (1987), pp. 111–15.

44. *America*, pp. 23, 1.
45. *Ibid.*, p. 9.
46. *Ibid.*, pp. 21, 123.
47. *Ibid.*, p. 104.
48. 'It is then that art enters into its indefinite *reproduction*: all that reduplicates itself, even if it be the everyday and banal reality, falls by the token under the sign of art, and becomes esthetic. It's the same thing for production, which you could say is entering today this esthetic reduplication, this phase when, expelling all content and finality, it becomes somehow abstract and figurative. . . . Art and industry can then exchange their signs. Art can become a reproducing machine (Andy Warhol), without ceasing to be art, since the machine is only a sign' (*Simulations*, p. 151).
49. *America*, p. 17.
50. *Ibid.*, pp. 17, 15.
51. *Ibid.*, pp. 20, 21.
52. *Simulations*, p. 151.
53. *America*, pp. 21, 19.
54. *Ibid.*, p. 19. Breakdancing can spur the postmodern consciousness to some of its wilder flights of fancy in the search for models of svelte behaviour. 'Breakdancing is unquestionably the most awesome sign of The Eighties, and deserves a journalistic coup or two in our speculative offensive. Breakdancing embodies everything at once: street-wise authenticity, the expressiveness of the "submerged and rioting", funkiness, energy, supreme bodily achievement' (Adrian Martin and Gerard Hayes, 'The eighties (a fragment)', in Grosz *et al.*, *Futur Fall*, pp. 159–65 (p. 162)).
55. *America*, p. 36.
56. *Ibid.*, p. 37.
57. *Ibid.*, p. 39.
58. 'The year 2000', p. 23.
59. *America*, p. 39.
60. *Ibid.*, p. 23.
61. *Ibid.*, pp. 31, 29.
62. *Ibid.*, pp. 80, 104.
63. *Ibid.*, p. 97.
64. *Ibid.*, p. 96.
65. *Ibid.*, pp. 98, 99.
66. *Ibid.*, p. 28.
67. *Ibid.*, p. 98. Baudrillard's move towards faith and enthusiasm has something of the reconciliationist character frequently urged on poststructuralist and postmodernist theorists in recent years as a way out of the foundationalist deadlock. Such a reconciliationist imperative runs through many of the contributions to Fekete, *The Structural Allegory*. Andrew Wernick, for example, advises that 'the way toward a higher reconciliationism lies in dropping the strained doctrinalist mode, Marxist or otherwise, so as to grasp this new, and

in Nietzsche's sense Buddhized, *dispositif* of faith and reason, attitude and cognition, that French rationalism, through its structuralist dislocation, has now encountered' (Andrew Wernick, 'Structuralism and the French rationalist project', pp. 143–9 (p. 146)).

68. *America*, p. 101.

69. Richard Harland, *Superstructuralism: The philosophy of structuralism and poststructuralism* (1987), p. 183.

70. 'As the end of the century draws nearer he seems to be becoming more cynical, more exhausted, more iconoclastic and more burned-out. This disposition – quite widespread today – is reminiscent of fin de siècle exhaustion at the end of the nineteenth century, then associated with a period of cultural exhaustion, decadence and ennui' (*Jean Baudrillard*, p. 208).

71. There is an extensive literature on this genre, which flourished in seventeenth-century England and America, particularly amongst the sectarian movement. John Bunyan's *Grace Abounding to the Chief of Sinners* (and its fictional analogue, *The Pilgrim's Progress*) would be the outstanding example to quote. See Paul Delany, *British Autobiography in the Seventeenth Century* (1969) and Dean Ebner, *Autobiography in Seventeenth-Century England* (1971). I deal with some of the fictive implications of the genre in Stuart Sim, *Negotiations with Paradox: Narrative practice and narrative form in Bunyan and Defoe* (1990).

72. *Cool Memories*, pp. 10, 3. Kellner is particularly harsh in his judgement of what he refers to as 'this glaciated collection' (*Jean Baudrillard*, p. 201).

Chapter 11

1. 'Foucault, along with Jacques Derrida, is exemplary of an ideology now dominant among a certain sector of the Western radical intelligentsia: libertarian pessimism ... libertarian, because something of the old expression/repression model lingers on in the dream of an entirely free-floating signifier, an infinite textual productivity, an existence blessedly free from the shackles of truth, meaning and sociality. Pessimistic, because whatever blocks such creativity – law, meaning, power, closure – is acknowledged to be built into it' (Terry Eagleton, *The Ideology of the Aesthetic* (1990), p. 387).

2. *What's Wrong with Postmodernism?*, p. 182.

3. *Positions*, p. 12.

4. *America*, p. 15.

5. Israel Scheffler, *Science and Subjectivity* (1967), p. 19. Fish disputes Scheffler's conclusions about antifoundationalism on the basis that it does not really set the subject free, given the force exerted by social context and consensus: 'Rather than unmooring the subject, as Scheffler charges, antifoundationalism reveals the subject to be always and already tethered by the local or community norms and standards that constitute it and enable its rational acts' (*Doing What Comes Naturally*, p. 346). The trouble with such a reading is that it makes it difficult to see how consensus can ever be challenged.

6. 'In New York, the mad have been set free. Let out into the city, they are difficult to tell apart from the rest of the punks, junkies, addicts, winoes, or

down-and-outs who inhabit it. It is difficult to see why a city as crazy as this one would keep its mad in the shadows, why it would withdraw from circulation specimens of a madness which has in fact, in its various forms, taken hold of the whole city' (*America*, p. 19). One wonders whether the various outsiders listed here feel any the less alienated for being part of the end of history and the triumph of the hyperreal. As Kellner has observed, 'Baudrillard's nihilism is without joy, without energy and without hope for a better future' (*Jean Baudrillard*, p. 118).

7. *Philosophical Rhetoric*, p. 150. 'In many cases it is quite clear that the philosophical rhetoric concerned invites closure. The story has a conclusion and we are invited to accept it. In other writings, the "hot" ones, we are invited to keep the questions open and not fix upon a canonical interpretation. . . . The plain style is wary of rhetoric and poetry; the tropical style revels in them. A plain-style philosophical rhetoric works against speculation and flights of philosophical fancy. A tropical style encourages the use of the imagination, tries to stretch the audience's horizons' (*ibid.*).

8. As has been pointed out, we probably do the historical Plato a disservice by separating the arguments from the dialogue anyway: 'Plato philosophized in a period when the various intellectual activities which history was to resolve into separate academic disciplines distinct in object-matter and method were generally not yet separated and articulated . . . one substitutes for the historical Plato with his sometimes odd and uncomfortable concerns a sterilized and unhistorical figure who would be much more at home in a contemporary University department than would the author of the *Laws*' (David J. Melling, *Understanding Plato* (1987), pp. 17, 18).

9. *The Ideology of the Aesthetic*, pp. 396, 398. Eagleton's not unjustifiable hostility to Lyotard leads him to make an interesting misreading of *The Postmodern Condition*'s argument on legitimation: 'There is an interesting parallel in *The Postmodern Condition* between a "good" pragmatism and a "bad" one: just as those succeed best who tell the finest stories, so (as Lyotard himself remarks) he who has the fattest research grant is most likely to be right. The Confederation of British Industry, did they but know it, are postmodernists to a man' (*ibid.*, p. 396). Lyotard is in fact *deploring* the latter state of affairs where institutional finance controls research opportunities, and it is in order to *correct* just such abuses that he argues for an opening up of the data banks to the general public. Eagleton's polemic rather runs away with him here. For an interesting sociologically based defence of naïveté in thinkers like Lyotard and Baudrillard, see Jacques Leenhardt, 'The role of the intellectuals in France' (*ICA Documents* 4 and 5, pp. 63–5), in which naïveté is seen as a rhetorical gesture adopted by intellectuals in response to the threat posed by totalizing systems. Leenhardt traces the gesture back to Albert Camus: 'The reversal to which Camus then invites his friends Aron and Sartre means abandoning Hegelian historical reason in favour of an approach which he, himself, qualifies as *naïve*. By a naïve approach, he does not mean a stupid one, but rather one which seizes reality in its immediacy and not through the code of a totalizing vision. Against a major totalizing synthesis, Camus suggested a minor approach. . . . In the seventies, when the intellectuals hit against the conceptual walls which they had themselves erected, they rediscovered – some of them with a surprising ingenuity – the philosophical and sociological sources of this "other approach" to which Camus had alluded . . . the master-thinkers

vanish' (*ibid.*, pp. 64, 65). Lyotard's *petit récit* bears all the hallmarks of this 'minor approach'.

10. Jonathan Ree makes a similar general observation about the claims of the antifoundationalist school: 'One may doubt, of course, whether anti-founda-tionalism really is the theme of our times. . . . If we are punting on cultural trends and the signs of the times, then the rise of religious fundamentalism in the 1980s suggests that if anyone is a "throwback to antiquity" it may be the postmodernists rather than the foundationalists' ('Timely meditations', p. 39).

11. Jacques Derrida, with Geoff Bennington, 'On colleges and philosophy', *ICA Documents*, 4 and 5, pp. 66–71 (pp. 69, 70, 68). GREPH (*Groupe de Recherche sur l'Enseignement philosophique*) was a research group that Derrida was associated with at one time.

12. *What's Wrong with Postmodernism?*, p. 70.

13. For an argument claiming the beneficial effects for socialism of little narrative challenges (feminism, ecology, disarmament, ethnic rights, etc.) to socialist grand narratives and class politics, see Paul Browne, 'Reification, class and "new social movements"', *Radical Philosophy*, 55 (1990), pp. 18–24.

14. See Derrida's various attacks on such enthusiasts in *Ear of the Other*: 'this word [deconstruction] which I had only written once or twice . . . all of a sudden jumped out of the text and was seized by others who have since determined its fate in the manner you well know. Faced with this, I myself then had to justify myself, to explain, to try to get some leverage. . . . But for me "deconstruction" was not at all the first or the last word, and certainly not a password or slogan for everything that was to follow' (*ibid.*, p. 86). For all his ostensible radicalism about meaning and undecidability, it is interesting to note of Derrida that, as David Wood has remarked, 'he too is obsessed with having his intentions properly read' (David Wood, 'Derrida and the paradoxes of reflection', *Journal of the British Society for Phenomenology*, 11 (1980), pp. 225–38 (p. 233)).

15. *What's Wrong with Postmodernism?*, p. 50. For a discussion of the implications of the 'Kantian turn' in later Lyotard, see Stephen H. Watson, 'The adventures of the narrative: Lyotard and the passage of the phantasm', in Hugh J. Silverman (ed.), *Continental Philosophy I: Philosophy and non-philosophy since Merleau-Ponty* (1988), pp. 174–90.

16. 'On colleges', pp. 69, 70.

17. 'We are not, I believe, bound to decide. An interpretive decision does not have to draw a line between two intents or two political contents. . . . There can always be a Hegelianism of the left and a Hegelianism of the right, a Heideggerianism of the left and a Heideggerianism of the right, a Nietzscheanism of the right and a Nietzscheanism of the left, and even, let us not overlook it, a Marxism of the right and a Marxism of the left. The one can always be the other, the double of the other' (*Ear of the Other*, p. 32). Derrida also deals with the question of Heidegger's politics in 'Of spirit', trans. Geoff Bennington and Rachel Bowlby, *Critical Inquiry*, 15 (1989), pp. 457–74.

References

Books

Abrams, M. H., and James Ackerman, *Theories of Criticism: Essays in literature and art* (Washington: Library of Congress, 1984)

Althusser, Louis, and Étienne Balibar, *Reading Capital*, trans. Ben Brewster (London: NLB, 1970)

Arac, Jonathan, Wlad Godzich and Wallace Martin (eds.), *The Yale Critics: Deconstruction in America* (Minneapolis: University of Minnesota Press, 1983)

Baker, Nicholson, *The Mezzanine* (New York: Viking Penguin; Cambridge: Granta, 1989)

Barthes, Roland, *Image-Music-Text*, trans. Stephen Heath (Glasgow: Fontana/ Collins, 1977)

Barthes, Roland, *S/Z*, trans. Richard Miller (New York: Hill and Wang, 1974)

Baudrillard, Jean, *America*, trans. Chris Turner (London and New York: Verso, 1988)

Baudrillard, Jean, *Cool Memories*, trans. Chris Turner (London and New York: Verso, 1990)

Baudrillard, Jean, *Seduction*, trans. Brian Singer (Basingstoke and London: Macmillan; New York: St Martin's Press, 1990)

Baudrillard, Jean, *Simulations*, trans. Paul Foss, Paul Patton and Philip Beitchman (New York: Semiotext(e), 1983)

Bennington, Geoffrey, *Lyotard: Writing the event* (Manchester: Manchester University Press; New York: Columbia University Press, 1988)

Bernstein, Richard J. (ed.), *Habermas and Modernity* (Cambridge, Mass.: MIT Press; Cambridge: Polity Press, 1985)

Bloom, Harold, *et al.*, *Deconstruction and Criticism* (London and Henley: Routledge & Kegan Paul; New York: Seabury Press, 1979)

Booth, Wayne, *Critical Understanding: The powers and limits of pluralism* (Chicago and London: University of Chicago Press, 1979)

Bunyan, John, *Grace Abounding to the Chief of Sinners*, ed. Roger Sharrock (Oxford: Clarendon Press, 1962)

Bunyan, John, *The Pilgrim's Progress*, ed. J. B. Wharey, rev. Roger Sharrock (Oxford: Clarendon Press, 1928, 1960)

Butler, Christopher, *Interpretation, Deconstruction, and Ideology* (Oxford: Clarendon Press, 1984)

Callinicos, Alex, *Against Postmodernism: A Marxist perspective* (Cambridge: Polity Press, 1989; New York: St Martin's Press, 1990)

Chapman, A. J., and H. C. Foot (eds.), *It's a Funny Thing, Humour* (Oxford: Pergamon, 1977)

Culler, Jonathan, *On Deconstruction: Theory and criticism after structuralism* (Ithaca, N.Y.: Cornell University Press, 1982; London: Routledge & Kegan Paul, 1983)

Culler, Jonathan, *Structuralist Poetics: Structuralism, linguistics and the study of literature* (London and Henley: Routledge & Kegan Paul, 1975)

Delacoste, Frédérique, and Priscilla Alexander (eds.), *Sex Work: Writings by women in the sex industry* (London: Virago Press, 1988; San Francisco: Cleis Press, 1987)

Delany, Paul, *British Autobiography in the Seventeenth Century* (London: Routledge & Kegan Paul; New York: Columbia University Press, 1969)

Derrida, Jacques, *Dissemination*, trans. Barbara Johnson (Chicago: University of Chicago Press; London: Athlone Press, 1981)

Derrida, Jacques, *The Ear of the Other: Otobiography, transference, translation*, trans. Peggy Kamuf, ed. Christie McDonald (Lincoln, Neb., and London: University of Nebraska Press, 1988)

Derrida, Jacques, *Edmund Husserl's 'Origin of Geometry': An introduction*, trans. J. P. Leavey (New York: Hays, 1978)

Derrida, Jacques, *Glas*, trans. J. P. Leavey and R. Rand (Lincoln, Neb., and London: University of Nebraska Press, 1986)

Derrida, Jacques, *Limited Inc*, trans. S. Weber and J. Mehlman (Evanston, Ill.: Northwestern University Press, 1988)

Derrida, Jacques, *Margins of Philosophy*, trans. Alan Bass (Chicago: University of Chicago Press; Brighton: Harvester, 1982)

Derrida, Jacques, *Of Grammatology*, trans. Gayatri Chakravorty Spivak (Baltimore and London: The Johns Hopkins University Press, 1976)

Derrida, Jacques, *Positions*, trans. Alan Bass (London: Athlone Press; Chicago: University of Chicago Press, 1981)

Derrida, Jacques, *The Post Card: From Socrates to Freud and beyond*, trans. Alan Bass (Chicago and London: University of Chicago Press, 1987)

Derrida, Jacques, *Signeponge/Signsponge*, trans. Richard Rand (New York: Columbia University Press, 1984)

Derrida, Jacques, *Speech and Phenomena and Other Essays on Husserl's Theory of Signs*, trans. David B. Allinson (Evanston, Ill.: Northwestern University Press, 1973)

Derrida, Jacques, *Spurs: Nietzsche's styles*, trans. Barbara Harlow (Chicago and London: University of Chicago Press, 1979)

Derrida, Jacques, *The Truth in Painting*, trans. Geoff Bennington and Ian McLeod (Chicago and London: University of Chicago Press, 1987)

Derrida, Jacques, *Writing and Difference*, trans. Alan Bass (London and Henley: Routledge & Kegan Paul; Chicago: University of Chicago Press, 1978)

Descartes, René, *Philosophical Writings*, trans. Elizabeth Anscombe and Peter Thomas Geach (London: Thomas Nelson, 1970)

Descombes, Vincent, *Modern French Philosophy*, trans. L. Scott-Fox and J. M. Harding (Cambridge and New York: Cambridge University Press, 1980)

Dews, Peter, *Logics of Disintegration: Post-structuralist thought and the claims of critical theory* (London and New York: Verso, 1987)

Doney, Willis (ed.), *Descartes: A collection of critical essays* (London and Basingstoke: Macmillan, 1968; New York: Doubleday, 1967)

Eagleton, Terry, *The Ideology of the Aesthetic* (Oxford and Cambridge, Mass.: Basil Blackwell, 1990)

Ebner, Dean, *Autobiography in Seventeenth-Century England* (The Hague: Mouton, 1971)

Ellis, John M., *Against Deconstruction* (Princeton, N. J.: Princeton University Press, 1989)

Engels, Friedrich, *Anti-Dühring (Herr Eugen Dühring's revolution in science)* (Peking: Foreign Languages Press, 1976)

Fekete, John (ed.), *Life After Postmodernism: Essays on value and culture* (Basingstoke and London: Macmillan; New York: St Martin's Press, 1988)

Fekete, John (ed.), *The Structural Allegory: Reconstructive encounters with the new French thought* (Manchester: Manchester University Press; Minneapolis: University of Minnesota Press, 1984)

Feyerabend, Paul, *Against Method: Outline of an anarchistic theory of knowledge* (London: Verso; New York: Schocken Books, 1978)

Fischer, Michael, *Does Deconstruction Make Any Difference?: Poststructuralism and the defense of poetry in modern criticism* (Bloomington, Ind.: Indiana University Press, 1985)

Fish, Stanley, *Doing What Comes Naturally: Change, rhetoric and the practice of theory in literary and legal studies* (Oxford: Clarendon Press, 1989)

Fish, Stanley, *Is There A Text in This Class?: The authority of interpretive communities* (Cambridge, Mass.: Harvard University Press, 1980)

Fitch, Frederick Brenton, *Symbolic Logic: An introduction* (New York: Ronald Press, 1952)

Foster, Hal (ed.), *Postmodern Culture* (London and Concord, Mass.: Pluto Press, 1985; *The Anti-Aesthetic* (Port Townsend, Wa.: Bay Press, 1983))

Freud, Sigmund, *Complete Psychological Works*, I–XXIV, trans. J. Strachey *et al.* (London: Hogarth Press, 1953–74)

Gadamer, Hans-Georg, *Philosophical Hermeneutics*, trans. David E. Linge (Berkeley, Los Angeles and London: University of California Press, 1976)

Gardner, Howard, *The Quest for Mind: Piaget, Lévi-Strauss and the structuralist movement* (London: Quartet Books, 1976; New York: Alfred A. Knopf, 1972)

Gasche, Rodolphe, *The Tain of the Mirror: Derrida and the philosophy of reflection* (Cambridge, Mass.: Harvard University Press, 1986)

Gleick, James, *Chaos: Making a new science* (London: Sphere Books, 1988; New York: Viking, 1987)

Grosz, E. A., Terry Threadgold, David Kelly, Alan Cholodenko and Edward Colless (eds.), *Futur Fall: Excursions into post-modernity* (Sydney: Power Institute Publications, 1986)

Habermas, Jürgen, *Communication and the Evolution of Society*, trans. Thomas McCarthy (London: Heinemann; Boston: Beacon Press, 1979)

Habermas, Jürgen, *The Philosophical Discourse of Modernity*, trans. Frederick Lawrence (Cambridge: Polity Press, 1987)

Harland, Richard, *Superstructuralism: The philosophy of structuralism and poststructuralism* (London: Methuen, 1987; London and New York: Routledge, 1988)

Hartman, Geoffrey, *Criticism in the Wilderness* (New Haven, Conn.: Yale University Press, 1980)

Hartman, Geoffrey, *Saving the Text: Literature/Derrida/philosophy* (Baltimore and London: The Johns Hopkins University Press, 1981)

Hegel, G. W. F., *Phenomenology of Spirit*, trans. A. V. Miller (Oxford: Oxford University Press, 1977)

Hegel, G. W. F., *The Philosophy of History*, trans. J. Sibree (New York: Dover, 1956)

Heidegger, Martin, *Being and Time*, trans. John Macquarrie and Edward Robinson (London: SCM Press; New York: Harper, 1962)

Hirsch, E. D., *The Aims of Interpretation* (Chicago: Chicago University Press, 1976)

Hirsch, E. D., *Validity in Interpretation* (New Haven: Yale University Press, 1967)

Hobbes, Thomas, *Leviathan*, ed. C. B. Macpherson (Harmondsworth: Penguin, 1968)

Hooker, Michael, *Descartes: Critical and interpretive essays* (Baltimore and London: The Johns Hopkins University Press, 1978)

Hume, David, *An Enquiry Concerning Human Understanding*, ed. L. A. Selby-Bigge, rev. P. H. Nidditch (Oxford: Clarendon Press, 1975)

Hume, David, *A Treatise of Human Nature*, ed. D. G. C. Macnabb (Glasgow: Fontana/Collins, 1962)

Husserl, Edmund, *The Idea of Phenomenology*, trans. William P. Alston and George Nakhnikian (The Hague: Martinus Nijhoff, 1964)

Husserl, Edmund, *Phenomenology and the Crisis of Philosophy*, trans. Quentin Lauer (New York, Evanston and London: Harper & Row, 1965)

Jardine, Alice, and Paul Smith (eds.), *Men in Feminism* (New York: Methuen, 1987)

Jay, Gregory S., and David L. Miller (eds.), *After Strange Texts* (University, Al.: University of Alabama Press, 1985)

Kellner, Douglas, *Jean Baudrillard: From Marxism to postmodernism and beyond* (Cambridge: Polity Press, 1989)

Kirk, G. S., and J. E. Raven, *The Presocratic Philosophers* (Cambridge and New York: Cambridge University Press, 1957)

Kuhn, Thomas, *The Copernican Revolution: Planetary astronomy in the development of western thought* (Cambridge, Mass., and London: Harvard University Press, 1957)

Kuhn, Thomas, *The Structure of Scientific Revolutions* (Chicago and London: University of Chicago Press, 1970)

Lakatos, Imre, and Alan Musgrave (eds.), *Criticism and the Growth of Knowledge* (Cambridge and New York: Cambridge University Press, 1970)

Leitch, Vincent B., *Deconstructive Criticism: An advanced introduction* (London: Hutchinson; New York: Columbia University Press, 1983)

Lévi-Strauss, Claude, *The Raw and the Cooked: Introduction to a science of mythology, I*, trans. John and Doreen Weightman (London: Jonathan Cape; New York: Harper & Row, 1969)

Llewelyn, John, *Derrida on the Threshold of Sense* (Basingstoke and London: Macmillan, 1986)

Locke, John, *An Essay Concerning Human Understanding*, ed. A. D. Woozley (London and Glasgow: Fontana/Collins, 1964)

Lyotard, Jean-François, *The Differend: Phrases in dispute*, trans. George Van Den Abbeele (Manchester: Manchester University Press; Minneapolis: University of Minnesota Press, 1988)

Lyotard, Jean-François, *The Lyotard Reader*, ed. Andrew Benjamin (Oxford and Cambridge, Mass.: Basil Blackwell, 1989)

Lyotard, Jean-François, *The Postmodern Condition: A report on knowledge*, trans. Geoff Bennington and Brian Massumi (Manchester: Manchester University Press; Minneapolis: University of Minnesota Press, 1984)

Lyotard, Jean-François, *Tombeau de L'intellectuel et autres papiers* (Paris: Galilee, 1984)

Lyotard, Jean-François, and Jean Loup Thébaud, *Just Gaming*, trans. Wlad Godzich (Manchester: Manchester University Press; Minneapolis: University of Minnesota Press, 1985)

McHale, Brian, *Postmodernist Fiction* (London: Methuen, 1987; London and New York: Routledge, 1989)

Macherey, Pierre, *A Theory of Literary Production*, trans. Geoffrey Wall (London, Henley and Boston: Routledge & Kegan Paul, 1978)

Magliola, Robert, *Derrida on the Mend* (West Lafayette, Ind.: Purdue University Press, 1984)

Magnus, Bernd, *Nietzsche's Existential Imperative* (Bloomington, Ind., and London: Indiana University Press, 1978)

Marx, Karl, and Friedrich Engels, *The Communist Manifesto*, trans. Samuel Moore, ed. Frederic L. Bender (New York and London: W. W. Norton, 1988)

Mason, Jeff, *Philosophical Rhetoric: The function of indirection in philosophical writing* (London and New York: Routledge, 1989)

Melling, David J., *Understanding Plato* (Oxford and New York: Oxford University Press, 1987)

Mitchell, W. J. T. (ed.), *Against Theory: Literary studies and the new pragmatism* (Chicago and London: University of Chicago Press, 1985)

Nehamas, Alexander, *Nietzsche: Life as literature* (Cambridge, Mass., and London: Harvard University Press, 1985)

Nietzsche, Friedrich, *Thus Spake Zarathustra*, trans. R. J. Hollingdale (Harmondsworth: Penguin, 1969)

Nietzsche, Friedrich, *The Will to Power*, trans. Walter Kaufmann and R.J. Hollingdale (London: Weidenfeld & Nicolson, 1968; New York: Random House, 1967)

Norris, Christopher, *The Contest of Faculties: Philosophy and theory after deconstruction* (London and New York: Methuen, 1985)

Norris, Christopher, *The Deconstructive Turn: Essays in the rhetoric of philosophy* (London and New York: Methuen, 1983)

Norris, Christopher, *Derrida* (London: Fontana, 1987)

Norris, Christopher, *What's Wrong with Postmodernism?* (Hemel Hempstead: Harvester Wheatsheaf, 1990)

Pears, David, *Wittgenstein* (Glasgow: Fontana/Collins, 1971)

Pivčević, Edo, *Husserl and Phenomenology* (London: Hutchinson & Co., 1970)

Plato, *The Republic*, trans. Francis MacDonald Cornford (London, Oxford and New York: Oxford University Press, 1941)

Quine, W. V. O., *Word and Object* (Cambridge, Mass.: MIT Press, 1960)

Reader, Keith, *Intellectuals and the Left in France Since 1968* (Basingstoke and London: Macmillan; New York: St Martin's Press, 1987)

Richards, I. A., *Principles of Literary Criticism* (London and Henley: Routledge & Kegan Paul, 1960)

Rorty, Richard, *Consequences of Pragmatism* (Brighton: Harvester; Minneapolis: University of Minnesota Press, 1982)

Rorty, Richard, *Contingency, Irony and Solidarity* (Cambridge and New York: Cambridge University Press, 1989)

Rorty, Richard, *Essays on Heidegger and Others: Philosophical papers volume 2* (Cambridge and New York: Cambridge University Press, 1991)

Rorty, Richard, *Philosophy and the Mirror of Nature* (Princeton, N. J.: Princeton University Press; Oxford: Basil Blackwell, 1980)

Ryan, Michael, *Marxism and Deconstruction: A critical articulation* (Baltimore and London: The Johns Hopkins University Press, 1982)

Sallis, John (ed.), *Deconstruction and Philosophy: The texts of Jacques Derrida* (Chicago and London: University of Chicago Press, 1987)

Sartre, Jean-Paul, *Being and Nothingness*, trans. Hazel E. Barnes (London: Methuen, 1958)

Sarup, Madan, *An Introductory Guide to Post-structuralism and Postmodernism* (Hemel Hempstead: Harvester Wheatsheaf, 1988)

Saussure, Ferdinand de, *Course in General Linguistics*, eds. Charles Bally, Albert Sechehaye and Albert Reidlinger, trans. Wade Baskin (London: Peter Owen, 1960)

Scheffler, Israel, *Science and Subjectivity* (Indianapolis: Bobbs Merrill, 1967)

Shakespeare, William, *Love's Labour's Lost*, ed. Richard David (London and New York: Methuen, 1951)

Silverman, Hugh J. (ed.), *Continental Philosophy I: Philosophy and non-philosophy since Merleau-Ponty* (New York and London: Routledge, 1988)

Silverman, Hugh J. (ed.), *Continental Philosophy II: Derrida and deconstruction* (New York and London: Routledge, 1989)

Sim, Stuart, *Negotiations with Paradox: Narrative practice and narrative form in Bunyan and Defoe* (Hemel Hempstead: Harvester Wheatsheaf, 1990)

Smyth, Edmund J. (ed.), *Postmodernism and Contemporary Fiction* (London: B. T. Batsford, 1991)

Speake, Jennifer (ed.), *Dictionary of Philosophy* (London: Pan Books, 1979)

Staten, Henry, *Wittgenstein and Derrida* (Lincoln, Neb.: University of Nebraska Press, 1984; Oxford: Basil Blackwell, 1985)

Trotsky, Leon, *On Literature and Art*, ed. Paul N. Siegel (New York: Pathfinder Press, 1970)

Ulmer, Gregory L., *Applied Grammatology: Post(e)-pedagogy from Jacques Derrida to Joseph Beuys* (Baltimore and London: The Johns Hopkins University Press, 1985)

Wimsatt, W. K., and M. C. Beardsley, *The Verbal Icon: Studies in the meaning of poetry* (Lexington, Ky.: University of Kentucky Press, 1954; London: Methuen, 1970)

Wittgenstein, Ludwig, *Philosophical Investigations*, trans. G. E. M. Anscombe (Oxford: Basil Blackwell, 1968)

Wood, David, and Robert Bernasconi, *Derrida and Différance* (Evanston, Ill.: Northwestern University Press, 1988)

Articles

Browne, Paul, 'Reification, class and new social movements', *Radical Philosophy*, 55 (1990), pp. 18–24

Deckers, L., and P. Kizer, 'Humour and the incongruity hypothesis', *Journal of Psychology*, 90 (1975), pp. 215–18

Derrida, Jacques, 'Of spirit', trans. Geoff Bennington and Rachel Bowlby, *Critical Inquiry*, 15 (1989), pp. 457–74

Derrida, Jacques, with Geoff Bennington, 'On colleges and philosophy', *ICA Documents*, 4 and 5 (1986), pp. 66–71

Foucault, Michel, 'Interview with Bernard-Henry Levy', *Oxford Literary Review*, 4 (1980), pp. 3–14

Frampton, Kenneth, 'Some reflections on postmodernism and architecture', *ICA Documents*, 4 and 5 (1986), pp. 26–9

Giles, H., and G. S. Oxford, 'A multidimensional theory of laughter causation', *Bulletin of the British Psychological Society*, 23 (1970), pp. 97–105

Habermas, Jürgen, 'Work and Weltanschauung: The Heidegger controversy from a German perspective', *Critical Inquiry*, 15 (1989), pp. 431–56

Jay, Martin, 'In the empire of the gaze', *ICA Documents*, 4 and 5 (1986), pp. 19–25

Kearns, James, and Ken Newton, 'An interview with Jacques Derrida', *Literary Review*, 14 (1980), pp. 21–2

Kenny, D. I., 'The contingency of humor appreciation on the stimulus-confirmation of joke-ending expectations', *Journal of Abnormal and Social Psychology*, 51 (1955), pp. 644–8

Leenhardt, Jacques, 'The role of the intellectuals in France', *ICA Documents*, 4 and 5 (1986), pp. 63–5

Lyotard, Jean-François, 'Defining the postmodern', *ICA Documents*, 4 and 5 (1986), pp. 6–7

Lyotard, Jean-François, 'Rules and paradoxes and svelte appendix', trans. Brian Massumi, *Cultural Critique*, 5 (1986), pp. 209–19

McRobbie, Angela, 'Postmodernism and popular culture', *ICA Documents*, 4 and 5 (1986), pp. 54–8

Maier, Norman R. F., 'A gestalt theory of humour', *British Journal of Psychology*, 23 (1932–3), pp. 69–74

Newman, Michael, 'Revising modernism, representing postmodernism', *ICA Documents*, 4 and 5 (1986), pp. 32–51

'Pass notes', *The Sunday Correspondent*, 15 April 1990, p. 53

Plant, Sadie, 'The situationist international: a case of spectacular neglect', *Radical Philosophy*, 55 (1990), pp. 3–10

Porphyrios, Demetri, 'Architecture and the postmodern condition', *ICA Documents*, 4 and 5 (1986), p. 30

Prior, A. N., 'The runabout inference-ticket', *Analysis*, 21 (1960), pp. 38–9

Rapp, A., 'Toward an eclectic and multilateral theory of humour and laughter', *Journal of General Psychology*, 36 (1947), pp. 207–19

Ree, Jonathan, 'Dedicated followers of fashion', *The Times Higher Educational Supplement*, 916, 25 May 1990, pp. 15–17

Ree, Jonathan, 'Proletarian philosophy: a version of pastoral?', *Radical Philosophy*, 44 (1986), pp. 1–7

Ree, Jonathan, 'Timely meditations', *Radical Philosophy*, 55 (1990), pp. 31–9

Rose, Margaret A., 'Post-modern pastiche', *British Journal of Aesthetics*, 31 (1991), pp. 26–35

Sage, Lorna, review of Jacques Derrida, *Dissemination*, *Observer*, 10 January 1982

Schaff, Adam, 'Marxist dialectics and the principle of contradiction', *Journal of Philosophy*, 57 (1960), pp. 241–50

Searle, John R., 'Reiterating the differences: a reply to Derrida', *Glyph*, 1 (1977), pp. 198–208

Shultz, T. R., and M. B. Scott, 'The creation of verbal humour', *Canadian Journal of Psychology*, 28 (1974), pp. 421–5

Soper, Kate, 'Feminism, humanism and postmodernism', *Radical Philosophy*, 55 (1990), pp. 11–17

Whiteley, C. H., 'Epistemological strategies', *Mind*, 78 (1969), pp. 25–34

Wood, David, 'Derrida and the paradoxes of reflection', *Journal of the British Society for Phenomenology*, 11 (1980), pp. 225–38

Wood, David, 'Style and strategy at the limits of philosophy', *The Monist*, 63 (1980), pp. 494–511

Wyver, John, 'Television and postmodernism', *ICA Documents*, 4 and 5 (1986), pp. 52–4

Index